The Complete Photo Guide to

# NEEDLEWORK

**Creative Publishing international**

First published in the United States of America by
Creative Publishing international, Inc., a member of
Quayside Publishing Group
400 First Avenue North
Suite 300
Minneapolis, MN 55401
1-800-328-3895
www.creativepub.com or www.Qbookshop.com

Visit www.Craftside.Typepad.com for a behind-the-scenes peek at our crafty world!

ISBN: 978-1-58923-641-7

Printed in China
10 9 8 7 6 5 4 3 2 1

Library of Congress Cataloging-in-Publication Data

Wyszynski, Linda.
    The complete photo guide to needlework / Linda Wyszynski.
      p. cm.
    ISBN-13: 978-1-58923-641-7 (pbk.)
    ISBN-10: 1-58923-641-6 (soft cover)
    1. Embroidery–Pictorial works. 2. Needlework–Pictorial works. I. Title.

TT770.W97 2012
746.44–dc23

2011023809

Copy Editor: Catherine Broberg
Proofreader: Karen Ruth
Cover and Book Design: Kim Winscher
Photo Coordinator: Joanne Wawra
Page Layout: Heather Parlato
Illustrations, graphs, and stitch photographs: Dennis Wyszynski

The Complete Photo Guide to

# NEEDLEWORK

Creative Publishing
international

# CONTENTS

# Introduction

This book will open the door to the world of needlework for you. There are always new threads, beads, and fabrics available that are saying "come explore with me." Discover all the wonderful ways you can enjoy creating with stitches. Once you learn the stitches, anything is possible. Beautiful fabrics and threads are just waiting for you to pick them up and create.

There are no do's or don'ts in today's world of needlework. The ABCs will describe the equipment available, how to transfer designs, and how to start creating designs of your very own. You will find descriptions of different types of supplies that are available today. It is up to you to decide what you want to purchase. Some stitchers become collectors of tools, while others are attracted to threads, embellishments, or fabrics. You may be the stitcher who only purchases what is needed to complete the project at hand and then discover your weakness along the way. I've never found my single weakness, I love it all.

At the beginning of each technique chapter, different types of fabric are discussed that are suitable for that technique. Once you learn the basic skills outlined in each chapter, you'll be able to create any of the stitches found within those pages. A full-size photograph and a stitch graph will show in clear steps how the needle is to travel. The projects are simple enough for a novice to enjoy, yet intriguing enough to entice the advanced stitcher.

In many of the technique chapters, I often say keep the stitch straight or use the same height for each stitch. While this is important to follow if possible, it's also essential that you as the stitcher enjoy stitching. When my grandmother taught me to stitch when I was eight, it was important to her that each stitch be worked the best it could be. I was to remove the stitch and rework it if it wasn't perfect. Over the years I've tried—without success—to eliminate that reminder from my brain. Even today I hear Grandmother Coggins saying it could be a little straighter or the loops need to be the same height. Thanks to her I am able to create stitching works of art. But what your eye and hand create is a work of art each time you pick up a needle and thread—whether or not it is "perfect." Stitch for relaxation and have fun doing it!

I have given you the information needed to become a needle artist. As you look over the projects, think about how you, as the stitcher, can complete a project as shown or be adventuresome and take my challenge. The challenge is to use the ideas given but choose your own stitches, fabric, threads, and embellishments. Use the stitch guide sections as a resource when choosing new stitches or surfaces for the projects. Use whatever fabric, thread, or embellishment you fancy. The choice is yours to make.

Get started by taking a shopping trip, and you will see the gorgeous colors of threads and fabrics along with the various tools that are available today. You only need a few basic supplies to create your first project. The world of needlework is waiting for you to create whatever your imagination can conceive. Create a project using one or multiple techniques shown in this book. The ideas that come to mind are endless—from home décor to embellished jeans to jeweled cuffs. You are in the driver's seat for one of the wildest creative journeys of your life.

*Linda*

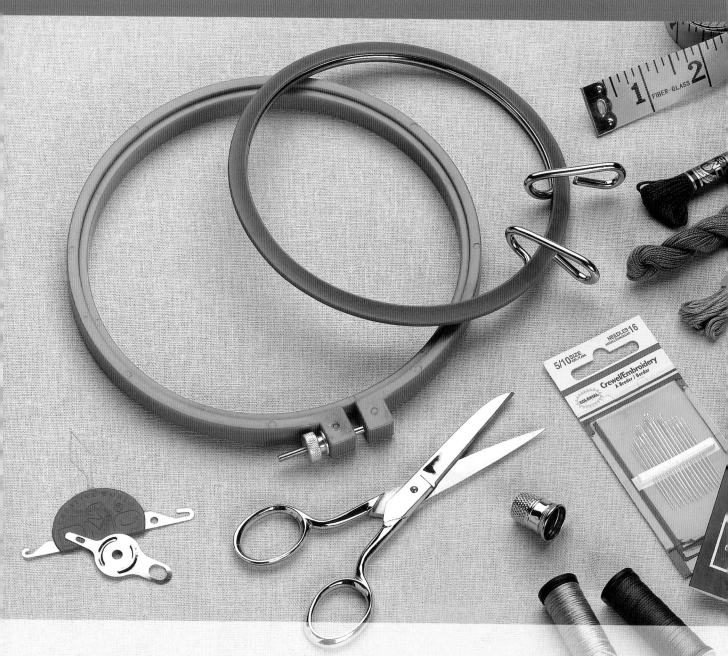

# ABCs OF NEEDLEWORK

All you need to get started is a needle, thread, fabric, pair of scissors, and an idea. The correct equipment enhances the needlework experience and makes stitching much easier. The information in this section will be used as a reference for choosing the correct equipment and supplies. You will refer to the information time and time again.

# Stitching Equipment and Supplies

Needlework requires a very low investment in equipment and supplies, yet there are many options to consider. Many tools, fabrics, threads, and yarns can be used for more than one type of needlework, and those items are introduced here. Specific information is provided in each needlework section.

## NEEDLES

Needles are the most important tool required to create a beautiful piece of needlework. The type and size of needle you choose depends on the fabric or canvas and the type of thread or wool to be used for the stitching.

A needle needs to fit your hand and feel comfortable when stitching. Choose a needle with an eye large enough for the thread or wool to move freely through but not larger than needed. This is especially true when working with silk ribbon which will become tangled and difficult to work with if the eye is not large enough.

When you stitch, the threads of the fabric move, allowing the needle to slide through the weave. Once the needle passes through, those threads move back into place. But when you work with a needle that is too large, it leaves a hole in the fabric or enlarges the canvas hole.

### Beading Needles

Beading needles are long and thin with small eyes and sharp points. Sizes range from 10 (largest) to 15 (smallest). Use them with beading thread or thread that has been run several times over beeswax. Choose a size that can pass through a bead along with several threads. If the needle and thread are too thick, the glass bead may break and the needle may bend. Although they have a sharp point, beading needles can be used on even-weave fabric and needlepoint canvas after the stitches are in place.

Sizes 10, 13, and 15

### Chenille Needles

Chenille needles are thick with large eyes and sharp points. Sizes range from 18 (largest) to 28 (smallest). Used for creative embroidery, crewel, and silk ribbon; the larger sizes are used for wool and crewel threads, size 3 and 5 pearl cotton, metallic braids, and silk ribbon. The smaller sizes are used for embroidery floss, over-dyed thread, combination threads (wool and silk), smaller sizes of metallic braids, and size 12 and 8 pearl cotton. The size 28 can be used for beading. When using these needles for silk ribbon stitches, the size of needle used depends on the width of the ribbon used. This needle can be used on any fabric that has a plain weave.

Sizes 18, 22, and 26

### Crewel Needles

Crewel needles are thin with long eyes and sharp points. Sizes range from 1 (largest) to 10 (smallest). The larger sizes are used for wool and larger metallic braids. The smaller sizes are used for strands of cotton, silks, rayon thread, and smaller metallic braids. This needle can be used on any plain weave fabric. Size 7 or 8 can be used for beading after the stitches are in place.

Sizes 1, 5, and 10

## Embroidery Needles

Embroidery needles have long medium eyes and sharp points. Sizes range from 1 (largest) to 10 (smallest). They are used for creative embroidery and crewel, with stranded threads, silks, rayon, metallic thread, and braid. This needle can be used on any plain weave fabric or for general hand sewing.

Sizes 5, 7, and 10

## Sharps

Sharp needles are thin and short with small eyes and sharp points. Sizes range from 1 (largest) to 12 (smallest). These needles are excellent for finishing seams by hand or securing an appliqué. The thin needle allows you to take small running stitches and to hide a slip stitch between the folds of fabric.

Sizes 6, 7, and 10

## Milliners

Milliners are long and thin with very small eyes and sharp points. Sizes range from 1 (largest) to 10 (smallest). This needle is the same diameter down the length of the needle. Use a milliner to work a bullion knot that has a smooth even appearance. This needle can be used on any plain weave fabric. It also works well for attaching beads with beading thread if a longer beading needle is not required.

These needles are excellent for finishing seams by hand or securing appliqués. The thin needle allows you to take small running stitches and to hide a slip stitch between the folds of fabric.

Sizes 3, 7, and 10

## Tapestry Needles

Tapestry needles are thick with large eyes and blunt points. They are slightly shorter than chenille needles and range in size from 18 (largest) to 28 (smallest). They are mainly used for cross-stitch and needlepoint and are perfect for working the whipped or laced portion of a crewel or creative embroidery stitch to prevent splitting the stitched thread. The larger sizes are used for wool, cotton thread, and crewel threads. The smaller sizes are used for embroidery floss, over-dyed, silk, and so on. The size 28 can be used for beading. This needle can be used on any even-weave fabric or needlepoint canvas.

Sizes 18, 22, and 28

# Lost Needle

Keep a magnet handy to easily locate needles that fall on the carpet or into the chair. For safety's sake, always rescue the needle.

# CUTTING TOOLS

Scissors or shears should be chosen for the task at hand. There are several types suitable for needlework. To keep scissors or shears sharp, use them only for what they were designated. When scissors are not in use, they should be put away for safety. Keep scissors covered with a sheath or place them in the case they came in to protect the sharp point.

Beading scissors

## Beading Scissors

Beading scissors are very small and sharp with a curved blade that allows a ½" (1.3 cm) blade cut. You can find them at beading stores. They should only be used to cut beading threads like Silamide or Nymo. Never cut beading wire with them. Wire cutting scissors are also available in beading stores. Cuticle scissors are similar to but less expensive than beading scissors.

Needlepoint canvas shears

## Needlepoint Canvas Shears

Canvas shears are the same as fabric shears with a 6" (15.2 cm) or 8" (20.3 cm) blade. Use old shears, or purchase inexpensive shears to cut canvas. Canvas is hard on shears and will dull the blade over time.

## Embroidery Scissors

Embroidery scissors

Embroidery scissors are small and sharp and have a tapered point with a 1" (2.5 cm) blade cut. There are many different kinds available in a wide range of prices. These scissors are used to cut lengths of cotton, silk, or wool threads. When cutting thread lengths, it is recommended that you cut close to the base of the blade.

# Stay Sharp

Use older embroidery scissors for cutting synthetic fibers and metallic braids to keep your newer embroidery scissors sharp.

## Fabric Shears

Fabric shears are large and sharp and have a straight 8" (20.3 cm) blade. They are used for cutting all types of fabric.

Fabric shears

## Paper Scissors or Shears

Paper scissors or shears are available in many sizes. Cut tissue paper and tape with these.

## Cutting Board, Wide Ruler, and Rotary Cutter

This equipment is often thought of more for quilting than needlework. Although they are not necessary for this type of stitching, these tools ensure clean accurate cuts on all types of fabric. If you have a clean cut on the edge of your fabric, you have a well-finished project.

Paper scissors or shears

# Multiple Scissors

Use certain scissors or shears for specific items, so when you want a clean cut of thread or a smooth edge on the cut fabric you get what you expect. You do not need all the types of scissors discussed in this section to create a beautiful piece of needlework.

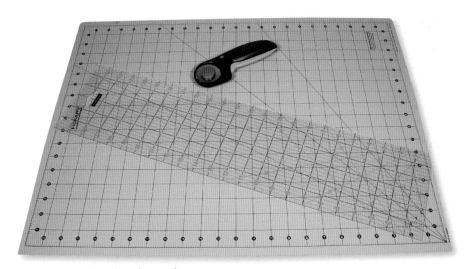

Cutting board, wide ruler and rotary cutter

# HOOPS OR FRAMES

Creative embroidery, cross-stitch, crewel, silk ribbon, and bead embroidery are usually worked in a hoop or frame, though some stitchers prefer not to use them. Hoops and frames hold the work taut, making stitching easier and stitches more uniform. The size and type of hoop or frame will depend on the project and your preference. The information below will help you decide which type will work best for you.

When using a hoop, 2" to 3" (5.1 to 7.6 cm) of excess fabric should extend beyond the hoop or frame, before the fabric has been secured. This will help to keep the fabric taut once the hoop or frame has been tightened. When working on premade clothing, it is not always possible to have this much extra fabric. In such cases, you may find it easier to work the project without a hoop or frame.

If the hoop allows the fabric to slip during stitching, readjust the fabric as needed. When working on particularly delicate fabric, try wrapping the hoop with muslin fabric strips to lessen the stress on the needlework fabric. Cut ½" (1.3 cm) strips of fabric to wrap around each of the hoop circles. Secure the end of the wrapped fabric with a small tack stitch.

Always remove the needlework from the hoop, clamp, or snap frame when not stitching. If they are left in place for longer than the stitching time, a permanent mark may develop on the fabric and thread. Or, frame up a larger piece of fabric than called for to keep the project area away from the frame or loop edges. This allows you to keep the fabric in the frame until the project is completed.

## Wooden and Plastic Hoops

Wooden hoops have a screw tension. Plastic hoops come with a screw or spring tension. Both types of hoops have two round circles, one smaller than the other. To use a screw-tension hoop, separate the two circles and place the fabric over the smaller circle so it lies smoothly. Place the larger top circle over the fabric, pressing it into place. Gently screw the tension device to hold the work securely in place between the circles. The fabric needs to be taut across the bottom circle.

If using a hoop with a spring tension, be sure the fabric is smooth over the smaller circle before carefully placing the larger hoop on top. The spring-load tension will adjust automatically.

## Scroll Frame (with a split)

Slots in the dowel rods of this frame hold the fabric securely. You can adjust the tension so the fabric is taut for stitching. When you need to reposition the work, simply loosen the screws and roll to the desired area.

This type of frame makes it easy to quickly frame up and start the project without needing to tack or baste the work to the frame. It can be used for cross-stitch, crewel, silk ribbon, bead embroidery, and creative embroidery.

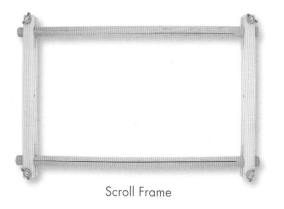

Scroll Frame

## Ratchet Frame

This is a lightweight frame that works similarly to the wooden scroll frame. This new system allows the fabric to scroll back and forth effortlessly on the two-way ratchets. The fabric is held at the correct tension between the two split rails without leaving marks on the fabric. Small or large projects can be worked on it without having to baste the fabric to the frame. The lightness of the frame makes it perfect for stitching and for traveling. It can be used when working cross-stitch, crewel, silk ribbon, bead embroidery, and creative embroidery.

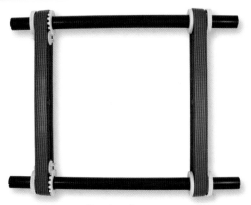

Ratchet Frame

## Handi Clamp

This frame functions like the scroll frame, but it has two plastic clamps to hold the fabric in place. It does not require thumb tacks or staples and there is no basting. Simply lay the fabric over the dowel rod and snap the half-circular fastener in place on one end. Repeat for the other end. Use the knobs to roll up and tighten the fabric, making it taut in the frame. The company does recommend placing a piece of quilt batting (4" [10.2 cm] wide by the length of the scroll bar) between the frame and fabric to avoid marking the fabric with the frame bar. This frame is easy to use and is suitable for cross-stitch, needlepoint, crewel, silk ribbon, bead embroidery, and creative embroidery.

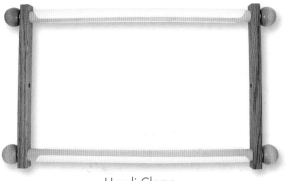

Handi Clamp

## Q-Snap Frame

The Q-Snap is square. Place the fabric over the square and snap the half-circular fasteners in place on each side of the frame. Once the fasteners are in place, rotate them slightly away from you to tighten the fabric so it is taut in the frame. This frame works well for traveling.

Q-Snap Frame

## Stretcher Bar Frame

These frames (not shown) are used for needlepoint canvas and are discussed in the needlepoint chapter (page 210).

# Keeping Clean

If you use a frame, slide your work into a pillowcase when you stop stitching to keep the work clean.

## SUPPLIES

### Beeswax

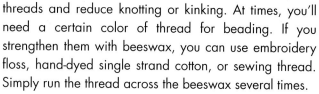

Available in needlework shops, beeswax is used to strengthen threads and reduce knotting or kinking. At times, you'll need a certain color of thread for beading. If you strengthen them with beeswax, you can use embroidery floss, hand-dyed single strand cotton, or sewing thread. Simply run the thread across the beeswax several times.

### Masking Tape

After cutting your needlepoint canvas to the proper size, tape the edges with masking tape to prevent raveling.

### Iron and Ironing Board

It is important to remove all wrinkles from fabric before stitching. If fabric has been folded for long, lightly spray with water mixed with a teaspoon of white vinegar before light pressing. Batik fabric should be washed before spraying with vinegar water.

### Press Cloth

This type of cloth is needed when fusing stabilizers to the wrong side of fabric. It is also handy when pressing a dark colored or synthetic fabric to avoid creating a shine on the fabric.

## Tip

Did you know you have a built-in needle threader? Cut the thread with good scissors and hold the thread tightly between your thumb and index finger. Slide the needle between your fingers and push the hand holding the thread forward. The thread will slide into the needle.

### Light Source

Good lighting is important when stitching. Ideally, the light should come from over your shoulder. The best types of lighting are natural window light, daylight bulbs, and daylight fluorescent lamps.

### Magnification

Several types of magnification work well. These include lighted floor stands, table lights with magnifiers, magnifiers that hang on a cord around the neck, and magnifiers that fit on your head allowing your glasses to remain in place.

My favorite is the magnifier that fits on your head. You can adjust it low enough to see the needlework while still being able to see above the top edge of the magnification. This allows you to watch TV or observe other people in the room.

### Needle Threader

The needle and thread you choose will determine the kind of needle threader needed.

### Quilter's Tape

This is a tape with a light adhesive that will not leave a residue on fabric. Use it to hold tissue paper on the right side of the fabric until basting it in place. Mark the tape every ¼" or ½" (0.6 or 1.3 cm) to help keep your border stitches evenly spaced. Remove the tape when you're done stitching for the day—do not leave tape on the fabric for more than a few hours. Read all product instructions before using.

## Ruler and Measuring Tape

Keep a measuring tape handy to locate the center of your fabric before placing your design. A small ruler is handy for measuring the length of a stitch or for accurately placing patterns.

## Laying Tool or Stiletto

Either of these tools can be used to enlarge needlepoint canvas holes when working an eyelet stitch that several threads will share. They can also be used to lay a metal thread or stranded thread so it does not twist as it enters the canvas. When these tools are not in use, secure the stiletto tip or place the laying tool in its case. Store this tool out of the reach of children.

## Straight Pins and Pin Cushion

Use straight pins to hold fabrics together or to mark a starting point on canvas or stitchery. Straight pins can be used to straighten out a knot in your thread. If you have a kink in a creative embroidery thread that doesn't want to lie smoothly against the fabric, just use the pin as a laying tool.

## Thimbles

Using a thimble is entirely optional. When used, it is normally worn on the middle finger to help push the needle through heavier fabrics. You may find the feel of a thimble awkward at first. It will take time to learn to stitch using one, but it prevents pricking a finger.

## Magnets

Placing a magnet on each side of your fabric creates the perfect spot to place your needle while stitching.

## Thumb Tacks, Brass Tacks, or Staple Gun

Tacks or staples are used to hold the needlepoint canvas taut on the stretcher bar. This will be discussed in more detail in the needlepoint section.

## Tweezers

These little jewels are a must in every needlework basket. They help to remove threads that have been clipped, extract bits of tissue paper that are stuck under a stitch, and pick up a needle that is buried deep in the carpet.

# Charts, Diagrams, and Patterns

## DESIGN CHARTS

Cross-stitch and needlepoint are worked from a chart and are referred to as counted work. Creative embroidery, crewel, and bead embroidery are normally considered free-form techniques. If worked using a chart and even-weave fabric, they would then become counted work. The creative embroidery, crewel, and bead embroidery techniques are shown in a free-form style in this book, which allows more freedom when working the stitches.

### Cross-stitch Charts

Cross-stitch charts are shown on a square grid. Each stitch is represented by a square on the chart. The color key and chart have corresponding symbols that indicate the color, type of thread, and amount of thread needed for each stitch. Information is given if the cross-stitch is worked over one or two threads on even-weave fabric. Some patterns will give sizes of the design when worked on more than one type of fabric and fabric count. Others indicate the fabric size needed for that project. When counting cross-stitch, count each square on the pattern for correct placement on the fabric. For more information refer to the Cross-Stitch chapter (page 186).

### Needlepoint Charts

Needlepoint charts show where each stitch is placed on the weave of the canvas. Some needlepoint patterns have a color key along with instructions and others simply give written instructions. In needlepoint, stitches are often shown over more than one intersection (grid line) to indicate how the stitch is worked. For counted needlepoint stitches, there will be a stitch graph showing how to work each stitch. The graph will have numbers and letters indicating where the needle comes up from the back of the canvas and where it should travel before it goes back down into the canvas. When counting needlepoint, count each grid line on the chart to determine where to place

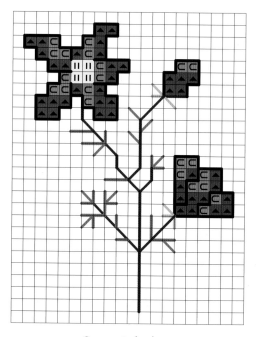

Cross-stitch chart

Needlepoint chart

the stitch on the canvas. The chart usually indicates where the center is located. For more information, refer to the Needlepoint chapter.

## Stitch Diagrams

Cross-stitch and needlepoint have diagrams that show a grid line with arrows and/or numbers to indicate where to place the stitch. Creative embroidery, crewel, silk ribbon, and bead embroidery have diagrams that show how the stitch is worked without a grid. These diagrams have arrows and numbers, but the stitch length is up to the stitcher.

## Design Patterns

Patterns for creative embroidery and crewel come in the form of line drawings, pattern books, kits, and stamped pattern packs. For the line drawings and pattern books, you'll need to transfer the pattern onto the fabric to be used. This information is discussed under Transferring Patterns (page 20). Stamped patterns are purchased in pattern packs and come in a wide range of themes. The stamped design is ironed directly to the fabric. Follow the manufacturer's instructions to transfer the pattern onto the fabric.

Hand drawings are really patterns that you can transfer using any of the methods discussed in this section. Create a keepsake for your child by turning one of their drawings into a finished piece of needlework.

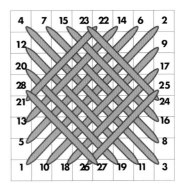

Needlepoint stitch

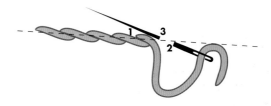

Embroidery diagram

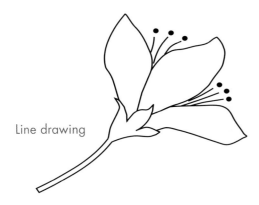

Line drawing

Drawing by Rileigh Pack, age 11

# Transferring Patterns and Stabilizing Fabric

Once you have the design and fabric, you will need to decide how to transfer the design to the fabric and how to stabilize the fabric, if necessary. The subjects of design transfer and stabilizers are closely related, and the stabilizer information is included with the pattern transfer discussion.

There are several ways to transfer an original design or pattern to your fabric. The fabric and stabilizer used often determines which transfer method to use. With a little experimentation, you will soon decide the type of transfer method and supplies you prefer. I use the basting method with tissue paper or the nonfusible stabilizer more than any other method. I like the transfer results of the basting.

## TRACING

Tracing is a key technique when transferring designs. There are many considerations when selecting an appropriate marker or pencil for use when tracing.

### Permanent or Waterproof Pens

Use these pens to trace the pattern onto the stabilizer or tissue paper. Once the pattern is traced, it's best to let the ink dry for a few minutes before placing it next to the fabric and basting the design. These two types of pens should not rub off on the thread or ribbon when the stitches pass through the traced area.

Here are some examples of pens: Pigma Micron black fine pen, which is a micro pigment ink waterproof pen purchased in art stores, and Sharpie permanent black fine pen available in drug stores, discount stores, and so on. Be sure the Sharpie says that it is permanent. Do not use either of these types of pen directly on fabric because the lines will not come out when the fabric is washed.

### Pencils

A mechanical, #4 hard, or marking pencil can be used to trace the pattern onto the stabilizer or tissue paper. If using white or very light colored threads, ribbons, or silk, the pencil lead could leave a slight discoloration on the threads or fabric surface. Most pencil lines marked directly on fabric will come out when washed, but there is always the chance they will remain visible.

### Vanishing or Water-erasable Marking Pens

These widely available pens can be used to draw a pattern directly onto the fabric. They work especially well for children, who can draw their own pattern and then execute the stitches of their choice. If using the water-erasable pen, be sure to wash the project after the stitching is completed to remove the marked lines. The vanishing pen lines should indeed simply vanish. Follow the product directions carefully. Also, try to keep fabric marked with these pens out of the direct sun, as heat could set the marks permanently.

## Tracing on Fabric Method

Use a sunny window or light box to trace directly onto the fabric. Place the fabric over the pattern, centering the pattern in the correct position. Pin the pattern to the fabric. Recheck placement by holding the fabric up to the sunny window or placing it on the light box. When you are satisfied with the placement, tape the fabric to the light box or window, using ¼" (6 mm) quilter's tape. Trace the pattern using an appropriate marker or pencil. This is a quick and easy way to transfer the pattern.

Tracing on fabric

## Tracing Using Transfer Paper and Stylus Method

This method uses colored tracing or transfer papers to trace the pattern directly onto the fabric. The papers are available in several colors, and the color should not smear or come off on the thread. If the pattern has writing on the back, trace the pattern onto tracing paper or tissue paper before transferring it to fabric or stabilizer. Simply place the traced pattern in correct position over the fabric. Slip the transfer paper under the design, carbon against the fabric. Use the stylus as you would a pencil, bearing down on the stylus with a little pressure. Trace over the pattern, transferring it to the fabric.

These are some of the transfer papers available: DMC wax-free tracing paper that is less powdery than others on the market. It will wash out. Clover's tracing paper does not smear, and it will wash out, but it does transfer a stronger color to the fabric. This paper comes in brighter colors. Loew Cornell transfer paper is greaseless, wax free, erasable, and smudge proof. It's best to test the product on a scrap of fabric to be sure you like the results before using it on your project fabric. Always read the product instructions.

Transfer paper

# Small Details

When tracing a design that has small details like embellished beads or small lazy daisies, use a straight line or small dot to indicate where they are to be placed. Every mark you make on the fabric must be covered with a stitch or it will show. For beads used for embellishment, rather than indicate it on the transfer, use the pattern as a guide for placement.

## IRONING METHOD

### Heat Transfer Pencil

Heat transfer pencils, available in craft and fabric stores, allow you to transfer patterns directly to the fabric. The lines are permanent, so they should only be used if the needlework will cover the lines entirely. This method transfers the mirror image of the pattern, so trace the pattern onto tissue paper first using plain pen or pencil, then flip the paper over and trace the lines with the heat transfer pencil. Center the pattern facedown on the right side of the fabric, and pin in place. Transfer the pattern to the fabric with a heated iron, following the pencil manufacturer's directions.

## BASTING METHOD

With this method, the pattern is transferred to stabilizer or tissue paper before basting it onto the fabric. The basted stitches remain on the fabric until you stitch over them or remove them. They will not disappear, require washing, or discolor the fabric or threads. This method gives you the truest transfer. Although it does require a few more minutes to baste the pattern onto the fabric, the results are well worth it, especially when transferring larger patterns.

To baste the pattern in place, use either sewing thread or one strand of embroidery floss that matches the colors of threads to be used to complete the pattern. For ease in removing basting thread, do not knot ends. Instead, take two small backstitches to begin and end the basting thread. When the stitching of the project is completed, remove any basting threads that show. As you stitch the project, you will cover most if not all of the basting stitches, saving you the extra time it would take to remove the basting stitches.

Basting through tissue paper on right side

### Basting Using Tissue Paper

This method works well for all types of projects, especially for small designs on clothing. Use a low-temperature iron to press out any wrinkles in the paper. Trace the pattern onto the tissue paper using a fine-tip black permanent pen or pencil. Then center the traced pattern faceup on the right side of the fabric, and pin in place. Baste the pattern onto the fabric, stitching through the tissue paper and fabric. When the entire pattern has been basted, run the tip of the needle along the basting lines to score the tissue paper; then carefully tear the paper away. Use tweezers to remove any little pieces of tissue paper that remain.

# Small Designs

If stitching a small area on clothing, baste close to the tissue pattern to secure it to the fabric. Then bypass the basting step and work the decorative stitches through the tissue paper onto the fabric. This does not work well for large areas because the tissue paper will tear and the pattern will be unusable.

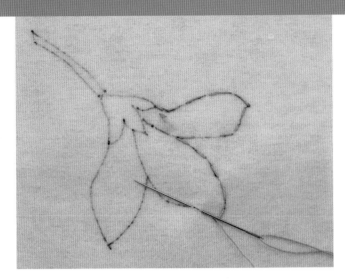

Basting through stabilizer on wrong side

## Basting Using Fusible Stabilizer

This method works well for medium-weight fabrics like corduroy, twill, and home décor items. Be sure your fabric choice can withstand the temperature required for fusing. Pellon's featherweight fusible stabilizer is a good choice. Using an appropriate marker or pencil, trace the pattern onto the stabilizer. Then center the traced pattern facedown on the wrong side of the fabric, and pin in place. The pattern can easily be seen through the stabilizer. Fuse the stabilizer to the fabric, following the manufacturer's instructions, and allow to cool. Working from the wrong side, baste the pattern onto the right side, stitching thorough the stabilizer and fabric so the pattern shows clearly on the right side.

## Basting Using Non-fusible Stabilizer

This method works well for light- to medium-weight opaque home décor and clothing items. Pellon #30 non-fusible stabilizer is easy to use and gives the finished work a little body. Using an appropriate marker or pencil, trace the pattern onto the stabilizer. Then center the traced pattern facedown on the wrong side of the fabric, and pin in place. The pattern can easily be seen through the stabilizer. Working from the wrong side, baste the pattern onto the right side, stitching thorough the stabilizer and fabric so the pattern shows clearly on the right side. For clothing, trim away excess stabilizer after the needlework is finished.

## OTHER STABILIZES

The following stabilizers are opaque, making it necessary to use one of the transferring methods that transfer to the front of the fabric. Suggestions include, Basting Using Tissue Paper, Heat Transfer Pencil, and Tracing Using Transfer Paper and Stylus.

### Fusible Fleece (Pellon)

Fusible fleece works well to stabilize lighter weight fabric. For bead embroidery, it gives the needed support behind the fabric for the weight of the stitches. It does require that you transfer the pattern using one of the transfer methods discussed in this chapter.

The fleece gives body to the fabric while adding padding between the fabric and the back of the work. It helps to keep the fabric from wrinkling. The down side of the product is that it can leave small bits of batting on the front of the fabric if stitches need to be removed. This product works well with creative embroidery, crewel, and bead embroidery.

### Cotton Flannel

When working bead embroidery, place a piece of flannel behind your fabric to support the fabric to hold the beads in place. This is especially useful when working a design with heavier beads. It gives a good support to the fabric being used to work the design on.

# Straight Lines

Baste a guide line or place a piece of quilter's tape straight across the area to be stitched on the plain weave fabric. Measure from the bottom edge of the fabric up to the guide to be sure it is straight.

# Special Information on Stitching

This general information is needed before stitching the techniques described in this book. Combined here for easy reference, this information will be used again and again as you become familiar with stitching. When the term "thread" is used, it refers to thread or yarn unless other specified.

## GLOSSARY OF TERMS

Here are the meanings of some of the common terms and phrases used for needlework:

**Bead embroidery stitches.** Adding beads within an embroidery stitch to enhance it.

**Bead stitches.** Beads stitched on fabric using a beading thread.

**Clean hole.** Canvas hole that has not had a previous stitch worked through it.

**Compensating stitch.** A portion of a stitch in a given area where there is not enough room to complete the stitch unit. Compensating stitches are placed after the area is stitched to even up the sides of the area.

**Dirty hole.** A dirty canvas hole is where a previous stitch has been worked.

**Even-weave fabric.** Cloth in which the number of warp (vertical) threads equals the number of weft (horizontal) threads in a square inch.

**Hole.** Open area between the canvas threads.

**Intersection.** An intersection is where the canvas threads cross on the mesh of the needlepoint canvas.

**Plain weave fabric.** An over-under motion is used to weave the fabric without a definite thread count.

**Rhythm.** How the needle goes through the canvas/thread to complete the stitch.

**Shared hole.** A canvas hole that two or more threads use.

**Sewing method.** To stitch by sliding the needle in and out of the fabric on the front side of the fabric in one motion.

**Snug.** To pull a thread secure against the fabric or canvas.

**Stab-stitch method.** To stitch by moving the needle up through the fabric or canvas and down through the fabric or canvas in two motions.

**Strand (ply).** A single thread as it comes from the skein or spool. An individual thread separated from a stranded thread. A single strand is sometimes referred to as a ply.

**Taut.** To keep the stitching thread or canvas mesh firm to the touch.

**Travel or traveling.** The path or direction the stitch will cover.

**Stitch path.** The area where the stitches are to be placed.

**Unit or stitch unit.** A stitch unit is a completed stitch pattern. It can be comprised of several stitches or a single stitch.

## FABRIC PREPARATION

Before using washable fabric for creative embroidery, crewel, silk ribbon, bead embroidery, and cross-stitch; wash, dry, and iron fabric following the manufacturer's instructions. If you do not prewash the fabric, it may shrink when it is washed later, distorting the stitches.

If your finished project will not be washed, it is not necessary to prewash the fabric. Washing removes sizings which are used in some fabrics to give the fabric a crisp look that enhances the finished project.

When using a loosely woven fabric, overcast (zigzag) the edges. Some stitchers prefer to always overcast or serge the edges or run a quick basting hem along the edges.

Any of the fabrics discussed in the Creative Embroidery, Crewel, Silk Ribbon, and Bead Embroidery chapters can be used for any of these techniques. If you find a fabric you like that was not discussed, ask for a small sample of it to work a few stitches on. Then answer the following questions to determine if the fabric is suitable for the stitching technique. Did the needle slide easily in and out of the fabric? Did the fabric lie flat after the stitches were in place? Do you like the effect of the stitches and thread with the fabric?

## SPECIAL INFORMATION ABOUT THREAD

For easy stitching, thread should be cut in 14" to 16" (35.6 to 40.6 cm) lengths for stitching. Metallic thread and braids should be cut in 12" to 14" (30.5 to 35.6 cm) lengths. Some types of thread and most yarn become fuzzy if the length is longer than 16" (40.6 cm). Even strand cotton will start to become worn looking if a longer length is used.

The nature of thread is to become twisted as you stitch. To counter this, form a habit of twisting your needle clockwise one turn after every few stitches to keep the thread straight. You can also let the needle and thread dangle downward from the fabric to allow the thread to untwist.

Some thread manufactures indicate how many strands to use for the different sizes of needlepoint canvas and even-weave fabric. There are so many threads on the market, it is impossible to list them all and give the number of strands to use for each fabric count. You will need to determine if the thread is covering the canvas, plain weave, or even-weave fabric. Some stitchers prefer a heavy thread look to their needlework while others like a lighter look. Play around with the thread and see which look you like best.

### Stranded Thread

All threads that are stranded should be separated and then plied back together unless otherwise noted in a pattern. This gives you better coverage when stitching. Hold the cut length between your thumb and index finger, leaving a small amount of thread exposed above the fingers. Separate one strand from the rest and pull that thread straight up. Continue until the number of strands needed have been separated. Use the number of strands called for by putting the plies back together.

### Braids (Metallic)

Stitching braids come on spools. When you cut a length, it likes to slightly curl. To smooth out the thread, simply run your fingernail down the cut length.

## Silky Floss

Six-strand embroidery floss and stranded satin thread take on a more silky look and are easier to handle when they have been dampened and dried. Cut strands 14" to 16" (35.6 to 40.6 cm) long, and run them one at a time over a slightly damp sponge. Lay the dampened threads aside to dry (some colors will bleed onto the fabric or canvas if not dry). Then join the desired number of plies before stitching.

## Stab Stitch/Sewing Stitch

If you chose to use a hoop or frame, you will need to use the stab stitch method to stitch your project. This simply means you place one stitch at a time. You bring the needle up from the wrong side and go down into the fabric or canvas from the right side to work the stitch.

If not using a hoop, you can use the sewing method. Simply slide the needle in and out of the fabric using shallow stitches.

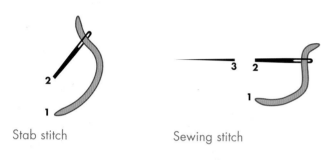

Stab stitch          Sewing stitch

## Thread Tension

Thread tension is a concern for every stitcher. Try to keep the tension consistent on all your stitches. Hold your fabric or canvas so you have a side view (front and back) of the stitches. Are any stitches of the same type, and with the same thread, higher or lower than the rest? If they are uneven, the tension is not consistent. Do your stitches appear the same? Do they appear to be pulling the fabric so it is wrinkling around the stitches or the canvas threads so they buckle? Does the stitching surface still lie flat? Are the stitches too loose? If you can run your needle under the thread and pull the stitch away from the fabric or canvas, it is too loose and you will need to pull your stitches a little tighter. Are the stitches too tight? Is it difficult to run your thread under your stitches on the back when ending your thread? This would indicate too tight a tension. If this happens, loosen your tension just a little. Your stitches should be somewhere between too tight and too loose. Perfect tension requires patience and practice. One thing that does help is to learn to look at

your needlework on the front and on the back every few stitches. If you make this a habit, you will be able to recognize when you are pulling the thread too tightly or leaving it too loose. The tension of a stitch is important in the finished needlework piece. You can be an advanced stitcher or a beginning stitcher and not have a quality piece if the tension isn't correct.

## Compensating Stitches

Compensating stitches are needed when a complete stitch pattern will not fit into a given area. You, the stitcher, will need to fit the stitch into the area. Use a small scrap of fabric or canvas to work several of the stitches in question. Learning to work the stitch pattern will help you figure out the compensating portion of the stitch.

If it is necessary to compensate a stitch to fit a pattern section and you are having trouble visualizing the complete stitch or a portion of the stitch, mark the outline of the area on graph paper. Graph out the stitch in its entirety, lightly marking over the given area. Use an eraser to remove the portion of the stitch that does not fit into the area. This will help you see how to compensate when you stitch the area.

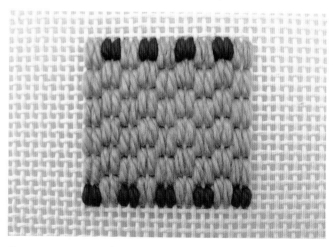

Compensating stitches are in red

### Laying the Thread

Although it is optional when stitching, laying thread with a laying tool creates a smoother look. Using a laying tool can be as simple as guiding the thread with your finger as it goes down into the fabric or canvas. You can also use a darning needle, stiletto, or a laying tool sold in needlework shops. Keeping the thread straight and smooth gives the stitch a nicer appearance. Stranded threads should lie next to each other without twisting over themselves.

To lay threads, bring the thread to the front side of the work. Place the laying tool under the thread. Take the thread to where it goes down into the fabric or canvas. Use the tool to gently work the thread in one direction as it goes into the hole of the canvas or the even-weave fabric. In order to have the thread lie correctly, it must be smooth as it goes down into fabric or canvas and comes up out of the fabric or canvas.

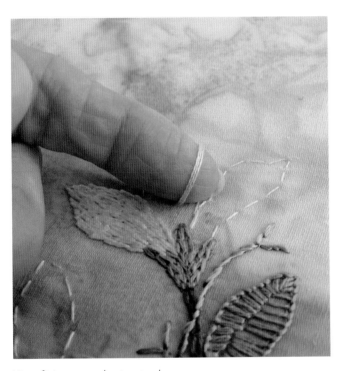

Your finger as a laying tool

Using a laying tool

# Tension

If you find you are a stitcher who consistently pulls the stitches too tightly, always use a hoop or frame when stitching. Having a consistent tension and being sure your threads lie flat and are not twisted will help ensure a beautiful piece of needlework.

## Beginning and Ending Threads

### Small Knot

Creative embroidery, crewel, and bead embroidery can all be started using a small knot.

Thread the needle and bring the tip end of the thread length up along the side of the needle so the end of the thread is toward your body and the point of the needle is straight up in the air. Hold the thread firmly next to the needle between your thumb and forefinger with your stitching hand grasping the middle of the needle. With the other hand, wrap the loose thread at the tip of your thumb around the end of the needle two or three times. (The number of wraps determines the size of the knot). Catch the end of the wrapped thread between your thumb and needle, and adjust the loose length of thread so it hangs downward along the needle. Hold the thread gently but firmly and pull the needle straight up with your stitching hand. The wrapped thread will slide down along the length of thread to form a small even knot at the tip end. Clip the tail of the thread near the knot. Hold the knot between your thumb and forefinger, and pull on the knot to be sure it is secure.

### Easy Knot

Thread the needle. Moisten the end of your index finger. Wrap the end of the thread around the index finger. Roll the thread between your index finger and thumb until twisted together, and slide the loop to the tip of your index finger. Grip the top of the loop between your index finger and thumb, and pull it down to the end of the thread to form the knot.

### Waste Knot

This type of knot can be used for any technique that uses plain or even-weave fabric as well as for needlepoint. Use a waste knot in areas where your stitches will cover the fabric or canvas. Put the needle down through the front side of your fabric or canvas in the area you will travel over. The knot should be 1" to 1½" (2.5 to 3.8 cm) away from the starting point. Bring the needle up from the back at your starting point and begin stitching, working over the thread toward the knot. When you reach the knot, clip it off and continue stitching.

Once the knot is clipped, it may be necessary, on the back, to clip the thread closer to the last stitch placed. This will keep the fuzzy end of the thread from pulling to the front with the next stitch placed.

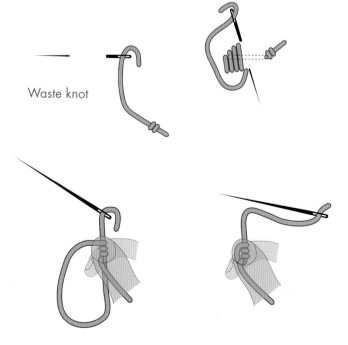

Waste knot

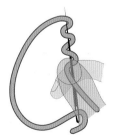

Small knot

### Away Waste Knot

Cross-stitch and needlepoint can be started with an away waste knot.

Tie a knot in the end of your thread and move 2" or 3" (5.1 or 7.6 cm) away from the stitching area. Put the needle down through the front of the fabric or canvas. Come up from the back of the fabric or canvas with your needle at the starting point and begin stitching. When you have finished stitching, clip the waste knot on the front of the fabric or canvas, and weave the thread under the stitching on the back to secure. This knot is the same as a waste knot, only it is placed further away from the working area.

Once you have an area stitched, this method can be used for any of the techniques. Simply weave the new thread length into the previously stitched work for about an inch (2.5 cm) to secure. Then begin stitching, being careful for the first couple of stitches so you don't pull the thread tail out. If this project is one that will be washed many times, use a different method to begin so the thread is more secure.

### Weaving Under to End

Use this method to end thread for crewel, silk ribbon, creative embroidery, cross-stitch, and needlepoint. If the project isn't going to be washed or have heavy use, you can simply weave the thread under several previously placed stitches on the back of the fabric. If the project is going to be washed, use a loop knot before clipping the thread.

### Ending Slippery Threads

To secure metallic, metallic braids, satin, and cotton pearl thread, run the thread under several stitches on the back of the fabric or canvas, and then take two backstitches over the thread of previously worked stitches. Be careful not to disrupt the stitches on the front.

### Loop Knot

For a more secure ending, use a loop knot to end the thread. On the back of the fabric, weave the thread under several previously placed stitches. Then take the needle and thread around the stitch, slipping the needle through the looped end of the thread. Pull thread to secure the knot.

Loop knot

### Removing Stitches

All stitchers at some point decide to rip out thread. This is simply part of the life of a stitcher. You may decide you do not like a type or color of thread. Or you feel you can do nicer stitching on the project. Whatever your reason, when you rip, use a blunt needle to help pull the stitch out of the fabric or canvas. As you pull the stitches out, clip the thread to shorten it if it is long; this will make it easier to pull out. It is never a good idea to use scissors to cut out thread, as you run the risk of cutting the fabric or canvas in addition to the thread. Use a new piece of thread to stitch the ripped area.

# Hand Work

If you do not want to rip, my best advice is to learn to love the stitches you create. As my mother used to tell me, it is, after all, hand work.

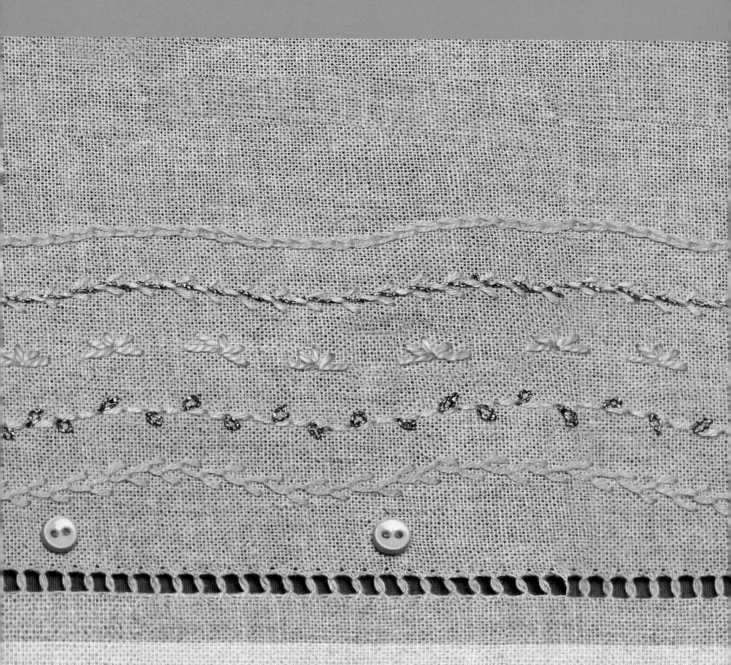

# CREATIVE EMBROIDERY

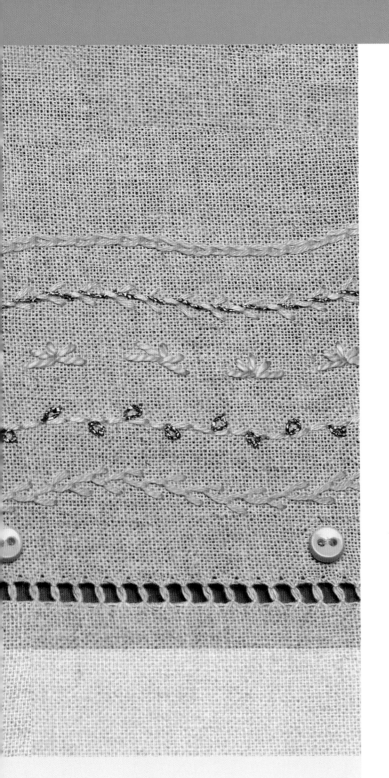

Creative embroidery is a free form of embroidery that does not require counting. It is both easy to learn and fun to stitch. The stitches have soft appeal, as they flow freely across the fabric.

If this is your first venture into needlework, this form of embroidery is an excellent place to start. The stitches in this chapter are easy to learn and the projects work up quickly.

Use a line-drawn pattern, or create bands of stitches, or just sit down and create your own pattern on the fabric. See the ABCs of Needlework (page 8) for basic information on choosing equipment, transferring patterns, and other tips on getting started.

# Fabric

Creative embroidery can be worked on any surface that a needle can slide through. Plain weave fabric with a higher thread count gives a nice crisp finish to a project. All types of premade items can be embellished with embroidery, from kitchen towels to clothing to fabric shoes.

When planning your project, choose a fabric that is suited to the pattern and the finished design. Use a neutral colored fabric to enhance the threads used to stitch the design, or use a colorful fabric with neutral or pastel colored threads. Fabric that has a lot of give or stretch does not work well for this technique. It is difficult to maintain an even tension, resulting in stitches that do not lie flat.

Use a stabilizer with the fabric to give the fabric body. Stabilizers are discussed in the ABCs section of the book (page 23). If you prefer not to use a stabilizer, use two layers of your project fabric. The following fabrics are used most often for this technique.

## COTTONS (PLAIN WEAVE)

Cotton fabrics are available in an array of beautiful, lush solid colors. The batiks make a wonderful background for embroidery. They come in a wide range of colors, along with some that have more than one color tone.

White on white and cream on cream prints or stripes (patterns on the fabric are of like color) give just a hint of texture to the background for embroidering. In the quilting world, this type of fabric is used for the quilt pattern background. I love stitching on this type of white fabric. The threads bring the color to the project.

Muslin—unbleached or bleached white—is a lightweight fabric. It comes in 100 percent cotton or a 50/50 blend. The 100 percent cotton is a good choice for embroidery. Available in different thread counts (a higher thread count works best), it is a nice surface for kitchen towels, aprons, and pillows. Muslin also works well with transfer paper, window tracing, or iron-on pencil.

## SHEER

This transparent fabric is slippery and can be a little difficult to work with. Layer two pieces together to create a little more weight to the fabric. You can choose a darker tone of the same color, or use a contrasting color under the sheer. Adding a piece of stabilizer under the solid fabric would give the two pieces of fabric even more stability. This fabric is beautiful when used by itself or in combination with a piece of solid colored fabric. It is well worth the effort once the project is complete.

# Quick Gift

Need a gift for tomorrow? Pick up a baby bonnet, guest towel, or a blouse—then work your magic with the needle during the evening.

## SILK NOIL

This natural silk has a nubby texture that enhances your stitchery. Wonderful for purses or picture frames, the fabric comes in a wide range of colors. Black or off-white colors are wonderful backgrounds for colorful stitchery

## SHANTUNG

This textured fabric has a silk look. It works especially well for home décor projects.

## FELT

Felt comes in wool blends, bamboo, and 100 percent wool. The wool blends and bamboo are widely available, and the 100 percent wool can be found in specialty shops or online. Felt is easy to use and does not ravel. Projects can quickly be finished by using one of the edging stitches.

## LINEN

Linen fabric found in fabric stores comes in several colors along with a natural color that is sold in the home décor area. The natural color is thinner than linen found in needlework shops. It can be used with a stabilizer. Linen from needlework shops is used for even-weave stitching but can also be used for freeform without counting. The higher the fabric count, the easier it is to work the stitches.

## PAPER

Embroidery stitches can also be worked on all types of paper found in scrapbook and paper stores. Transfer your design to the paper and then place the paper over a computer mouse pad. Using a sewing needle, poke tiny holes through the paper into the pad where you want to place stitches. Then simply stitch the design. Instead of knotting the thread ends, tape them to the back of the paper.

# Thread

The threads discussed in this section are just a few of the many threads that can be used for this technique. Others are available in local needlework shops and on the Internet.

When choosing thread for a project, consider what the project will be used for. Choose a thread that can be washed if the project will require it. Most thread today can be washed by hand, while others will need to be dry-cleaned.

When purchasing over-dyed, hand-dyed, and variegated threads, buy the full quantity the project requires at the same time, and be sure that all of the threads are from the same dye lot; threads from a different dye lot may vary slightly in color. Even silks and stranded cotton could have a slight difference in color, although the difference is not usually noticeable on a project. These threads do not list a dye lot on the package. A very slight difference would only be detectable if stitching a large background with one color. If you are working such a project and find you are running short on thread, stop stitching and purchase the new thread. Then alternate cut strands from each of the skeins of thread to blend the new color with the previous color.

## PEARL COTTON (COTON PERLÉ)

This cotton thread is slightly twisted and is used as a single strand. It has a beautiful sheen with many colors to choose from along with several sizes. Sizes used for creative embroidery are 5, 8, and 12. Size 12 is used for very fine work, and 5 can be used as a laid thread for couching.

## SIX STRAND EMBROIDERY FLOSS

Made with 100 percent cotton, this six-strand embroidery floss thread is available in solid and variegated colors. There is a large range of solid colors to choose from and many of these colors come in a range of shaded tones. Cotton threads are very versatile and easy to use. You will need to watch your tension when stitching with cotton, as there is no stretch or give to the thread.

## LINEN

Linen is a six-strand thread that comes in soft colors that work well for a pastel palette. It is easy to work with, although the strands have slightly coarse texture.

## SATIN AND RAYON

These six-strand threads have a very silky, shiny sheen. They work best for flat, straight stitches or satin stitches but can also be used in place of stranded cotton with careful manipulation. Although they are slippery to work with, these threads are well worth the effort when the end result is viewed. These threads are manmade but contain some natural fiber so they do not fall into the synthetic thread range.

## SYNTHETIC THREAD

These polyester threads are beautiful when stitched. Varieties include tubular threads that have a nice shiny appearance and work well for flat laid stitches to be couched down. There is also a single-strand thread that has a slight twist in the thread with a metallic fleck embedded along the thread. This thread works well for projects where just a little bit of sparkle is desired.

## COTTON HAND-DYED AND OVER-DYED

These threads come in a skein in six-strand embroidery floss and a single-strand thread. They are a joy to work with and are especially appropriate when filling an area. Once a pattern is worked with these threads, there can never be another exactly like it. The dyes create lovely shades of color along the thread. Use the thread as it comes from the skein. Knot the end of the thread that was previously cut before cutting a new length. By using the previous cut to begin stitching, you will match the color range of the thread you just ended.

*(continued)*

## SILK

Silk is available in hand-dyed and solid colors. It comes on a spool as a six- or twelve-stranded thread, a single thread card or skein, and in half skeins. It is an easy thread to work with and its lovely sheen sets it apart from other stranded threads.

## BRAID (METALLIC)

This metallic braid comes on a spool in many sizes. The very fine size 4 braid, fine size 8 braid, and tapestry size 12 braid work best for creative embroidery. The larger size 12 braid is great for using as a thread to couch over or for straight stitches where a touch of metallic is desired. This twisted braid is a dream to stitch with and a great way to add a little sparkle to your project. It is very flexible, which makes it ideal for working curved lines, and it can be used for any type of stitch.

## STRANDED METALLIC

This stranded thread can be used by itself or blended with another thread. It is a bit slippery, so watch your tension.

## MEMORY THREAD

This thread—which is really a flexible copper wire wrapped with a soft fiber—adds a dimensional appearance to a design. It works well on fabric or paper. Memory thread is wonderful for decorative stitches and embellishing. You can use it as a laid stitch to be couched.

When using as a laid stitch, place a couching stitch over the ends to hold the wrapped fiber on the wire in place. When working antennae on the butterfly you can use memory thread. If you want a coil, simply wrap the thread around a large needle. The bendable thread will allow you to secure one end of the length and leave the other end so it is slightly elevated above the fabric.

# Blending Threads

Looking for ways to blend thread for different effects?

- Use one strand of a non-metallic thread with a strand of metallic to create a little glitz. When working the blended stitches, the metallic may not show on every stitch, adding further interest to the area.
- Use one strand of a cotton thread with a strand of over-dyed or hand-dyed to add a touch of additional color to an area. Create a subtle look to an area of stitching by using a light and a dark shade of solid color threads with the same number of strands.

# Stitches

For the best results, work each stitch following the stitch graph numbers and arrows. When stitching, remember that the fabric should lie flat without pulling or wrinkling around the stitches. Refer to the information on tension (page 26).

Embroidery, crewel, and small chenille needles can be used for this technique. A tapestry needle works well to add the whipped or laced part of a stitch. If embellishing with beads, use a size 10 milliner or a short beading needle. For more information on needles, refer to page 10.

Stitches shown in creative embroidery, crewel, and silk ribbon are interchangeable. Combining stitches from the Bead Embroidery section with any of the stitches from these sections will add more interest to the finished work of art. All the stitches in this chapter can be worked on even-weave fabric.

## STRAIGHT

Straight stitches can be used to create motifs and darning patterns and can be worked in any direction. Bring the needle out at the starting point and take the needle and thread across the fabric for the desired stitch length of less than ¾" (1.9 cm). A longer stitch will give the appearance of an untidy loose stitch. This stitch does not conform to curved lines; avoid using it with even a short curved line, as you will lose the curve with a straight stitch.

You can use any type of thread for this stitch.

**Ways to use:** grass, leaves for small flowers, insect antennae, geometric patterns

**Also known as:** stroke stitch or single satin stitch

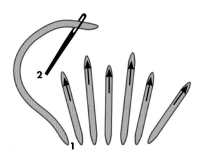

Different length straight stitches

## STEM

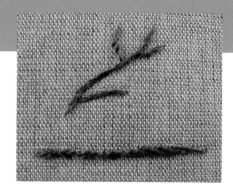

Travel from left to right, covering the pattern line. It is important to keep the thread below the needle, sewing the stitch by sliding the needle in and out of the fabric. The stitches are placed very close together to create the stem effect.

When working a curved line, place the stitches directly on the basted or drawn line. When using stranded thread, be sure that all the threads of each individual stitch are pulled using the same tension to maintain a smooth stitch. Pearl cotton will give this stitch a textured appearance.

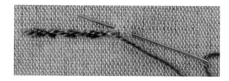

Keeping stitches close together

Vary the stitch length in different areas of a design. Small stitches will give a more delicate look while longer, larger stitches give a bolder look. Example: Use a long stitch for tree trunks, large branches, or house roofs. You can use any type of thread for this stitch.

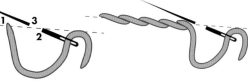

**Ways to use:** branches, flower stems, outlines, filling (leaves, flowers), lettering

**Also known as:** crewel, stalk

## SEED

This filling stitch works up quickly. It is an easy, mindless stitch to use. Work small, straight, even-length stitches. Place them randomly in different directions, without a given pattern. This stitch creates a light, airy effect in the desired shape. To vary the stitch pattern, make stitches of slightly different lengths. Keep the placement random. When using this stitch for filling areas, varying the length creates more charm.

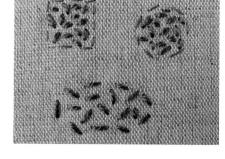

If a shaded effect is desired, use light and dark tones of the same color. For added texture, work some of the stitches in pearl cotton, leaving space between the stitches. Then fill in those areas with stranded floss stitches. You can use any type of thread for this stitch.

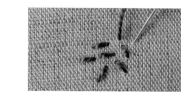

Random seed stitches

**Ways to use:** flower petals, leaves, background, shapes, monogram letters

**Also known as:** seed filling, speckling, rice grain, dot stitch

# Double Seed

To work a double seed stitch, make two stitches the same length, one just above the other, placing the stitches randomly.

## SPLIT

This is a versatile stitch that travels left to right. How you place the split in the stitch will determine how the stitch looks. You can work the stitch so the split comes in the center area, or the split can be placed closer to the end of the stitch. When working the curved areas, a smaller stitch should be used. When working around a curve, take care to place the split in the center area of the stitch between the strands of threads.

The split used as a filling stitch. It can be gradually shaded, or bands of one color in distinct shades can be used to create an attractive effect. For filling in areas, branches, or stems, split the stitch closer to the end of the stitch to give it a smoother look.

To achieve a smooth, even look in each stitch, use strands of a soft twisted thread or stranded thread. Use at least three strands of embroidery floss.

**Ways to use:** curved lines, straight lines, outlines, filling (closely worked rows) of flower petals, leaves, stems, branches, various shapes

**Also known as:** Kensington outline

Needle comes up through previous stitch

## HERRINGBONE

Travel left to right in a straight row. Although this stitch looks difficult, it is easy to work. Work the stitches as evenly and smoothly as possible. The small base horizontal stitches should be the same width, and the long slanted stitches should all be the same length. Use ¼" (6 mm) for the wide area of the stitch and ⅛" (3 mm) for the crossed area. You can use any type of thread for this stitch.

**Ways to use:** borders, bands, filling

**Also known as:** plaited, witch, catch, Mossoul, fishnet, Persian, Russian, Russian cross

Keeping stitches straight

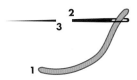
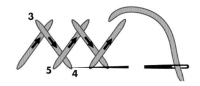

# JAPANESE DARNING

Work rows of the darning stitch using a sewing method. Travel right to left for the first row; then travel left to right for the second row. Continue to alternate the direction for each row. Leave the same amount of space between the stitches on each row and the same amount of space between the rows. You will notice that the second row is offset from the first and third row. This is important because it creates the slant of the vertical stitch that joins the three rows to create the pattern. For more of a slant to the vertical stitch, make the stitches on the offset row shorter. Place vertical stitches between rows 1 and 2. Turn work upside-down to place vertical stitches between rows 2 and 3.

This is a light lacy pattern, allowing the fabric to show through the stitch. Carefully follow the arrows and numbers for the correct travel path. This stitch is easy to work but hard to execute evenly and have the slight slant to the connecting stitches.

You can use any type of thread for this stitch.

**Ways to use:** wide borders, geometric bands, filling

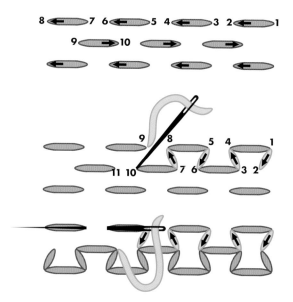

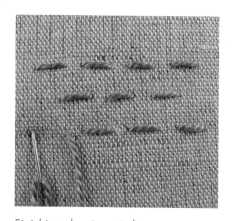

Finishing darning stitches

Starting second row after turning fabric

Completing stitch

# GUILLOCHE

This laced stitch travels left to right. Place sets of three straight stitches evenly spaced across the given area. As you work the laced stitches, adjust the thread so equal amounts of thread form the circles. If the thread is slightly loose, it is easier to form those circles.

If this stitch is being used on items that will be washed, you can couch down the laced thread by placing one couching stitch at the top of each loop of thread. Use a fine thread the same color as the lacing thread. Refer to the couching stitch (page 52).

The beauty of this stitch is being able to use more than one color or kind of thread. The stitch can be monotone or colorful. It's your choice.

For a more decorative stitch, add a French knot (page 63) in the center of each circle and place a border of the stem stitch (page 39) above and below the guilloche stitch.

You can use any type of thread for this stitch.

**Ways to use:** borders, bands

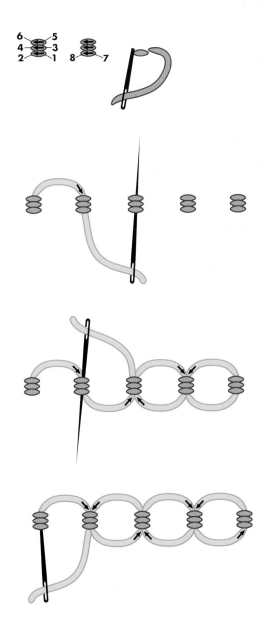

Lacing thread

End lacing

## STRAIGHT TIED HERRINGBONE

The added straight stitch is a simple embellishment for a beautiful stitch. Travel left to right. Work the herringbone stitch first, keeping the stitches as even and smooth as possible. When working the straight tied stitch, leave it a little loose. Use two colors and two types of threads to reveal the beauty of the stitch.

You can use any type of thread for this stitch.

**Ways to use:** borders, bands, filling

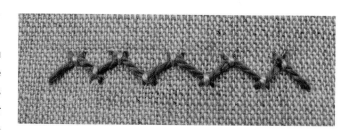

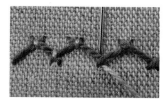

Working straight stitch

## TWISTED SATIN

This is a beautiful stitch that is easy and fun to work. Work this stitch diagonally, horizontally, or circularly, traveling left to right. Twisting the satin stitch gives a textured look to the stitch

Be careful not to pull the straight stitch too snug. For the twisted stitch, keep it slightly loose so the twist in the thread is visible.

Twisted threads work well for this stitch, but any type of thread can be used.

**Ways to use:** borders, motifs, filling, flowers, leaves

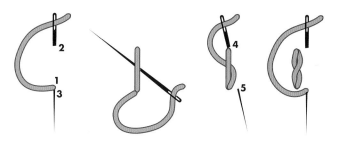

Threading the twist

Ending the stitch

## SATIN

Work this stitch diagonally, vertically, or horizontally, traveling left to right. It should be worked in small areas. If you would like to work a larger area, break it up into smaller sections. Place the stitches close together, keeping them flat as you work the area. When the stitching is completed, the threads should lie side by side, flat against each other. Hold the work at a slant to see if the threads are smooth and even across the top of the area.

Although the satin stitch looks like one of the simplest stitches, it is actually one of the most difficult stitches to work correctly. The challenge lies in keeping the tension correct and the stitches neat along the edges. The tension needs to be spot on, which is very difficult to maintain while working a border area or filling in a leaf or flower petal. While some stitchers do find this stitch easy to work, many are put to the test with this stitch. challenge. It's worth the effort to master because, when worked correctly, the satin stitch is one of the most beautiful stitches.

An alternative method for the satin is to work a split stitch around the area and then thread the stitch through these stitches, as shown in the Crewel chapter (page 81). This method was originally used for shadow work but has become popular to use for other techniques.

You can use any type of thread for this stitch. Silk and pearl cotton (smaller size) threads give the stitch a lovely glow.

**Ways to use:** monogrammed initials, small borders, especially filling flower petals and leaves

# Take a Break

If you are having trouble with a stitch, put the work down and take a break. When you return, you'll likely find that it's much easier.

Filling in a shape

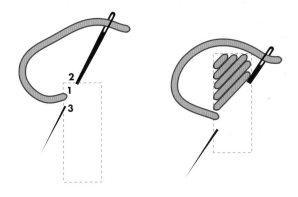

## LONG AND SHORT

This is a variation of a satin stitch with the stitches worked in an uneven pattern. Travel left to right. For the first row of stitches, alternate a short and long stitch across the top of the area to be filled in. For the remaining rows, work long stitches. The example shown is the traditional long and short stitch. To create the traditional look, keep the short stitches the same length; and work all the long stitches the same length throughout the area. For the long and short stitch to be effective, there needs to be a distinct difference between the two sizes of stitches.

After the first row is in place, work down the shape to be filled in. Place the outside stitches first; then fill in the area between these stitches. Work small sections of the area this way as you work down the shape.

For working uneven shapes (flower petals with curves), adjust the size of your stitches to fit the shape. Place some shorter and some longer stitches when working down a flower petal, especially if the petal is long and narrow. You can also vary the length of the stitches to give more texture to the area when using embroidery floss. If worked this way, you will not have the set pattern look of the long and short stitch.

Shading the area is what gives this stitch its beauty. Shade the chosen color light to dark and divide the shape into two or three sections. The traditional way is three sections with three shades. If working more than one flower in a design, use only two colors for one of the flowers, giving that flower a slightly different look.

You can use any type of thread for this stitch. Pearl cotton and embroidery floss work well.

**Ways to use:** filling

**Also known as:** embroidery stitch, shading stitch, plumage stitch

 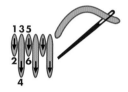

Alternating long and short stitches

Placing long stitches

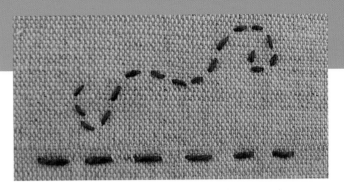

# RUNNING

This simple stitch is worked by sliding the needle in and out of the fabric in a sewing motion. Travel right to left across the area. If using an even-weave fabric, each stitch should be the same length and spaced evenly along the line stitched. If using plain weave fabric, make the stitch on the top side of the fabric longer than the stitch on the back, keeping the stitch length as even as possible. The length of the stitch will depend on the texture of the fabric and the thread being used. For straight-line stitch work, use a stitch length that is ¼" (6 mm) or less. If it is an outline stitch, it should be a small stitch to conform to the line being covered and stitches should fit evenly along the line, as in the swirl shown at right. You can use any type of thread for this stitch.

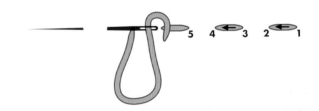

Keeping the stitches straight

**Ways to use:** outlining, borders, foundation for other stitches, bands, straight lines, curved lines

# CHECKERBOARD RUNNING

This running stitch travels right to left, starting with the center row. When working bands of this stitch, work the next set of three rows approximately ¼" (6 mm) above or below the first set.

This stitch is striking when different colors or shades of a color and the same weight of thread are used for each of the rows, as shown above. Experiment with threads to determine the thread weight and color you like best. You can also vary the stitch length on alternating rows to create a slightly different look to the stitch pattern.

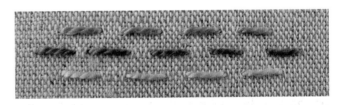

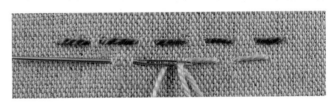

Middle of bottom row

You can use any type of thread for this stitch. Pearl cotton and single-strand cotton work especially well.

**Ways to use:** borders, filling bands of zigzag, wavy, or straight lines

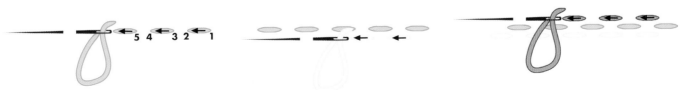

## LACED RUNNING

This is a variation of the running stitch. Work the running stitch, then the laced stitches. Both stitches should be worked right to left, and all rows worked should travel right to left.

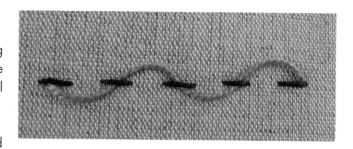

Use a tapestry needle to work the laced thread to avoid picking up material or splitting the running stitch. The same loop height should be used for each laced stitch.

The same weight of thread can be used, or use a slightly heavier thread for the lacing. Use two colors of thread for a richer look. A single row of this stitch makes an effective border around a stitched motif. For borders on towels, several rows of the stitch placed ¼" (6 mm) apart make a very interesting border. If this stitch is being used on items that will be washed, you can couch down the laced thread by placing one couching stitch at the top of each loop of thread. Use a fine thread the same color as the lacing thread. Refer to the couching stitch (page 52).

You can use any type of thread for this stitch.

**Ways to use:** bands, borders, corner bracket borders

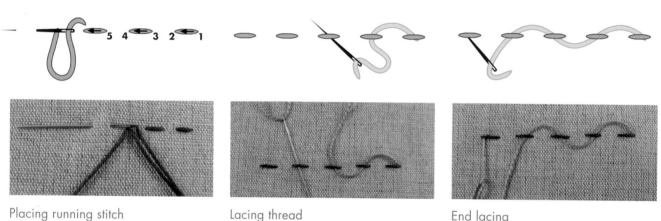

Placing running stitch            Lacing thread            End lacing

# BACKSTITCH

Although the individual stitch goes to the left, the travel path goes from left to right—hence the name backstitch. Begin stitching a stitch length from the starting point. Work the first stitch back over to the starting point and down into the fabric. Each additional stitch is started a stitch length away from the previous stitch. When the area is completed, all stitches are snug against each other. The stitches should resemble a machine-sewn stitch.

This is a very versatile stitch and can be used in decorative ways. It is easiest worked on an even-weave fabric. It is a stunning stitch when worked on plain weave. Do keep the stitches on plain weave as straight and neat as possible, with each stitch the same length. It is best not to use a nubby or fuzzy thread. Twisted threads give the most textured look to the stitch. You can use any type of thread for this stitch.

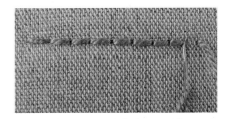

Traveling left to right

**Ways to use:** outline (shown), stems, filling in branches (to add texture), details within motifs, flower petals

**Also known as:** Point De Sable, stitching, darning pattern

# ZIGZAG BACKSTITCH

This stitch travels left to right. Although it is worked in a slightly different way, it has the rhythm of the backstitch. Stitch length can vary according to the fabric or canvas used. Follow the numbers when working the stitch to keep the back threads from showing through on sheer fabrics or open weaves. When using this stitch for a band, use a ¼" (6 mm) stitch length.

For a border stitch, as shown above, turn the fabric upside down after working the first row. Work a second row, placing the bottom tip of the stitches of this row of zigzags snug to the first row to create a diamond. Do not split the thread of the previously placed stitches as you work. After the diamond effect is created, you can add a French knot (page 63) in the center and a row of the split stitch (page 38) ¼" (6 mm) or so from the top and bottom of the diamonds so it becomes a lovely border stitch. You can use any type of thread for this stitch.

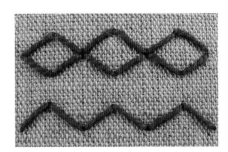

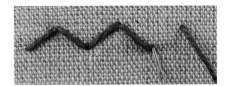

Sharing hole with previous stitch

**Ways to use:** bands, borders, background filling

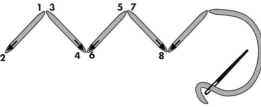

## TRIPLE BACKSTITCH

Work the stitch using a sewing motion, traveling from left to right to work the three straight lines of each completed stitch. Leave a small space between each set of the three stitches. As you work the stitch, if the numbers are followed, a cross-stitch will form on the backside of the fabric. Keep the stitches as straight and even as possible.

This stitch is at its best when worked with a thicker thread like size 5 or 3 pearl cotton. Use size 3 pearl cotton for heavier fabrics.

The border stitch is shown above. When used as a band stitch, work several rows of the stitch pattern close together using a different color for each of the rows. This is a sweet delicate stitch and one of my favorites.

You can use any type of thread for this stitch. I like to use embroidery floss, laying the threads.

**Ways to use:** bands or borders, corner bracket borders

**Also known as:** Hungarian

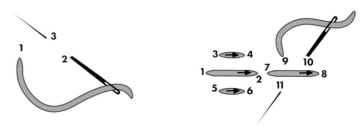

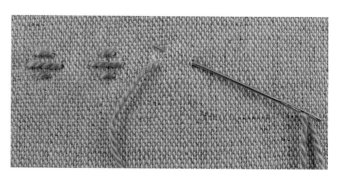

Starting the next stitch

## CLOSED TRIPLE BACKSTITCH

This stitch travels left to right and is worked by sliding the needle in and out of the fabric using a sewing motion. A wider band can be stitched by placing several rows of this stitch one on top of the other. Place a compensating stitch on the alternate rows for even ends. Use a stab-stitch motion to keep stranded floss smooth. If using pearl cotton or other heavy thread, use the sewing motion.

You can use any type of thread for this stitch.

For a nice, smooth effect, use four to six strands of embroidery floss, as shown. Pearl cotton also works well for this stitch. If you would like a shaded or variegated look, use hand-dyed or over-dyed thread.

**Ways to use:** bands, borders, filling

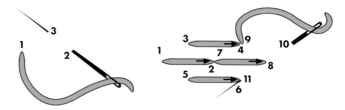

Continuing to next stitch

# PEKINESE

Legend has it that this stitch was worked so small by the Chinese stitchers centuries ago that many of the stitchers went blind. They used this stitch as a filling stitch for their floral work.

This stitch gently flows across the fabric. It is a beautiful stitch, especially when worked in two colors using silk or satin. When using this stitch as a filling for a flower, you can shade each petal by using different shades of the same thread. Keep the stitches small when filling an area.

This stitch travels left to right for the backstitches and the lacing. Work the backstitches first. Use a tapestry needle for the lacing. Be careful not to pierce the fabric or thread as you weave the laced stitches. Keep the laced loops as even as possible.

You can use any type of thread for this stitch.

**Ways to use:** bands, outlines, corner borders, filling

**Also known as:** Chinese, forbidden, blind

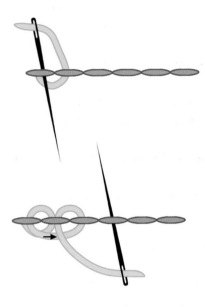

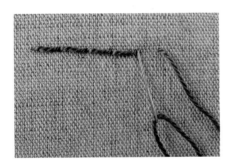

Placing backstitches

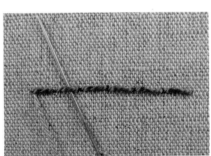

Start lacing

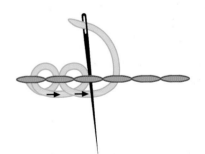

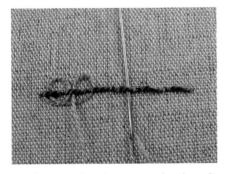

On lower side, skip over a backstitch

End lacing

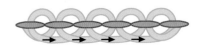

## BLANKET

This stitch travels left to right. When working on a plain weave fabric, keep the vertical stitches straight and the same height, and place the horizontal stitches the same distance apart. Keep the bottom loop of the thread pulled at the same tension. The stitch height is determined by how the stitch is used. Decorative stitches can be slightly longer or shorter, as shown above. If using the stitch to close two pieces of fabric or felt to create a pillow, a smaller stitch length will be necessary.

Set your imagination loose when working this stitch. Use different heights to form a peak or rounded look to the stitch. Or simply place three short stitches together before repeating the pattern. On a piece of paper draw variations of the stitch. It's fun to play around with this stitch.

You can use any type of thread for this stitch. Pearl cotton and single-strand threads work best.

**Ways to use:** edgings, filling for flowers and leaves, bands, outlines

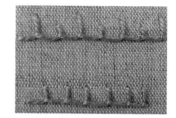
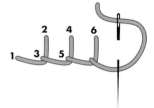
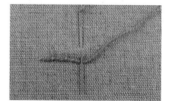
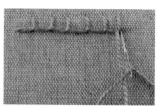

Keeping thread under needle    Ending the row

## Tip

If you find working the overlapping, up and down, or closed blanket stitch difficult, learn the blanket stitch first. This will give you the rhythm of the stitch, making the others easier.

## OVERLAPPING BLANKET

Work one row of the blanket stitch, traveling left to right. Then turn the fabric upside down to work the second row, going left to right. Place the second row of stitches between the stitches of the first row. For the beginning horizontal part of the stitch of the first row and the ending horizontal stitch of the second row, make a shorter stitch to give the appearance of a closed stitch. The stitched example shows two ways to begin and end this stitch when using it as a border stitch: two short stitches on one side and one long stitch on the other.

You can use any type of thread for this stitch. Pearl cotton and single-strand threads give this stitch a nice look.

**Ways to use:** borders, edgings, decorative stitches on clothing, straight or curved lines

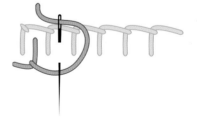

Second row with fabric turned

## UP AND DOWN BLANKET

This stitch travels left to right. Make the vertical part of the stitch slightly longer than a normal blanket stitch.

For some stitchers this stitch looks complicated. Yet once you learn the rhythm of the stitch, you will find it is easy to work. The second vertical stitch adds beauty to the blanket stitch. Just remember not to pull too tightly when making the horizontal part of the stitch, because the second vertical stitch needs to slip down behind it.

This beautiful stitch can be worked in a circle to create a flower or motif.

You can use any type of thread for this stitch.

Satin thread gives this stitch a stunning smooth raised look when it is used as an edging. Pearl cotton adds texture.

**Ways to use:** borders, bands, edgings, filling, decorative hems

**Also known as:** double blanket

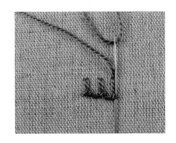
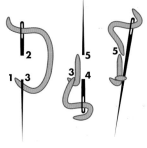

Sliding needle under stitch

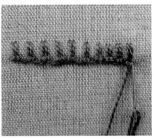
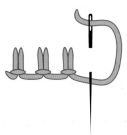

Ending the row

## CLOSED BLANKET

This stitch, which travels left to right, is worked similarly to the blanket stitch. The vertical stitches of each set of stitches share a hole without piercing the thread of the first stitch placed. The right stitch is placed at a slight angel to connect over to the first vertical stitch in each stitch. As you work the stitch, always keep the thread under the needle on the downward stitch. Keep the stitches the same distance apart as you work across the area.

You can use any type of thread for this stitch.

Pearl cotton and single-strand threads work well for this stitch.

**Ways to use:** decorative hems, borders, bands, edgings

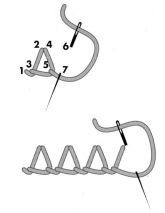

Slant the needle to create the closed stitch

## COUCHING

This stitch travels left to right around the area to be couched. A couching stitch is a straight stitch placed over the laid thread or threads to be secured to the fabric. If possible when working the couching stitch, come up and go down in the same hole or area under the laid thread.

Metallic braids add a touch of sparkle to the couching. If the couching thread is not used for a decorative purpose but to simply hold the thread or braid in place, use the same color of thread or braid for the couching stitches.

To create a fancy couching effect for decorative braids, use a cross-stitch (page 81), zigzag back (page 47), or lazy daisy (page 58) to hold the braid in place.

Pearl cotton and single-strand threads work best.

**Ways to use:** decorative swirls, filling shapes, secure lacing threads and decorative braids

**Also known as:** basic couching, plain couching

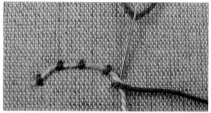

Couching over laid thread

## FLY

This is a simple but effective stitch. It can be worked in a vertical, horizontal, circular, or a curved direction. Travel top to bottom.

It's great to use to fill in a leaf shape. The tie-down stitch can be long or short in length depending on how you are using the stitch. It can be worked as a wide or narrow stitch giving it a V or Y shape.

You can use any type of thread for this stitch.

**Ways to use:** bud and flower sepals, filling, borders, leaf veins, grass

**Also known as:** tied, Y, open loop

Working the loop

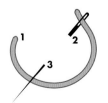

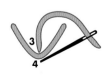

# INTERLACED FLY

This stitch can travel in a vertical, horizontal, circular, or curved direction. Work the stitch top to bottom.

Slide the lacing up from the back at the beginning of the tied stitch, keeping it as close to the thread as possible without disrupting the placed fly stitch. The lacing stitch does not pierce the fabric. It is best to use a tapestry needle so you do not pierce the other stitches.

For best effect, use a different color and type of thread to work the lacing. This stitch works well in combination with other stitches when working a band pattern. Two rows of the interlaced fly look nice worked across a towel. Place the rows very close together so the tips of the V part of the stitch almost touch. For a different look, work the rows going in different directions from each other to give added interest to the band.

You can use any type of thread for this stitch. Metallic braid, pearl cotton, or hand-dyed single-strand thread work well for the lacing of this stitch.

**Ways to use:** bands, borders, pillow edging, appliqué stitch

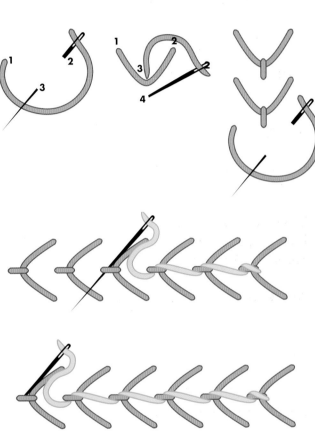

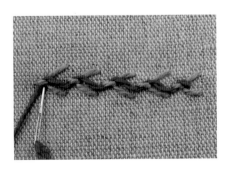

Stitching the fly

Lacing thread

End lacing

## FISHBONE

Work this stitch from the top to bottom for a leaf or from left to right for bands or borders. This stitch conforms to the shape it is filling and has a slight slant to the straight stitches. When the stitches are in place, the center area has a slight V shape similar to the fly. When working these slanted stitches, be sure that they cross over each other in the center area. If you do not cross the stitches, the fabric will show. A basted center line down the middle of the shape to be filled, makes placing the crossed stitches much easier. You can place the stitches close together, as shown, or leave a small space between the stitches, as shown in the Crewel chapter (page 89). Notice the straight compensating stitch at the tip of the leaf to give the leaf a more defined shape. For a shaded fishbone, use different shades of the same thread color as you work the shape. For a straight band across a towel or edge of a pillow, baste the center line to help with the crossing of the stitches. For best results, watch the tension on this stitch.

You can use any type of thread for this stitch. Pearl cotton or stranded threads work especially well.

**Ways to use:** filling, bands, leaves, feathers

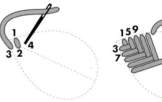

Placing stitch over center base line

## FERN

This is a fun stitch to use! You can travel in any direction, working the stitch from top to bottom. The straight stitches can be worked as a single unit or in a length of stitches. If you find the sewing method uncomfortable to find the rhythm of the stitch, use the stab method. The length of the stitches can be worked evenly or as required for the area. When working around a tight curve, as shown, the side diagonal stitches should be worked at slightly less of an angle. In some places, the center straight stitch will need to be slightly shorter to fit within the area.

You can use any type of thread for this stitch.

**Ways to use:** borders, filling, foliage, motifs, scrolling background patterns, veins of leaves

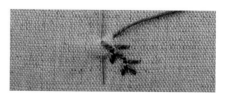

Working side stitch

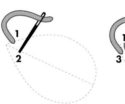

# LEAF

Work this stitch from the bottom upward. If working a band or border, travel left to right. This stitch conforms to the shape it is filling and has a slight slant to the straight stitches. It is worked similarly to the fishbone stitch.

This is a beautiful flat leaf stitch to use when you would like to have a leaf that appears translucent. When working this stitch, it is important to leave space enough between the stitches. Each stitch has a slant and the stitches cross over each other in the center. The hardest part of working this stitch is being careful to crisscross the thread over far enough in the center area. For best results, practice this stitch on a scrap of fabric to learn the rhythm of the stitch in the center area.

To use as a border stitch on plain fabric, you many want to baste three lines parallel to each other and spaced an equal distance apart. Work the stitches between the lines in the same manner as shown for the leaf.

You can use any type of thread for this stitch. Pearl cotton or hand-dyed single-strand threads give a smooth look to the stitch.

**Ways to use:** filling, leaf shapes, borders

**Also known as:** fir

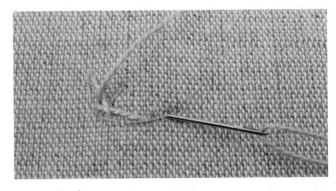

Starting leaf

Keeping crossover consistent

Ending leaf

# FEATHER

There are many feather stitches with this stitch as their foundation. Travel in a vertical, horizontal, circular, or curved direction, working top to bottom. It is important to keep both sides even in height. Keep the stitch size the same or vary the size, depending on the desired look. The rhythm of this stitch works well with the sewing method as you place the stitches on alternate sides. Use your finger to hold the thread in place while completing the stitch.

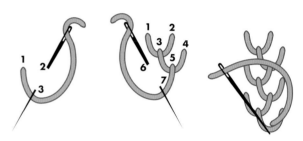

You can use any type of thread for this stitch.

**Ways to use:** light filling, borders, outlines, circular motifs, grass, ferns, leaves, embellishment on clothing, as an appliqué stitch, bird feathers

**Also known as:** single coral, briar, plumage

Working curved shape

# FEATHERED CHAIN

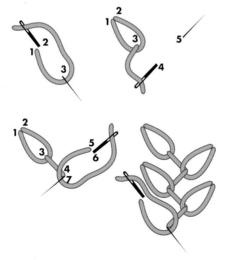

This stitch is worked in a zigzag motion starting on the left side and working left to right and top to bottom. This stitch can be tricky to work until you find the rhythm; easiest to work in a sewing motion. Use your finger to hold the thread in place while completing the stitch. If you have difficulty working it as a freehand stitch, baste two parallel lines to work the stitch between.

You can use any type of thread for this stitch. Pearl cotton or single-strand twisted work especially well.

**Ways to use:** bands, border, vines, appliqués

**Also known as:** chained feather

Working chain

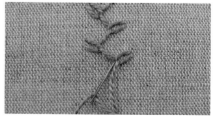

Ending chain

# CHEVRON

If you have not worked this stitch before, use a small scrap of fabric and practice the stitch until you are comfortable with the rhythm.

This stitch can be worked at different heights. The thickness of the thread will determine the height. The single chevron row above was worked with size 5 pearl cotton; the filling rows of chevron were worked with size 8 pearl cotton.

On a plain weave fabric, basting horizontal lines across the fabric area to be stitched will be helpful in keeping the stitches straight. Work this stitch from left to right, keeping the horizontal and slanted stitches as even in length as possible. Notice that the first and second horizontal stitches are worked differently. The first horizontal stitch of the pattern has one slanted stitch and the second horizontal stitch has two slanted stitches. When you take the second small stitch from 6 to 7, you are sharing a hole with 4. On the illustration it will say 4/7. Follow the numbers and arrows carefully.

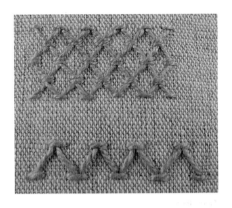

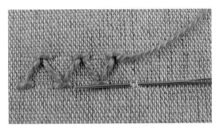

Starting horizontal portion of stitch

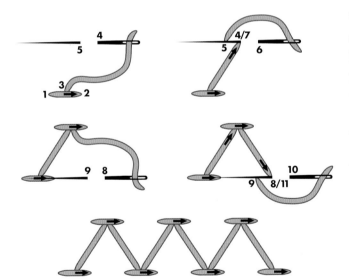

When working this stitch as a filling stitch, baste three straight horizontal lines across the area to be filled in. Place the lines apart vertically for the height of the stitch you are planning to work. Once you have those rows in place, it will be easier to work the other rows and you may find it unnecessary to baste more rows. The rhythm of the stitch will guide you in placing the stitches.

This is an intriguing stitch, especially when worked with a twisted thread like pearl cotton or a satin thread. You can use any type of thread for this stitch.

**Ways to use:** borders, bands, filling

## LAZY DAISY

This stitch can be worked in any direction. It is worked like a chain stitch and is anchored with a small vertical tie-down stitch. For a neater stitch, keep the ends of the loop together where they meet at the top. When working a flower petal, use the same hole for the two ends of the loop. How you work this stitch will depend on the look you want to achieve. You'll need to use your finger to hold the left side of the loop in place while you complete the stitch. Add a straight stitch in the middle of the loop for a filled lazy daisy.

This versatile stitch can be used alone or grouped together. You can use any type of thread for this stitch.

**Ways to use:** filling, flower petals, buds, leaves, bands

**Also known as:** detached chain, tail chain, knotted knot, daisy, loop, picot, tied loop

Working loop          Filling in loop

## LONG-TAILED DAISY

This stitch can be worked in any direction. It is worked the same as the lazy daisy. Simply work the daisy and add a long stitch for the tail. It can be worked alone or in a circle, with the tails all coming to the middle of the area. For a variation, add a straight stitch or a French knot in the center of the loop.

You can use any type of thread for this stitch. Twisted or single-strand threads show off the beauty of this stitch.

**Ways to use:** single flower stems, circular motifs, filling

Stitching the long tail

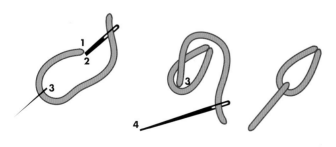

## CHAIN

Travel in any direction, working top to bottom. Keep the ends of the loop even or share the same hole. It is worked similarly to the lazy daisy. If you are working the stitch correctly, only backstitches should be visible on the back. Use your finger to hold the thread in place while completing the stitch. The stitch should lie flat against the fabric, and the fabric should not pucker.

When using this stitch as a filling stitch for flowers or leaves, start each row at the tip of the leaf or petal, working all the rows in this manner. For border stitches, work different size chains together. Work a short stitch, a long stitch, and repeat pattern. This variation is shown. You can also vary the stitch by working a long stitch and two short stitches; then repeat pattern. You can use any type of thread for this stitch.

**Ways to use:** borders, curved motifs, circular shapes, filling, outlines

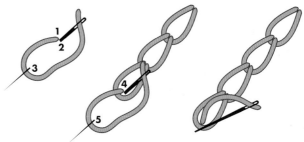

Working chain      Ending chain

**Also known as:** tambour, point de chainette

## LACED CHAIN

Travel in any direction. Work the chain stitch first; then place the lacing. Slide the lacing up from the back on the right at the beginning stitch, keeping it as close to the thread as possible without disrupting the chain stitch. Use a tapestry needle for lacing.

You can use any type of thread for the chain stitch. Metallic braid and pearl cotton work especially well for lacing. This stitch is most effective if two colors are used.

**Ways to use:** bands, outlines, clothing, edging on pillows, borders

Lacing chain

End lacing

## BACKSTITCHED CHAIN

Travel in any direction, working top to bottom. Keep the ends of the loop even or share the same hole. Work the chain stitch first; then place the backstitches. Use your finger to hold the thread in place while completing the stitch. The backstitches inside the chain can be worked with small stitches, as shown, or with stitches that touch each other and fill the area. This stitch is most effective if two colors and two textures of thread are used.

You can use any type of thread for the chain stitch. Metallic braid and pearl cotton work especially well for backstitches.

**Ways to use:** bands, outlines, clothing

Working chain

Working backstitch

## CABLE CHAIN

This is a variation of the chain stitch. It is a beautiful stitch with a small knot at the end of each loop. Travel in any direction, working top to bottom.

When the thread is wrapped around the needle, it should form an S. Use your finger to hold the thread in place while completing the knot portion of the stitch. Watch the tension when working the knot. It is better to have the knot a fraction too loose than too snug.

You can use any type of thread for this stitch.

**Ways to use:** embellishing clothing, filling, borders, bands, outlining leaves and motifs

**Also known as:** cable, knotted cable

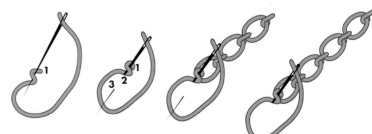

Completing knot and starting next loop

Ending stitch with knot

## OPEN CHAIN

Travel in any direction, working top to bottom. This stitch is worked the same as the chain stitch only the ends of the loop remain open. Use your finger to hold the thread in place while completing the stitch. As you work the loops, watch your tension. It is easy to pull them too snug. Use your finger to widen the loop to work the right side of the loop. Vary the width and length of the stitch, as desired. If you have difficulty working this stitch freehand, you can baste lines to work within.

You can use any type of thread for this stitch.

**Ways to use:** couching thread for ribbons or cords, outlines, bands, borders

**Also known as:** Roman chain, square chain, ladder

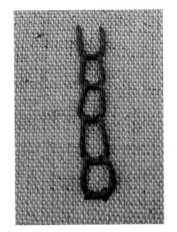

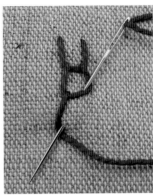

Working left side of chain

## SPINE

This is a quick and easy decorative version of the chain stitch. Travel in any direction, working top to bottom.

Keep the stitch flat against the fabric. When you work the angled spine, work it slightly above the bottom of the chain stitch. The next chain stitch will be placed below the straight spine stitch.

The straight spine part of the stitch can be worked on every other chain stitch, as shown above, or worked all on one side or both sides.

You can use any type of thread for this stitch.

**Ways to use:** borders, outline, filling

Working straight spine

   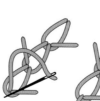 

# ROSETTE CHAIN

This stitch can be worked in a circle or straight line, traveling right to left. The rosette is beautiful on cuffs and collars of clothing. However, some stitchers feel it is too loose a knot to use this way. If you would like to use it for clothing embellishment, place a tack stitch with matching sewing thread to hold the bottom loop of the stitch. It is worth the extra time it takes to use it as an embellishment.

This stitch needs to be worked gently and not pulled too snug. Use your thumb to hold the thread in place, and follow the numbers and arrows. Be careful that the thread loops correctly for the first part of the stitch where you slide the needle and thread carefully under the thread next to where the stitch was started. Keep the top and bottom threads the same height. Rosettes can be placed close together, as shown above, or spaced out.

Pearl cotton, twisted threads, and metallic braids show the stunning detail of the stitch.

**Ways to use:** embellishment on collar and cuffs, flower petals, borders, bands, edging for circles

**Also known as:** bead edging stitch

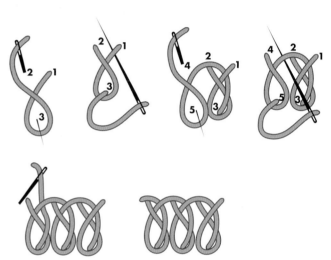

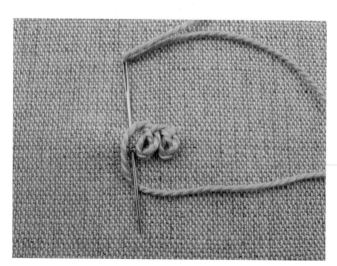

Starting new rosette

Ending rosette

THE COMPLETE PHOTO GUIDE TO NEEDLEWORK

# FRENCH KNOT

Place knot where desired. The size of thread and number of wraps will determine the knot size produced. Use one, two, or three wraps depending on your desired knot size. Once the thread is wrapped on the needle, it is important to keep the needle straight and the thread taut as it enters the fabric. Use your other hand to hold the thread taut. Practice this stitch on a scrap of fabric using a thick thread. When you master the knot this way, you can use any type of thread in your projects. For best results, work this stitch in a hoop or frame.

To create a sloppy knot, leave the wrapped thread loose as you pull it down into the fabric. You can change the size of the knot by adjusting the tension used when wrapping this knot. It is used for flower buds, centers of larger flowers, and to fill in areas. You can mix the two types of knots when filling areas to add texture. The lower right knot in the group of three is a sloppy knot.

You can use any type of thread for this stitch. French knots made with rayon or other synthetic threads are beautiful. Although this slippery thread is a little more difficult to use, the results are well worth the effort!

**Ways to use:** flower centers, filling, single row of knots spaced for outline of leaves or shapes

**Also known as:** French dot, knotted, twisted knot, wound

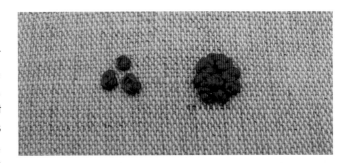

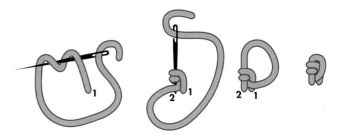

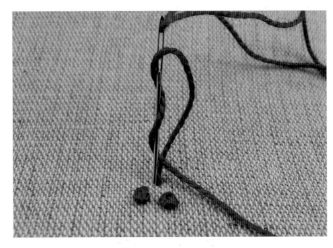

Starting needle into fabric

Keeping thread taunt

Pulling thread into fabric

## DOUBLE KNOT

This stitch works well on curved lines. Travel left to right, leaving ¼" (6 mm) between the knots. When taking the needle between the thread at 5, do not pierce the previously placed thread. Use the thumb of your other hand to hold the bottom of the knot as you gently pull the thread into place. To start the next knot, use the end of the long thread and start the knot at 2. Be sure to have the thread in the correct place for 4 and 5. To end this stitch, you can end it beside the knot or add the next long stitch.

You can use any type of thread for this stitch. Using a thick thread like pearl cotton will create a bold effect.

**Ways to use:** bands, outlines, curved lines, borders, around motifs

**Also known as:** Palestrina, tied coral, old English, Smyrna

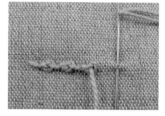
Starting knot

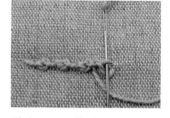
Sliding needle between threads to complete knot

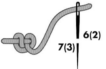 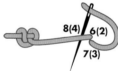 

## SCROLL

This is one of the easiest knots to work and the most beautiful with its gentle wave effect. Travel left to right, spacing the knots evenly either close together or at a distance.

After each knot is worked, reposition the thread so it surrounds the needle. A smaller circle works the best. To form the knot, pull gently downward on the thread until the knot forms. Resist pulling too snug or the knot will lose its beauty.

For added interest when using as a border or band stitch, work three lines of this stitch, alternating the knots so they fall in different places on the worked lines. You can use any type of thread for this stitch. Twisted or single-strand threads work especially well.

**Ways to use:** outlines, borders, bands, waves, filling

**Also known as:** single-knotted line

Forming knot

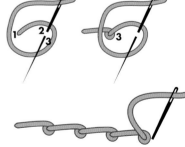

## PISTIL

This is an easy stitch to work and can be worked in any direction. It is a variation of a French knot with an added stem. This stitch is usually used in crewel work but it is too pretty to be limited to that technique.

When working this stitch, you can use any length of stem that works for the application. When using on a curved line, as you take the needle down into the fabric have the thread for the stem slightly loose to conform to the area. For a straight pistil, keep the stem thread and wrapped thread taut as it enters the fabric.

You can use any type of thread for this stitch. Twisted threads give a crisp look to the stitch.

**Ways to use:** flower stamens, flower petals, fillers

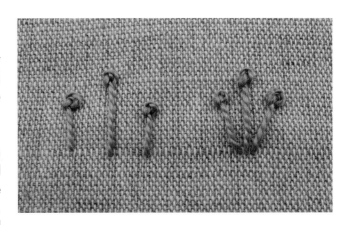

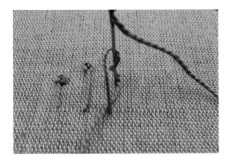

Starting needle into fabric

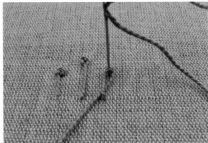

Keeping thread taunt

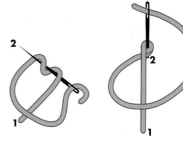

Pulling thread into fabric

# Going Solo

Work a single double knot in place of a French knot.

# Indigo Jacket

This simple design adds color to the deep indigo blue of the jacket. The embroidery embellishment gives the jacket a touch of elegance, making it perfect for a day at the office or an evening out. This pattern can be used as a border for pillowcases, on a small pillow, or on any garment. Increase the pattern for larger areas.

## YOU WILL NEED

• jacket, blouse, or vest

• hand-dyed single-strand cotton: guacamole

• six-strand embroidery floss: avocado green, very light topaz, medium electric blue

• embroidery or crewel needle

## STITCHES USED

• chain

• French knot

• lazy daisy

• stem

• straight

Design pattern (actual size)

## Stitching Information

**1** Transfer the design, using the tissue tracing method (page 22). Center and baste the pattern through the tissue paper onto the label of the jacket.

**2** Use one strand of the guacamole single-strand cotton and the stem stitch to work the flower stem.

**3** Use three strands of the avocado green embroidery floss and the straight stitch to work the flower leaves on the stem.

**4** Use two strands of the blue embroidery floss and the chain stitch to work the four-petal flowers.

**5** Use one strand of the topaz embroidery floss and the French knot to work the three knots in the center of each flower. Wrap the thread around the needle three times instead of the usual two times.

**6** Use four strands of the blue embroidery floss and the lazy daisy to work the bud flowers.

# Extra Touch

For added embellishment on the jacket, embroider a section of the pattern on the opposite side on the collar, above the lapel area. Or, work one bud, stem, and leaf under the pocket opening.

# Azalea Blaze Pillow

Sunshine yellow brings a blaze of color to any room with this cheerful design. Customize the flower colors to fit your décor. You can increase or decrease the pattern size to fit your pillow. A purchased pillow that includes a pillow sham makes finishing a snap.

## YOU WILL NEED

- 17½" x 13½" (44.5 x 34.3 cm) premade pillow with a sham cover

- 13" x 13" (33.0 x 33.0 cm) light blue batik fabric (adjust the fabric size if using hoop or frame), finished size 9" x 7" (22.9 x 17.8 cm)

- nonfusible stabilizer cut to size of fabric

- six-strand embroidery floss: lemon, light lemon, light avocado green, topaz, royal blue, very dark parrot green, medium parrot green, and bright canary

- stranded satin: ultralight avocado green

- pearl cotton, size 8: medium delft blue

- embroidery or crewel needle

## STITCHES USED

- blanket

- chain

- French knot

- lazy daisy

- long and short

- pistil

- stem

Design pattern (actual size)

## Stitching Information

**1** Transfer the design using nonfusible transfer method (page 23). Do not trace the small dots or stamens on the pattern. These will be worked freehand.

**2** Use three strands of the very dark parrot green embroidery floss and the chain stitch to work the flower stem, stopping at the five-petal flower and two sepals.

**3** Use three strands of the medium parrot green embroidery floss and the chain stitch to work the two sepals.

**4** Use two strands of the avocado green stranded satin and the stem stitch to work the stem and the short branches of the vine that wrap around the flower stem. Place two straight stitches at the tip of each branch.

**5** Use three strands of the medium parrot green embroidery floss and the blanket stitch to work the leaves on the flower stem. Start the blanket stitch at the tip of the leaf and work the straight horizontal part of the stitch over to the center vein. Keep stitches close together to cover the material.

**6** Use three strands of embroidery floss for the flowers and two strands for the bud. Work the long and short stitch shading as follows: Three-petal flower, use light lemon and lemon. Five-petal flower, use light lemon, lemon, and bright canary. Bud, use light lemon, lemon, and bright canary. Start with the lightest color at the flower tips and work toward the center of the flower. Refer to the photograph for shading on the flowers and bud.

**7** Use two strands of the topaz embroidery floss and the pistil stitch to work the stamens on the flowers.

**8** Use two strands of the light avocado green embroidery floss and the French knot stitch to work the base of the flowers on the vine.

**9** Use four strands of the royal blue embroidery floss and the lazy daisy stitch to work the vine flowers.

### Finishing

**10** Trim fabric to 9" x 7" (22.9 x 17.8 cm), following the grainlines as closely as possible. Place in the center of sham, and pin in place.

**11** Leave the edges of the fabric raw; gently remove any loose threads on fabric edges. Use the blue pearl cotton and the feather stitch to attach the fabric to the pillow.

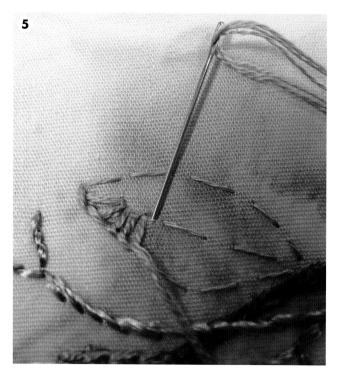

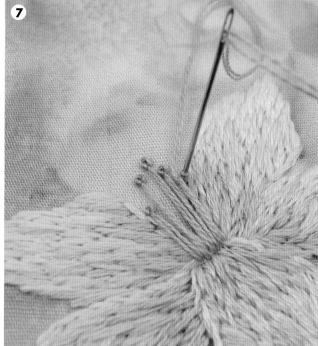

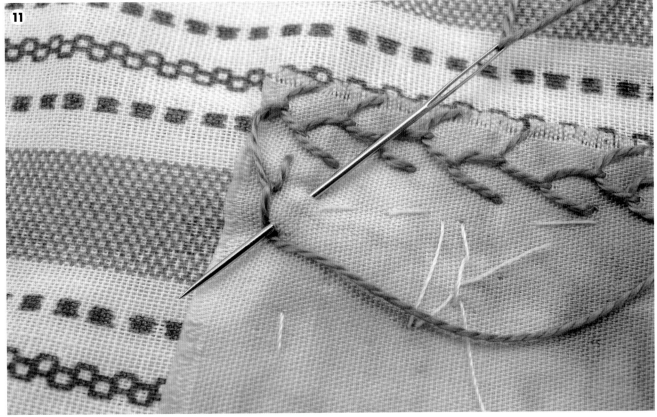

# CREWEL

Crewel is the sister of creative embroidery. The word "crewel" is derived from an old Welsh word meaning wool. Even in this century, crewel projects must include a wool thread, wool-blended threads, or wool yarn to be termed crewel.

The traditional crewel technique was and is worked with wool thread or Persian yarn on 100 percent linen twill. This very heavy fabric has a distinctive look with a diagonal pattern weave on both sides of the fabric.

# Fabric

The wide range of available fabrics has encouraged stitchers to use fabrics other than linen twill, making this a fun technique to stitch. Keep in mind that projects containing wool need to be dry-cleaned. These are some of the fabrics that work well for crewel work, although many other types of fabric can be used for this technique. When working with wool or wool-blend threads on lighter weight fabric, you'll need to use a stabilizer. Use either a nonfusible or fusible fleece. For the fusible, be sure the fabric can withstand the heat of the iron to fuse it in place. If you prefer not to use a stabilizer, use two pieces of the fabric and baste them together.

# Choosing Colors

When using a bright or colorful fabric for crewel, use soft, lighter tones for the threads and yarn.

## LINEN TWILL

Linen twill is not found in fabric stores but can be purchased online. It was used to cover furniture and became popular to use for crewel. Hundreds of years ago, stitchers hand-embellished yards of fabric with crewel work to cover furniture. In the early to mid-twentieth century, this was still popular among some crewel enthusiasts.

## LINEN

Even-weave linens from needlework shops can be used for crewel. The higher count linens work best for this technique. Loosely woven linens (gaps between threads) do not work well. The stitches will slide under the threads. Linen found in the home décor area of a fabric store can be used. It is thin and can be used with fusible fleece to stabilize. It works best for small projects like ornaments. Glasgow linen is a slightly heavier linen. It works well with wool or blends.

## UPHOLSTERY OR DRAPERY WEIGHT

There are stunning fabrics to be found in the home décor area of large fabric stores. I recently found a herringbone weave for upholstery that I am looking forward to using. Patterned, striped, textured, and silky fabrics work well for this technique. The type of fabric you choose to use will depend on the design and threads being used.

## DUPIONI

This interesting silk has a tight weave with irregular crosswise slubbed yarns that form ribs across the fabric. It is a light- to medium-weight fabric with a rough texture and dull sheen. It comes in natural or bleached white as well as bright dyed colors. This is a favorite choice for many crewel stitchers. The natural colored silk is beautiful when stitched using wool, silk, and cotton threads. The textures of the fabric and threads give the design an added elegance.

## CORDUROY

This fabric comes with a wide wale and fine wale. The wale gives the fabric a ribbed look that can add interest to the stitching. Choose the size wale that fits with the design you are stitching. A smaller detailed design would work better on a fine wale. For the wide wale, Persian yarn and pearl cottons work well. This is a seasonal fabric that is usually found in fabric stores in the fall.

## FELT

Felt is a great surface to use. Wool, wool blends, or bamboo thread all work well. Use a stabilizer to give the felt more body. This fabric does not ravel and the projects work up quickly. Edging stitches can be used for finishing the outside edges of the projects.

## SHANTUNG

This shiny fabric has crosswise ribs and slubs, giving character and texture to the fabric. Shantung has a fine texture and is woven from cultivated silk. There is also a synthetic fabric that looks like shantung. It is hard to tell the difference between the two. The synthetic is a slightly lighter fabric. Both types work but need to be stabilized.

## QUILTING COTTON

Cotton works well for crewel projects. This fabric comes in wonderful colors. Kona cotton is a little thicker than other brands on the market, making it a favorite. Do use a stabilizer with cotton.

## HAND OVER-DYED WOOL

This fabric comes in stunning over-dyed colors with the shades of color flowing over the wool fabric. Wool fabric with wool thread mixed with silks and single-strand cotton give an interesting textured look to any design. Wool does not ravel and can be finished with edging stitches.

# Thread

Today it is popular to use wool, wool-blended threads, and Persian yarns combined with other threads including metallics and silks. Wool blends and 100 percent wool single-strand thread are soft threads. Both of these threads are easy to work with. These types of threads are making it possible to stitch on silks and loosely woven fabrics, giving this technique a softer look. Using these combinations of threads gives the project a unique texture not found in other techniques. When stitching with wool or wool-blend yarns, leave a little more space between stitches than when you're working with a finer thread. You want the thread or wool to lie flat and smooth against the fabric.

Dye lots vary in color. If using over-dyed or hand-dyed thread, purchase all the thread needed for a project at one time. Additional information about some of the threads discussed in this section can be found in both the Creative Embroidery (page 34) and Cross-Stitch (page 191) sections. The threads discussed here are just a few of the many possibilities for this technique. Play around with all types of threads to see what you like to work with best. These are a few of the most common choices for crewel.

## CREWEL WOOL

This 100 percent wool yarn is single-strand soft wool. It is two strands twisted together to create one strand of wool and should not be separated. To work most crewel stitches, you will need to join several strands of this wool. The number of strands used depends on how thick a stitch you want for the area you are filling. This wool comes in a wide range of colors.

## PERSIAN YARN

This 100 percent virgin wool yarn is a three-ply yarn. You will need to separate the strands before stitching. It can be purchased in hanks, skeins, or by the pound. Some needlework shops also sell it by the three-ply strand. It comes in 230 shaded colors. Stitching with this yarn creates a slightly fuzzy appearance, adding an interesting texture to the stitched area.

## WOOL BLENDS

These blends come in single strand or three ply in fiber blends of wool/acrylic and wool/silk. The single-strand wool/silk blend is very easy to work with and seems to glide in and out of the fabric effortlessly.

## COTTON HAND-DYED AND OVER-DYED

These threads come in six-strand embroidery floss and a single-strand skein. The texture of the single strand works well for flower petals and leaves. The stranded works well for French knots, chain, or feather stitches. For more information on hand-dyed single-strand thread, refer to the Needlepoint chapter (page 218).

## SIX-STRAND EMBROIDERY FLOSS

This thread can be used for lacing stitches, French knots, and feather stitches.

## HAND OVER-DYED STRANDED COTTON

This is a six-strand cotton that can be used for couching, lacing stitches, French knots, and feather stitches. This thread has a soft blending of color that runs along the thread. It can add a touch of shading when working shapes or filling in areas.

*(continued)*

## TWISTED HAND-DYED

This three-ply pima cotton comes in many variegated colors. One strand can be used for crewel work. The three-ply strand (do not separate) can be used as a laid thread to couch over.

## SPECIALTY THREAD

This single-strand polyester with metallic flecks along the thread comes in many colors. It is easy to work with and can be used on fabric that is not a tightly woven. It works well on linen and silks.

## SILK

Silk comes in hand-dyed and solid colors, and is easy to stitch with. It is available on a spool in a six- or twelve-stranded thread, a single-thread card or skein, and in half skeins. It has a soft sheen, adding beauty to a design.

Silk also comes with metallic flecks scattered along the thread to give just a touch of bling to the stitches. This silk has a look of its own and is a very soft thread. The added metallic is a thread that is woven into the twisted strands. To see how it looks stitched, check out the fedora hat band project on page 106.

## BRAID (METALLIC)

This is a single-strand twisted braid. It should not be separated. It comes on a spool in many sizes. Very fine size 4 braid, fine size 8 braid, and tapestry size 12 braid—all of these can be used for this technique.

# No-no

Regular knitting yarns will not work for stitching crewel or needlepoint. Such yarn is stretchy and does not allow you to maintain the correct tension. The friction of the stitching motion will break down the fiber before the area is completed.

# Stitches

This technique includes a few nontraditional stitches. The chains and feather stitches are used mainly for creative embroidery or silk ribbon. They add charm to the crewel work and look simply beautiful when stitched in wool and wool blends.

Chenille or crewel needles work well. When stitching with 100 percent wool, wool blends, or Persian yarn, use a needle with a larger eye. A tapestry needle works well when working the whipped, laced, threaded, and woven stitches.

Take a quick review of the ABCs (pages 8 to 29) for equipment, needles, transferring patterns, or for questions about how to get started. If you have worked some of the creative embroidery stitches, the crewel stitches will be easy to master.

## STRAIGHT

This stitch can be worked in any direction, from top to bottom or bottom to top or even sideways. There is not a set way to work the stitch. A straight stitch does not conform to curved lines and should not be used for long stitches. When using yarn for small, short stitches, use a slightly loose tension so they do not become stubby.

You can use any type of thread for this stitch. Wool thread will give a smoother appearance to the stitch than a Persian yarn.

**Ways to use:** grass, leaves for small flowers, insect antennae, geometric patterns, anywhere a straight line is needed

**Also known as:** stroke stitch or single satin stitch

Completing stitch

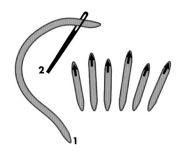

## SEED

Work these small stitches randomly in different directions, without a given pattern. For best results, work small, straight even stitches. This stitch works up quickly, creating a light airy effect in the desired shape. If a shaded effect is desired, use light and dark tones of the same color.

You can use any type of thread for this stitch. Wool thread creates a small stitch, as shown above.

**Ways to use:** flower petals, leaves, background, shapes, monogram letters

**Also known as:** seed filling, speckling, rice grain, dot stitch

Seeding an area

## DOUBLE SEED

Work small side-by-side stitches randomly across the area. Place the double stitches so they go in various directions without a set pattern. Keep them close together and as even in length as possible.

You can use any type of thread for this stitch. Wool thread creates a small stitch, as shown above.

**Ways to use:** flower petals, leaves, background, shapes, monogram letters

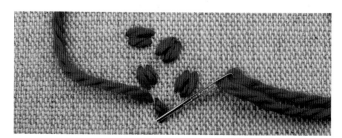

Keeping stitches parallel

## SPLIT

This is a flexible stitch that travels left to right. How you place the split in the stitch will determine how the stitch looks. You can work the stitch so the split comes in the center area, or the split can be placed closer to the end of the stitch. If using wool or Persian yarn, the thickness of the stitch is thinner if the split is closer to the end of the previous stitch.

**Ways to use:** curved lines, straight lines, outlines, filling (closely worked rows) of flower petals, leaves, stems, branches, various shapes

**Also known as:** Kensington outline

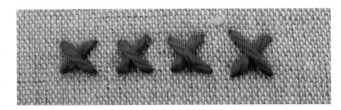

Splitting the thread

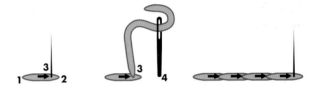

## CROSS

This simple stitch can travel horizontally, vertically, or diagonally, or place single stitches randomly over the area. It is beautiful when used as a couching stitch, randomly placed for a filling stitch, or worked as a border stitch. It can be used in all techniques in this book. This stitch is normally used on an even-weave fabric for the cross-stitch technique (page 195). Try to work the stitches evenly. This is not easy to do on plain weave fabric; the stitches may vary slightly on this fabric. Baste lines or use the quilter's tape marked with ¼" (6 mm) marks to keep the stitches even on plain weave fabric.

**Ways to use:** borders, bands, filling

**Also known as:** sampler stitch

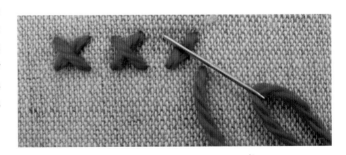

Completing the cross

## STEM

This is a very graceful stitch when worked in wool. Travel left to right across the line to be worked. When working curved lines or outlines, keep the stitch on the marked line. For all stem work, keep the thread below the needle at all times with the stitches close together.

You can use any thread for this stitch. For more texture, use pearl cotton, wool, or yarn.

**Ways to use:** branches, stems, outlines, filling, lettering

**Also known as:** crewel, stalk

Creating a straight stem

## CHEVRON

This stitch travels left to right. On a plain-weave fabric, baste horizontal lines across the fabric area to be stitched to help keep the stitches straight. Keep the horizontal and slanted stitches as even in length as possible. Notice that the first and second horizontal stitches are worked differently. When you take the second small stitch from 6 to 7, you are sharing a hole with 4 (printed as 4/7). Follow the numbers and arrows carefully.

You can use any type of thread for this stitch.

This is a great border stitch when worked with wool thread.

**Ways to use:** borders, bands, filling

Working horizontal stitch

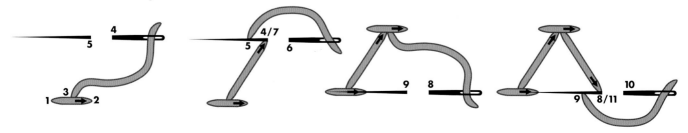

# THREADED BACKSTITCH

Travel left to right to work the backstitch over the area. For a stunning stitch, use two colors in different types of thread and different thread weights. Use a tapestry needle for the threaded stitch. Anchor the beginning threaded thread under an end stitch. End the thread in the same way on the other end of the line. When working the threaded loops, leave the thread slightly loose. The loops can be adjusted evenly after they are secured on each end.

**Ways to use:** bands, borders, outlines, clothing embellishment, lettering

**Also known as:** laced backstitch

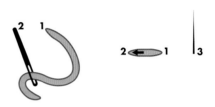

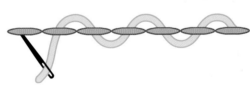

Working the backstitch

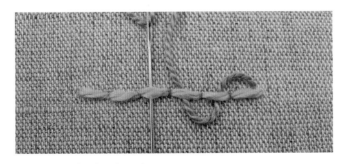

Threading the backstitch

End threading

## CURVED SATIN

This stitch should be worked in small areas. When stitching a large area, work small sections at a time. To work a small shape like this C, divide the area in half. When using wool thread or yarn, use a base stitch to slide the stitches through for a more even look. When using a base stitch, do not pierce the fabric with the satin stitch. Use the split stitch as a base stitch to work around the edge of the outline, keeping the stitches at a medium length. Use a tapestry needle to make it easier to slide under the split stitches that outline the shape. To begin the satin, come up from the back of the fabric on the outer top edge of the shape. Bring the thread over the top of the split stitch to the opposite side, and slide the needle/thread under the split stitch across from where you came up. Bring the needle/thread back over the split stitches to the lower side and repeat this process, working toward the end of the shape.

Sliding stitch under split stitch

As you slide under the stitch, be careful not to pick up threads of the previously placed split stitch.

You can use any type of thread for this stitch.

**Ways to use:** monogrammed initials, small borders, filling—especially flower petals and leaves

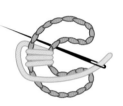

## ROMANIAN

This stitch is worked horizontally and travels top to bottom. It conforms well to filling shapes and works up quickly. It is simply a straight stitch with a small tie-down stitch in the middle. Although the tie-down stitch should be in the center of the area, a little variance adds interest.

You can use any type of thread for this stitch. Wool or twisted threads work especially well.

**Ways to use:** borders, bands, filling (small shapes), leaves, flower petals

**Also known as:** Oriental, Romanian couching, antique, Janina, Indian filling

Extending a border

## LONG AND SHORT

This is a variation of a satin stitch, with the stitches worked in an uneven pattern. Travel left to right. For the first row of stitches, alternate a short and long stitch across the top of the area to be filled in. For the remaining rows, work long stitches. For the long and short stitch to be effective, there needs to be a distinct difference in the length of the two stitches.

After the first row is in place, work down the shape to be filled in. Place the outside stitches first; then fill in the area between these stitches. Work small sections of the area this way as you work down the shape.

Shading the area is what gives this stitch its beauty. Shade the chosen color light to dark, and divide the shape into two or three sections. The traditional way is three sections with three shades. If working more than one flower in a design, use only two colors for one of the flowers, giving that flower a slightly different look. You can use any type of thread for this stitch. Wool thread or Persian yarns are very forgiving and give the stitch a beautiful appearance.

**Ways to use:** filling

**Also known as:** embroidery stitch, shading stitch, plumage stitch

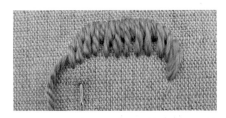

Starting row of long stitches

## BUTTONHOLE

Buttonhole stitches are worked very close together. The stitch travels left to right. The buttonhole is an excellent stitch to secure raw-edged motifs to other fabrics. It is beautiful both on curved lines and straight lines and can be worked around an area on the flat of the fabric or as an edging. The stitches can be worked side by side to create a tighter look to the stitch.

When working this stitch, keep the needle straight as you take the vertical stitch and keep the thread looped under the needle.

You can use any type of thread for this stitch.

**Ways to use:** edging, appliqué (raw edges), borders, filling

**Also known as:** button, close stitch, spaced blanket

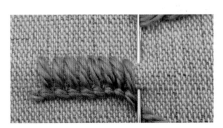

Placing vertical stitch over horizontal thread

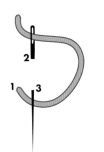 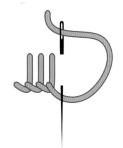 

## BLANKET LONG AND SHORT

This is a variation of the blanket stitch, and it travels left to right. Space the width and the height of the stitches for your desired look, keeping the alternating stitch slightly longer. This stitch creates a striking edging for cuffs and collars. It can also be used to secure fabrics together. Work rows of the long and short blanket stitch close together for an interesting filling stitch. Place the filling rows so the height of the longest stitch almost touches the horizontal stitch of the previous row.

You can use any type of thread for this stitch. Wool thread gives this stitch added beauty.

**Ways to use:** filling, borders, embellishment for clothing and home décor items, open buttonhole

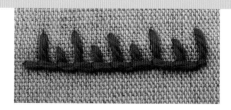

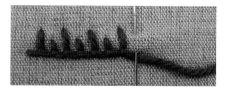

Placing short stitch

## BLANKET PINWHEEL

This is a variation of the blanket stitch and it travels left to right. Draw a circle on tissue paper and then use this pattern to baste the outline in the area desired. Once the basting is in place and the paper removed, define the center of the circle. Work the needle back and forth between two stitches in the center to enlarge the opening. This will make stitching easier. Work the stitch in the same manner as the blanket stitch.

With thicker threads, as you work the vertical stitch to the center hole, it will be impossible to place them all in the center. Let every other one drop down slightly outside the circle. The next thread will cover it going down into the center hole.

You can use any type of thread for this stitch. Wool threads and pearl cotton work especially well.

**Ways to use:** flower centers, flowers (add stem), borders, circles

**Also known as:** wheel, blanket wheel, circle

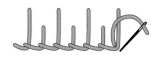

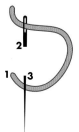

Working around circle

# Border Wheels

For an eye-catching border stitch, work half circles of the blanket pinwheel. You can space them out or let the outer stitches touch.

## KNOTTED BLANKET

This knotted variation of the blanket stitch travels left to right. It can be a little tricky to work, but it is worth learning. Keep the knot stitch secure on the needle while making the vertical stitch. The thread should be under the needle as you place the vertical stitch; at the same time pull the knot down into the fabric with the needle coming out and across the thread to make the horizontal part of the blanket stitch. The secret is to keep the thread taut around the needle. The height of the stitch can be worked even or varied. The stitches can be worked flat, in a circle, or on the edge of the fabric.

You can use any type of thread for this stitch. Wool threads work especially well.

**Ways to use:** filling, edging, bands, flower stamens, outlines

Working knot bringing needle out over horizontal thread

    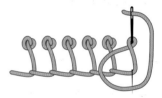

## FEATHER

This stitch can travel in a vertical, horizontal, circular, or curved direction, working top to bottom. The most important step when working this stitch is to keep both ends of the stitch (at 1 and 2) even in height. Keep the stitch width the same or vary the size depending on the desired look. The rhythm of this stitch works well using the sewing method as you place the stitches on alternate sides. Use your finger to hold the thread in place while completing the stitch.

You can use any type of thread for this stitch. Wool thread and pearl cotton work especially well.

**Ways to use:** circular motifs, borders, outlines, light filling, grass, ferns, leaves, embellishment on clothing, as an appliqué stitch, bird feathers

**Also known as:** single coral, briar, plumage

Working next stitch

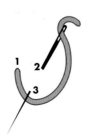 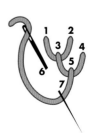 

## LONG ARMED FEATHER

This variation is worked similarly to the feather stitch. Travel in a vertical, horizontal, circular, or curved direction, working top to bottom.

The stitches between 1 and 2 are unevenly placed, with the outside arm being longer. Work the stitches alternately, left and right of an imaginary or basted center line.

You can use any type of thread for this stitch.

**Ways to use:** ferns, bands, borders, vines, filling, outlines, as an appliqué stitch

Placing long arm

 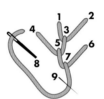 

## DOUBLE FEATHER

This variation is worked similarly to the feather stitch. Travel in a vertical, horizontal, circular, or curved direction, working top to bottom. Keep both ends of the stitch at 1 and 2 even in height. Stitches are worked diagonally downward, placing three or four stitches then alternating sides (left or right) of an imaginary or basted center line.

You can use any type of thread for this stitch. Silk, wool, and yarn work well.

**Ways to use:** ferns, bands, borders, vines, filling, outlines, as an appliqué stitch

Working third stitch

 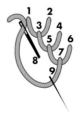 

# OPEN CRETAN

This stitch can be worked vertically or horizontally, traveling top to bottom. It has a simple rhythm that swings right to left using the sewing method. When worked horizontally it makes a beautiful border stitch. A plait forms in the center area as you work. As you work right to left, keep the needle straight across and the thread under the tip of the needle. These stitches can be worked close together or far apart. For filling of leaves or a flower petal, place them close together within the given shape.

You can use any type of thread for this stitch.

**Ways to use:** bands, borders, filling including leaves and flower petals

**Also known as:** Cretan, long-armed feather, Persian, quill

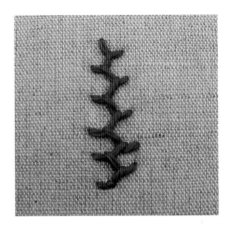

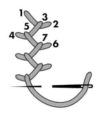
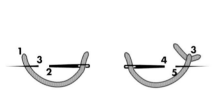

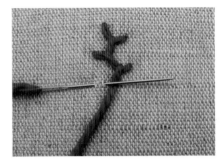

Placing left side of stitch

# FISHBONE

This stitch travels top to bottom down the shape or bottom to top up the shape. The stitches should cross slightly to create a thickness in the center area. This stitch conforms well to any shape. It is a great stitch for small treetops. It should lie smooth against the fabric. It works well for borders worked horizontally across an area.

Fishbone works up quickly and works well with all types of thread. For some leaves, begin by putting a straight stitch at the tip. Then put the first fishbone stitch at a slight angle so it covers the tip. You can use any type of thread for this stitch. Pearl cotton and wool thread give texture to the stitch.

**Ways to use:** bones, small treetops, bands, borders, leaves

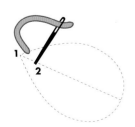
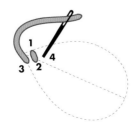

Sewing over for left stitch

## THORN

This stitch looks like thorns on a branch. Travel top to bottom. The center crossing of the diagonal thorn stitches can be crossed close to the center stem or at more of an angle, slightly out from the stem, as shown. How you work the crossed area of the left and right stitches will depend on the look you like. The long straight center stitch should be left slightly loose, the same as the laid stitch in couching. This stitch can be used as a fancy couching stitch.

You can use any type of thread for this stitch. Thicker threads like wool or pearl cotton add texture.

**Ways to use:** couching, ferns, foliage, filling

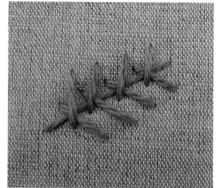

Starting new thorn

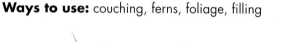

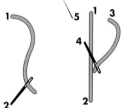

## CHAIN

This stitch travels in any direction, keeping the ends of the loop even or sharing the same hole. If you are working the stitch correctly, only a backstitch should be visible on the back. Use your finger to hold the thread in place while completing the stitch. Watch the tension to ensure that the stitch lies flat against the fabric with no puckering.

When using this stitch as a filling stitch for flowers or leaves, start each row at the tip of the leaf or petal working all the rows in this manner. It does take more time but creates a nicer appearance. When using as a filling stitch, use small stitches. This stitch works well for lettering.

You can use any type of thread for this stitch. If using this stitch to fill shapes, use a twisted or stranded thread. Wool, wool blends, or Persian yarns are too bulky.

**Ways to use:** borders, curved motifs, circular shapes, filling, outlines, lettering

**Also known as:** tambour, point de chainette

Completing a stitch

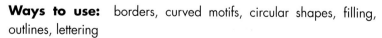

## ZIGZAG CHAIN

The stitches in this chain are worked at right angles to each other. You can travel in any direction—circular, swirl, horizontal, or vertical. For a filling pattern, place the rows of the zigzag either horizontally or vertically. Place the next row almost touching the previous row to create an interesting pattern. It is beautiful when worked on clothing with wool and silk stranded thread. Several colors can be used if placing more than one row of stitches next to each other. When working in rows, leave ¹⁄₁₆" (1.6 mm) or less between rows. You can use any type of thread for this stitch.

**Ways to use:** outlines, filling, zigzag lines, borders, bands, clothing embellishment, circular or swirl motifs

**Also known as:** Vandyke

Placing a zig

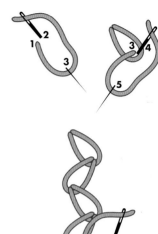

## CHECKERED (MAGIC) CHAIN

This is a chain stitch with a magical twist. Travel in any direction, working from top to bottom. Keep the ends of the loop even or share the same hole. Thread the needle with two contrasting colors or two tones of the same color. Follow the numbers on the chart carefully and be sure to have the thread placed as shown in the graph. Bring the needle out of the fabric with the threads together. Instead of looping both threads under the needle, loop only one of the threads. Make the loop and take the needle down into the fabric; both threads will follow the needle. Bring both threads up from the back, and then use the opposite color to make the next loop. Alternating colors, repeat this process until all stitches are in place.

You can use any type of thread for this stitch. Single-strand wool/silk blends or twisted threads work especially well.

**Ways to use:** borders, curved motifs, circular shapes, filling, outlines

Switching to red

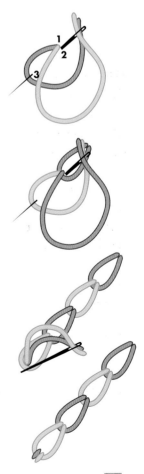

# HEAVY BRAIDED CHAIN

This simple stitch is two chains worked together without the tie-down stitch. Travel in any direction, working from top to bottom. Keep the ends of the loop even as you work these stitches. Anchor the first two chains by placing a straight stitch at the starting point of the area to be worked. Work the first two chains, sliding them through the straight stitch to anchor. For the remaining stitches, slide them under the previously worked chains to anchor. It may be necessary to help guide the stitches into place so they lie flat against the fabric and not on top of each other. Note that two loops are used to complete the stitch. You can use any type of thread for this stitch.

**Ways to use:** borders, curved motifs, circular shapes, filling, outlines

Threading behind previous stitch

# SINGLE-THREADED DETACHED CHAIN

This is a trail of single chain stitches worked across the area traveling in any direction. For a striking stitch, use two colors in different types of thread and different thread weights. Work a row of detached chain stitches over the area. Then thread the contrast thread through them using a tapestry needle. For added charm, work the chain stitches offset in a zigzag effect over the fabric.

You can use any type of thread for this stitch. Twisted threads work especially well for the threading thread.

**Ways to use:** swirled motifs, bands, borders, filling, embellishment for home décor

Stitching a chain

Threading chain

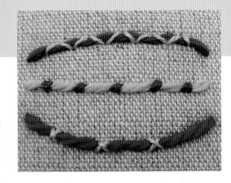

## FANCY COUCHING

This stitch travels left to right around the area to be couched. You can use any decorative stitch that can be worked across a laid thread as a fancy couching stitch. Shown are three fancy couching stitches: the cross-stitch, angled, and zigzag stitches. These stitches can be placed at random distances or you can space them ¼" or ½" (6 mm or 1.3 cm) apart, or any distance you prefer.

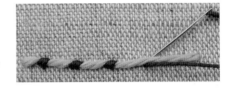

Work the long laid thread first, securing it in place; then work the couching thread over the laid thread. As you work over the laid thread, place the couching stitch carefully and do not pull it too snug.

Angled stitch

When couching over a larger area, use a longer thread and two needles. Use one needle for the laid thread, the other needle for the couching thread. Work small sections at a time.

You can use any type of thread for this stitch. Metallic braids add a touch of sparkle to the couching thread.

**Ways to use:** decorative swirls, filling shapes, secure lacing threads, and decorative braids

**Also known as:** basic couching, plain couching

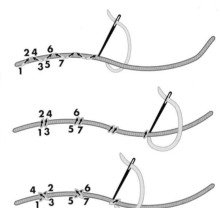

## FILLED LAZY DAISY

This stitch is the same as the lazy daisy or chain stitch with a straight stitch placed in the center of the loop. Work the stitch from left to right or in any direction desired. I prefer to keep the ends of the loop together (no space between) for a neat look and a flatter stitch. Filling the center area of the daisy creates more of a traditional flower look. This versatile stitch can be used singly or grouped together.

You can use any type of thread for this stitch.

**Ways to use:** filling, flower petals, buds, leaves, bands

Placing the filling stitch

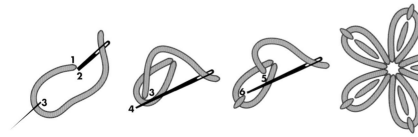

## TÊTE DE BOEUF

This charming filling stitch travels from the top to the bottom of the area to be filled. Work the single daisy stitch and place two straight stitches on either side. Place the first row across the area. Start the second row of stitches below the first row with the tête de boeuf positioned between the previously worked stitches. Offset each row in this manner. For borders and bands, use rows of three stitches offsetting the stitches, as discussed above.

You can use any type of thread for this stitch. A round thread like pearl cotton or a strand of hand-painted twisted thread will add more texture so the stitch stands out from the fabric.

**Ways to use:** filling, flower buds (worked singly), bands, borders

Placing straight stitch on left

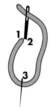

## DETACHED WHEATEAR

This stitch is worked individually, traveling in any direction. When the horizontal stitch is placed, do not pull it snug. There should be a slight give to the stitch to complete the wheatear. These stitches can be worked upright or placed at a slight angle when worked as a filling stitch.

You can use any type of thread for this stitch. Wool threads work especially well, and hand-dyed single-strand thread gives the stitch a slightly different appearance.

**Ways to use:** filling, borders, bands

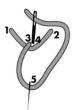

Placing ear

Working loop

 THE COMPLETE PHOTO GUIDE TO NEEDLEWORK

# WHEATEAR CHAIN

This stitch can travel in a horizontal, vertical, or circular direction. Although it appears to be the same stitch as the detached wheatear, it is not worked the same. Place two straight stitches at the starting point. Below the "ears," start the loop the same distance down as the width of the first stitches. Then take the needle up and slide the thread between the "ears" and the chain without piercing the chain thread to complete the stitch. Continue to work downward in this manner.

You can use any type of thread for this stitch. Wool or Persian yard adds texture to the stitch.

**Ways to use:** bands, borders, circular or swirl motifs

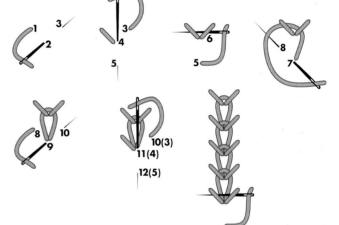

Threading under ears

Completing a stitch

# PETAL

This stitch is a combination of the daisy stitch and a straight or backstitch traveling right to left. It works well on straight or curved lines. Begin a stitch distance away from the starting point. Place the first stitch back toward that point. Come up halfway under the first stitch to make the daisy. Repeat this process across the area. End with the last daisy in the center or add an additional daisy at the tip of the last straight stitch for foliage.

**Ways to use:** stems, foilage, bands, circular or swirl motif, edging

**Also known as:** pendant chain

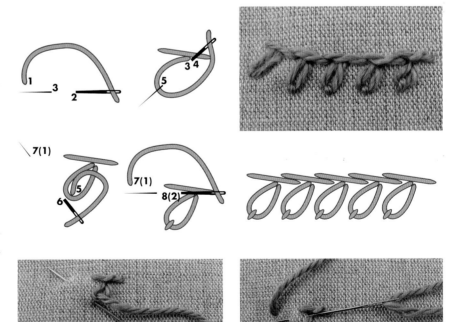

Completing first stitch

Starting second stitch

# FRENCH KNOT

Place knot where desired. The size of thread and number of wraps will determine the knot size produced. Use one, two, or three wraps depending on your desired knot size. Once the thread is wrapped on the needle, it is important to keep the needle straight and the thread taut as it enters the fabric. Use your other hand to hold the thread taut. Practice this stitch on a scrap of fabric using a thick thread. When you master the knot this way, you can use any type of thread in your projects. For best results, work this stitch in a hoop or frame. You can use any type of thread for this stitch. Wool thread or Persian yarn is beautiful when used to fill leaves and flowers for crewel.

**Ways to use:** flower centers, filling, single row of knots spaced for outline of leaves or shapes

**Also known as:** French dot, knotted, twisted knot, wound

Starting into fabric

Keeping thread taut

Completing knot

# PISTIL

This easy stitch is a variation of a French knot with an added stem. Use any length of stem that works for the application. When working on a curved line, as you take the needle down into the fabric have the thread for the stem slightly loose to conform to the curve. For a straight pistil, keep the stem thread and wrapped thread taut as it enters the fabric. You can use any type of thread for this stitch. Wool thread or Persian yarn gives a soft look to the stitch.

**Ways to use:** flower stamens, flower petals, filling

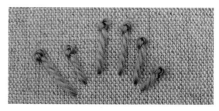

Placing needle into fabric

Pulling thread taut

Completing knot

# BULLION KNOT

These knots can be placed in any direction. Use a milliner or crewel needle with a small narrow eye.

It is important to place the base horizontal stitch of the knot correctly. Bring the needle back up at 1, sliding it through the same hole it originally came up at and keeping the needle on top of the original thread. Slide the needle out of this hole just far enough so you can wrap the thread. Holding the wrapped thread snug around the needle with your other hand, slide the needle straight through, pulling the thread gently in the direction the needle is sliding. Then pull gently in the opposite direction to tighten up the stitch. Use your nail or the tip of the needle to even out the looped threads. When making a flower, use French knots for the center; then place the knots clockwise around the center, placing two rows. You can also use yellow thread for the first knot, placing it where the center of the flower should be stitched. Then work bullion knots around the center knot.

You can use any type of thread for this stitch. Silk makes a beautiful knot.

**Ways to use:** roses, flower petals, flower stamens, leaves, flower buds

**Also known as:** coil, knot, caterpillar, worm, grub, Puerto Rico rose, port stitch, roll

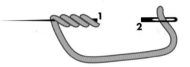

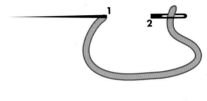

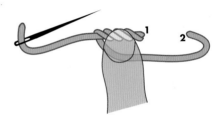

Needle over thread

Wrapped thread around needle

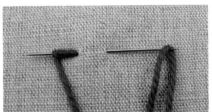

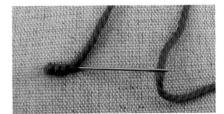

Pull needle away from knot

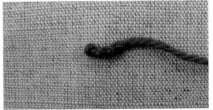

Pull in opposite direction

End stitch

# THREADED HERRINGBONE

This stitch travels left to right in a straight row. Work the stitches as evenly and smoothly as possible. The small base horizontal stitch should be the same width, and long slanted stitches should all be the same length. Notice that the start of the second stitch is even in placement to the last placed slanted stitch. Work the threaded stitch after the herringbone is in place. Begin and end the threading thread under the outside of the long slanted stitches.

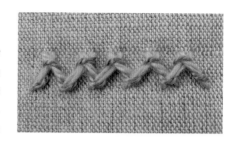

You can use any type of thread for this stitch.

**Ways to use:** borders, bands, filling

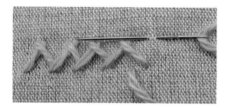

Working herringbone

Threading

Ending threading

# CORAL

This is the simplest of the knotted stitches and it travels right to left. Make the first knot very close to where you come up out of the fabric. Space the other knots at the same distance from each other across the area to be stitched. Do not pull the knot too snug or it will become distorted. When ending the stitch, place a long stitch at the end or end it next to the knot. The size of the vertical stitch (4–5) and the size of the thread determine the size of the knot.

You can use any type of thread for this stitch.

**Ways to use:** filling, outlines for motifs, leaves, flowers

**Also known as:** beaded knot, German knot, coral knot, snail trail, knotted outline

Forming knot

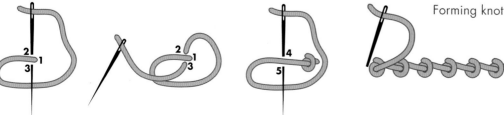

## SWORD EDGING

These small stitches can be worked randomly in any direction or in a straight line or rows for a border stitch. When working the stitch, be sure the first stitch is long enough and slightly loose so it will pull down into place when the longer tail stitch slides over and then under it. When working in rows, offset the stitches of each row.

You can use any type of thread for this stitch.

**Ways to use:** filling, borders, bands

First stitch

Threading under first stitch

## ROPE

This stitch has the look of a satin stitch when the area is completed. Worked from top to bottom, it is used for straight or curved lines. For a straight line, adjust the slant of the needle. The beauty of the stitch shows best on curved lines. As you work this stitch, keep the top of the stitch close to the same height so the stitch gradually works around the circle. If you want a smaller rope, use smaller stitches.

You can use any type of thread for this stitch. Wool thread shows this stitch beautifully.

**Ways to use:** curved lines, outlines, straight borders or bands

Extending rope

Ending stitch

## BOKHARA COUCHING

This versatile stitch can travel vertically or horizontally. It conforms well when filling shapes and works up quickly. It is worked the same as the Romanian stitch but is tied in several places. The number of tie-downs depends on the length of the base stitch.

Wool or wool blends, twisted or hand-dyed single-strand threads work best, but you can use any type of thread.

**Ways to use:** borders, bands, filling (small shapes), leaves, flower petals

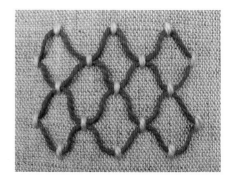

Completing couch stitch and lining up for next stitch

## CLOUD

This stitch travels right to left. Use two different types of threads in two colors. The small horizontal base stitches can be worked closer than shown. Adjust the space between stitches depending on how you are using the stitch.

Work the small straight base stitches first. Thread the second thread starting under the tip of the first small stitch on the right. When you reach the left side, go under the base stitch and through the fabric. Come back up under the lower half of the same stitch to work back across the area. Work all rows in this manner and begin and end under the stitches on the edge. You can use any type of thread for this stitch.

**Ways to use:** filling

**Also known as:** Mexican

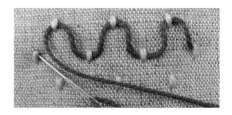

Ending first row of threading

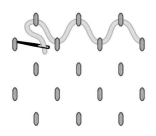
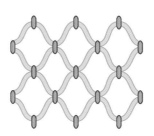

Starting second row

# HONEYCOMB FILLER

This stitch travels from top to bottom of the area. It can be worked in one color, shades of one color, or three complementary colors. Work the number of horizontal parallel lines needed to fill the area. Work the first set of diagonal stitches over the horizontal stitches. The last row of diagonal stitches can be the most difficult to place. Work this set of diagonal stitches by weaving them in and out of the horizontal and first row of diagonal stitches. Notice that in the upper right and lower left, the two diagonal woven stitches share the same space between the horizontal stitches. As you work this last row of stitches, use your finger to gently move the horizontal stitch over a little so the needle will slide down under the thread.

You can use any type of thread for this stitch. Wool or twisted threads work especially well.

**Ways to use:** filling

**Also known as:** net passing

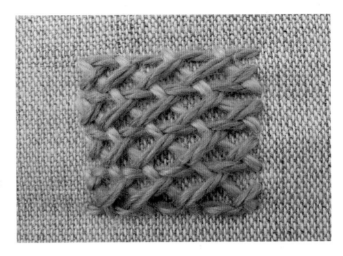

Placing last diagonal stitch

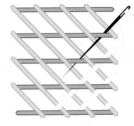
Weaving over stitches

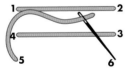

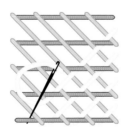

## SPIDERWEB WOVEN

This stitch travels in a circular direction. Stitch in a solid color or use two colors of thread or yarn. Try making different sizes of the spiderweb woven, but always use an *odd* number of spokes. Divide the area you are using into five even spaces and place the spokes. Make the spokes so they are not loose but not taut. Keep in mind that a good foundation stitch yields a good web. Start in the center, working clockwise, weaving the thread over and under the spokes.

You can use any type of thread for this stitch.

**Ways to use:** flowers, dots, circles, wheels, spiderwebs

**Also known as:** woven wheel, woven spot, woven spoke

Working last spoke

Weaving under and over

## SPIDERWEB WHIPPED

This stitch travels in a circular direction. Stitch in a solid color or use two colors of thread or yarn. Make the spokes so they are not loose but not taut. Keep in mind that a good foundation stitch yields a good web. Try making different sizes of the spiderweb whipped but always use an *even* number of spokes. Divide the area into eight even spaces and place the spokes. Start in the top center. Come up between two spokes, take a back stitch loop around one spoke, and go under two spokes. Continue to work in this manner until the spokes are covered. When you near the tip of the spokes, you may want to push the stitches closer to the center and place more stitches around the area. If you prefer to have space between the woven rows, leave the threads spaced slightly apart.

You can use any type of thread for this stitch. Wool thread makes a beautiful spiderweb.

**Ways to use:** flowers, dots, circles, wheels, spiderwebs

**Also known as:** backed stitch spiderweb, ribbed web

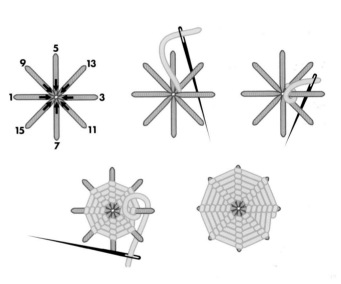

Completing foundation stitches

Working whipped stitch

# Paisleys and Pearls Pillow

This project combines charcoal-polished cotton with wool threads and Swarovski pearls, creating an elegant pillow that will add color and excitement to any room. By simply changing the colors to go with the décor, this paisley design can fit with any color scheme! For an alternate color choice, use an antique white pillow with three shades of blue or raspberry. The paisley pattern can also be worked on any garment or home décor item. A variegated thread can be used to add interest.

## YOU WILL NEED

- 18" × 12" (45.7 × 30.5 cm) premade pillow with a sham cover
- 100 percent wool thread: aqua, bright yellow, and orange red
- five pearls, size 6 mm: powdered almond
- sewing thread in aqua, red, and yellow
- Silamide bead thread, size A: medium gray
- crewel and beading needles

## STITCHES USED

- stem
- feather
- seed

## Stitching Information

**1** Remove the pillow insert. If not using a sham pillow, remove a few inches (cm) of stitches from the bottom seam and remove the stuffing from inside the pillow. Set insert or stuffing aside.

**2** Transfer the pattern using the tissue tracing method (page 22). Trace three paisley patterns.

**3** Lay the traced patterns on the pillow top and turn the paisleys, traced side down or up depending on the direction. Refer to photograph for placement. Pin the pattern in place and baste around the tissue paper.

**4** Use yellow sewing thread to baste the smaller inside line of the pattern onto the fabric. Use the red sewing thread to baste the middle line, and aqua sewing thread to baste the outside line. When basting is complete, remove the tissue paper.

**5** Use two strands of orange red wool and the stem stitch to stitch over the middle line of the paisley.

**6** Use two strands of sunny yellow wool and the feather stitch to stitch over the yellow basted line. Begin stitching at the tip of the paisley point, placing a feather stitch on each side of the basted line. Work down one side to the halfway point, and secure the last feather stitch on this side by placing a small stitch over the loop end. Work down the other side until your stitches meet. When the two feather rows meet, they will be back to back with the loops close together. End the last feather stitch by taking a slightly longer stitch that goes over the small stitch of the opposite loop, joining the sides for a finished look. If needed, adjust the size of the feather stitch as you near the area where the sides join so two feather stitches are not on the same side of the basting line.

**7** Use two strands of aqua wool and the feather stitch to work the outside line of the paisley. Work in the same manner as you did the yellow area.

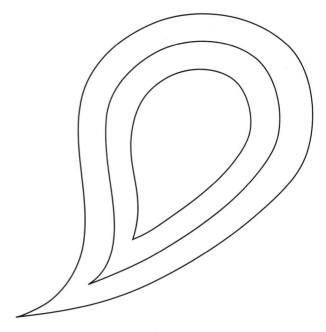

Paisley pattern (actual size)

**8** Use two strands of orange red wool and the seed stitch to fill in the center area of the paisley.

**9** Remove any remaining basting or tissue paper.

**10** Use two strands of bead thread to attach the five pearls, using a single bead stitch and spacing them evenly along the right side of the pillow front. If using a striped fabric, place the beads in the center of a stripe on the right side. Sew through each bead twice to secure, and take two small stitches on the back of the fabric. Tie off thread. Repeat for the other beads.

**11** Insert the pillow form. If necessary, stuff the pillow and sew the seam closed.

# Adjustable

Increase or decrease the pattern as needed to fit your project.

# Touch of Gold Fedora Hat

Crewel needlework can turn a classic hat into a fashion statement. This leaf and berry vine pattern is easy to work yet gives signature style to an otherwise ordinary accessory. White and metallic gold threads are striking against the gray felt. Switch it up with a lively color scheme to make a band for your favorite sun hat.

## YOU WILL NEED

- fedora hat: black
- bamboo felt: lava rock
- fusible fleece
- stranded (three-ply) silk and wool blend: white
- single-strand 100 percent silk shimmer: gold
- fine braid, size 8: gold
- six-strand embroidery floss: medium old gold
- crewel and chenille needles
- sewing thread: dark and light gray
- permanent adhesive
- rotary cutter and cutting board
- pressing cloth
- quilter's chalk pencil or tailor's chalk in white

## STITCHES USED

- straight
- fishbone
- French knot
- couching

Touch of gold design pattern (actual size)

## Stitching Information

**1** To determine the band length, measure around the base of the hat next to the brim and add 4" (10.2 cm).

**2** Cut the piece of felt using the rotary cutter and cutting board. Recheck the band length to ensure it is long enough to crisscross over in the back of the hat.

**3** Cut a piece of fusible fleece 1¼" (3.2 cm) wide and the same length as the band. Lay the piece of felt on a flat surface with the wrong side up. Place the piece of fleece, with the fusible side down, in the center of the wrong side of the felt band. Place the pressing cloth on top of the fleece, and fuse to the felt following the manufacturer's instructions. Fuse small sections at a time so the fleece does not slip out of place. Allow the felt band to cool.

**4** Working from the back, fold the side pieces of felt over the fleece, and pin in place. Use the gray sewing thread to lace the two pieces together. The band should remain flat and not curl upward.

**5** Use the tissue basting method to transfer the pattern. The pattern is a repeat pattern. It is laid out so the dashed lines on the pattern will overlap what is already traced once you trace the initial pattern. This will give a straight pattern line across the area. Center the pattern on the tissue strip.

**6** Center the tissue pattern on the front of the felt band. Baste the pattern using the light gray sewing thread.

**7** Use one strand of the white silk/wool blend and the fishbone stitch to work the leaves. Place a straight compensating stitch at the tip of each leaf to start the fishbone.

*(continued)*

**4**

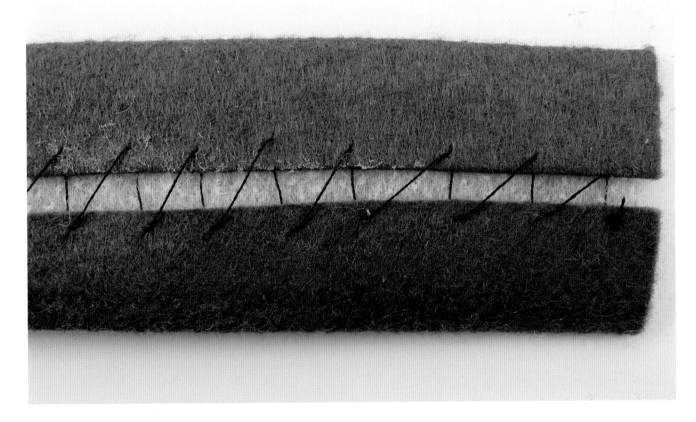

**8** Use the braid to work the French knots for the berries. Use a straight stitch for the three leaflets at the top of each berry. Work around the outside of the oval berry, and then fill in the center. Use a few sloppy knots in with the regular French knots.

**9** Use the shimmer silk to work the laid thread along the basted line of the vine. Couch the laid thread down with one strand of the gold embroidery floss. The silk is a soft round thread, so it should remain round as you couch over it. Watch the tension on the couching thread. You can carry the laying thread on the back going over the leaf and berry backs. The laying thread should not be pulled snug. You will need to shape it to conform to the basting line.

**10** Remove all basting thread. Use tweezers to remove any short stubborn pieces.

**11** Place the band around the hat with the ends crisscrossed in the back. Gently pull the band snug. Slide a straight pin into the two pieces of felt to secure the ends together.

Check to see if the band is still snug against the hat. Adjust if necessary and take a couple of basting stitches to hold the two pieces of band together. Do not pierce the hat.

**12** Remove the band from the hat, and trim the bottom piece of the band. Place the band back on the hat to check that enough of the bottom pieces has been trimmed away. Remove the hat and trim the top piece of felt. Place on the hat and check if additional trimming is necessary.

**13** Remove band from the hat and slip stitch the two pieces together along the cut edges, making sure your stitches do not show.

# Basting

For easy of removal of basting, be sure the basting stitches go all the way through the band to the back so the thread is visible.

**8**

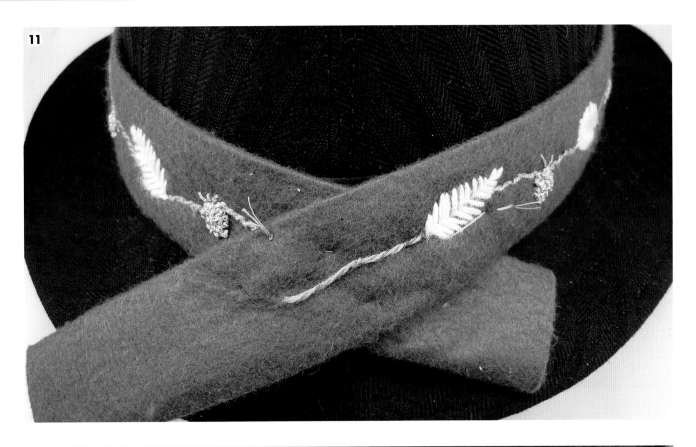

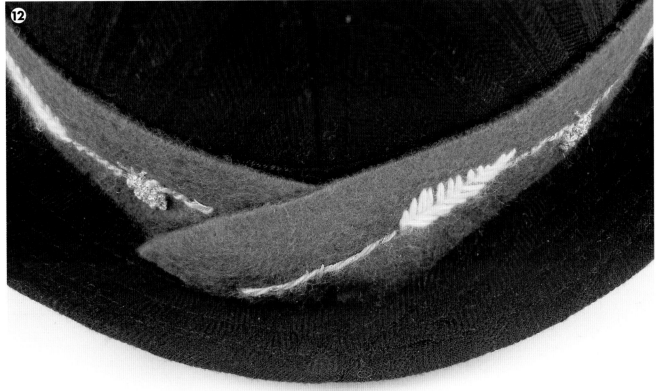

# SILK RIBBON EMBROIDERY

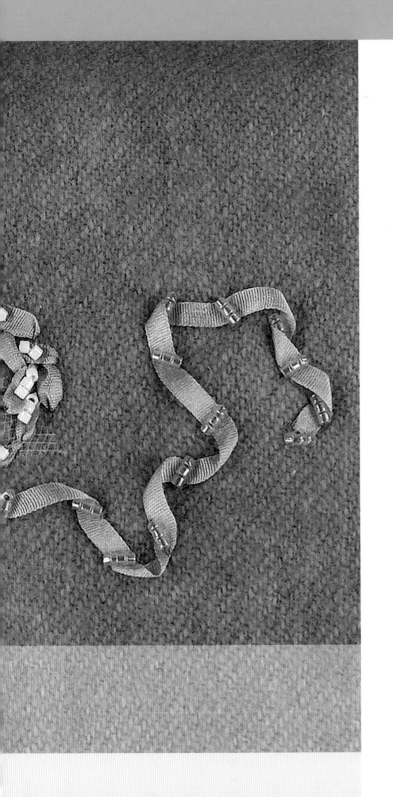

The rich silk colors and unique stitches used for silk ribbon designs make this technique exciting and fun to stitch. Projects can quickly be completed with minimum finishing. Silk ribbon embroidery can be used to embellish whatever the ribbon and needle can easily slide through. Working silk ribbon on premade items like clothing, home décor items, and accessories will give you a quick finished project. A pattern is not always necessary. Simply add a few flowers along the collar of a blouse to create a charming look.

The three-dimensional effects of this technique are perfect for floral work. Inspiration for silk ribbon embroidery can come from nature. Look around for fresh ideas of what you can stitch on fabric.

# Fabric

Fabrics with a high thread count are more difficult to use for this technique because the tightness of the weave puts extra strain on the silk ribbon. It is possible to stitch on purchased items such as cotton shower curtains and pillow cases, but it can be difficult to make the work look nice.

The following are some of the fabrics that work well for this technique.

## BATIK AND QUILTER'S COTTON

Cotton found in quilt shops works well for this technique.

## VELVET

Silk work is stunning on velvet. When working with this fabric, tape the edges (it sheds) and use a frame to keep the fabric from wrinkling.

## TULLE

This versatile fabric comes in many colors. It is a very fine mesh that is slippery and difficult to cut, but the end result makes it worth the time spent. There is a larger mesh called netting that does not work—the holes are too large for the stitches. Tulle can be used over a piece of fabric, even a cotton solid color. Baste the tulle to the fabric. Work the stitches through both fabrics. The project on page 140 has a small piece of tulle under the silk work, adding another texture to the design.

## SHEER

Like tulle, this fabric can be difficult to control, but it adds so much to the finished project. Baste the sheer over the fabric and stitch the design through both fabrics.

## OVER-DYED OR HAND-DYED 100% WOOL

This fabric comes in many beautiful colors and is easy to finish using one of the edging stitches shown in the various techniques discussed in this book. Silk ribbon embroidery worked on the wool fabric creates an interesting contrast of textures.

## 100% WOOL AND WOOL BLENDS

Pinstripe, herringbone, striped, checked, or solid color—it makes no difference. They all go beautifully with the silk ribbon stitches. These types of fabric add textural contrast to the silk work and provide added charm to the finished project.

## SILK AND RAYON BLENDS

The combination of silk fabric and silk ribbon stitches gives the finished piece a soft, gorgeous appearance. It is perfect for making a ring bearer's pillow for a wedding.

## OTHER TYPES OF FABRIC

Even-weave, linen, muslin, felt, and synthetics have been discussed in the Creative Embroidery, Crewel, and Cross-Stitch chapters. Refer to those chapters for information on these fabrics.

# Ribbon and Thread

## SILK RIBBON

Silk ribbon comes in a wide range of colors and in four widths: 2 mm, 4 mm, 7 mm, and 13 mm. All sizes may not be available in all colors. The color range depends on the brand of silk ribbon used. The 2 mm is not as widely used as the other sizes and is not available in many colors. The 4 mm is the most common size used by stitchers. Silk ribbon is available in quilt shops, needlepoint shops, and on the Internet.

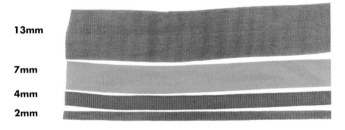

| 13mm |
| 7mm |
| 4mm |
| 2mm |

There are different types of silk ribbon. It is either woven with a finished selvage, or it is bias strips cut from silk cloth. For this type of silk ribbon work, use a ribbon with a selvage.

The finished project size and types of stitches used determine the sizes of ribbon you should use. When selecting a ribbon, keep in mind that the wider the ribbon the more room the stitch will take up on the fabric. If you prefer the daintier look of the stitches, work with the 4 mm width. Several sizes of ribbon can be used in a project to give the design more depth.

Learning to manipulate the ribbon is easy. Ribbon can endure handling, twisting, and being pulled in and out of the fabric. Ribbon can also withstand stitching, though it is fragile and can be easily damaged. It will fray on the ends and sometimes run. It works best to use pieces that are 10" to 12" (25.4 to 30.5 cm) or shorter. It is amazing how far the silk will go when stitching. If it becomes twisted or folded, silk ribbon can be ironed with a very low temperature iron.

## THREAD

Using threads to enhance the silk work will give the finished piece more texture and character. I love using wool blends, pearl cotton, metallic braids, tubular, silk, embroidery floss, and hand-dyed or solid color single-strand threads. A synthetic tubular thread can add a different texture than other threads when incorporated into stitching. Hand-dyed and over-dyed threads add charm to the piece. Memory thread adds a dimensional effect. Any of the threads discussed in the Creative Embroidery (page 34), Crewel (page 76), Cross-Stitch (page 191), or Needlepoint (page 216) chapters can be used in combination with the silk ribbon.

# Stitches

The secret to beautiful ribbon work lies in learning how to manipulating the silk. It often has a mind of its own. Some stitches have a twisted look, while other are more flat. The look is up to the stitcher.

For the twisted stitches, you can have the ribbon smooth as it comes out of the fabric or let it twist. For the flat stitches, as you work with the silk, keep the ribbon straight as it goes into the fabric. It is often necessary to straighten the silk before each stitch to ensure a smooth piece of ribbon. Lay the ribbon against the fabric and run your nail over the area where it comes out of the fabric to smooth and flatten the ribbon. This is easier than using a laying tool or needle. If you prefer a more wrinkled appearance, it is not necessary to straighten the ribbon.

Beginning and ending silk ribbon is different from what is done with other techniques. Thread the needle, leaving a ribbon tail. Take the tip of the needle and run it through the end of the short tail, and pull the needle so the ribbon slides through the tail until a knot forms next to the eye of the needle.

Once the ribbon is locked in the needle, begin the first stitch by leaving a ½" (1.3 cm) tail on the fabric's back. When the first stitch is complete, pierce the tail and slide the needle back through the ribbon tail on the fabric back to secure it in place. Be careful not to disrupt the stitch on the front.

To end the ribbon on the back of the fabric, run it under several previously worked stitches. You can also end it by sliding the needle and ribbon through the ribbon of a previously worked stitch and then sliding it back through the ribbon, forming a knot. Pull the ribbon taut without disrupting the stitches on the front.

A size 22 chenille needle works well for 4 mm ribbon; for wider ribbons use larger needles. Silk ribbon needs room to move in the eye of the needle. If you are having trouble working a stitch because the ribbon keeps bunching up, try a larger needle.

A stabilizer (page 23) should be used behind the fabric. The information in Laying the Thread (page 27) also applies to silk to help keep it straight and smooth going into and out of the fabric.

The stitched silk ribbon examples that follow were worked using 4 mm silk ribbon. They can also be worked using the wider 7 mm or 13 mm ribbon, unless otherwise noted in the stitch information.

Threading ribbon

Placing the first stitch

Securing the ribbon on the back

## LONG STRAIGHT

This stitch can be worked in any direction. For the beauty of the stitch to show, keep the bottom and top of the ribbon smooth as it goes in and out of the fabric. Straighten the ribbon by placing the needle behind it, and use the method shown for laying threads on page 27.

Stitches longer than 1¼" (3.2 cm) may need a couching stitch to hold them in place. This stitch works well for a longer straight leaf for a flower. Couch the stitch as needed for length, using one strand of matching embroidery thread.

This stitch does not conform to curved lines. It is, however, used as a slightly curved stitch for certain types of blossoms when used in combination with a tie-down stitch.

For a thicker leaf, use wider ribbon.

**Ways to use:** grass, leaves, flowers, tree branches, twigs

**Also known as:** stroke stitch, single satin stitch

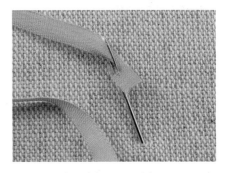

Keeping the ribbon straight

## STAB

This stitch is similar to but smaller than the long straight stitch and can be worked in any direction. The stitch can vary in length and width. Use the stab method to work the stitches. Keep the ribbon smooth and flat against the fabric. These stitches are worked at a ¼" (6 mm) to ¾" (1.9 cm) length.

**Ways to use:** flowers, buds, short grass

**Also known as:** straight

Creating a short stitch

## ROSE BUDS

These small flowers are usually worked vertically or slightly tilted to the right or left. A stem can be added if desired. Use the stab stitch to work the bud. For larger buds, use wider silk ribbon. Add short green stitches for the sepals, using two or three strands of embroidery floss or size 8 pearl cotton.

**Ways to use:** rose bush flowers, single roses, filling in areas

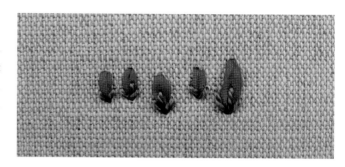

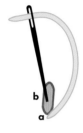

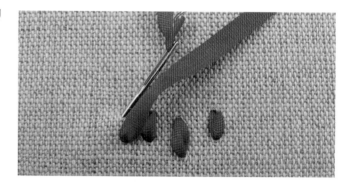

Taking a small stitch

## STEM

This stitch travels left to right. Keep the ribbon below the needle, sewing the stitch by sliding the needle in and out of the fabric. Keep the ribbon straight as it goes into the fabric, so it will lie flat. Place the stitches very close together to create the stem effect, but allow room for the width of the ribbon to lie flat against the fabric next to the previous stitch. When working a curved line, place the stitches directly on the basted or drawn line. Use 4 mm silk ribbon for small flowers; use 7 mm for larger flowers. Any type of thread can be used for the stem stitch for floral work. It adds a different texture, giving the flower more interest.

**Ways to use:** branches, flower stems, outlines

**Also known as:** crewel, stalk

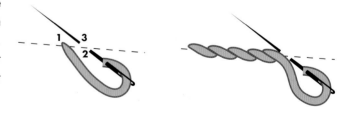

Keeping the stitch close

THE COMPLETE PHOTO GUIDE TO NEEDLEWORK

## SATIN

Work this stitch diagonally, vertically, or horizontally, traveling left to right. When used as a filling stitch, it works best in small areas. The ribbon should lie flat, side by side when the stitching is complete. For a more even looking stitch, straighten the ribbon as it goes in and of the fabric.

**Ways to use:** flower petals, leaves

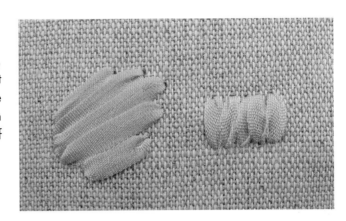

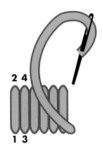

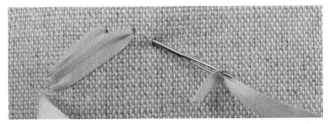

Placing ribbon for slight overlap

## COUCHING RIBBON

This stitch travels left to right across the area to be couched. A couching stitch is a straight stitch placed over a laid ribbon to secure it to the fabric. If possible when working the couching stitches, go down into the fabric near where you came out of the fabric. In this example, narrow ribbon is used for couching. Pearl cotton, embroidery floss, hand-dyed single-strand wool blends, or other types of embroidery threads can also be used.

**Ways to use:** decorative swirls, filling shapes, to secure other stitches

**Also known as:** basic couching, plain couching

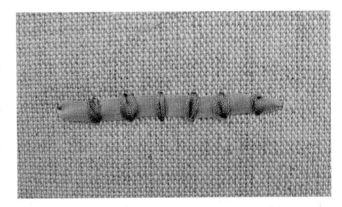

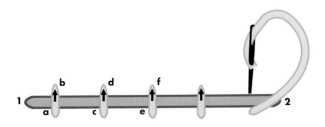

Couching the laid ribbon

## BEAD COUCHING OVER RIBBON

This easy-to-work stitch travels left to right around the area to be couched. I love the look of this type of couching. The ribbon can be laid in any direction or way. It can be folded in an accordion fashion or looped and twisted, as shown. Pin the ribbon to the fabric in the desired shape. Use bead thread to attach the beads over the ribbon slanting them in either direction. Three Delica beads fit across 4 mm ribbon; use more beads for wider ribbons.

For a different effect, use a French knot in place of the beads. The accordion-folded ribbon is beautiful with French knots to couch it down.

This stitch is used for the purse on page 140.

**Ways to use:** decorative swirls, filling shapes, embellishing clothing (collars or sleeves or along the hemline)

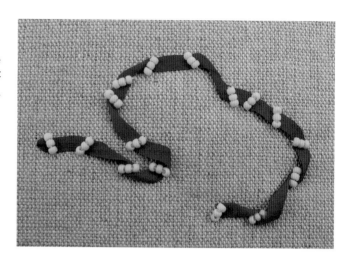

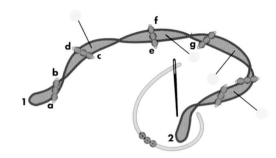

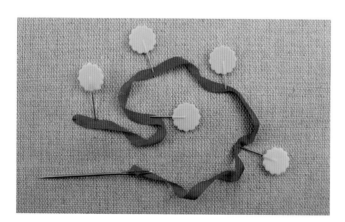

Pinning the ribbon in place

Securing laid ribbon with beads

## SIDE RIBBON

This stitch is worked either to the right or to the left. Use a gentle hand when pulling the ribbon down into the fabric. For each petal, bring the ribbon up from the back, lay the ribbon flat against the fabric for the desired length, and then take the needle straight down on either the left or right edge of the ribbon. Go through the ribbon, gently pulling the ribbon until it curls. The ribbon will curl on the opposite side of where the stitch is placed. If you pull too far, the ribbon will curl up in a thin line. Practice this stitch on a scrap of fabric before working on the project.

The piercing stitch can be placed on the left or right side for each petal, or you can vary the petals left to right as you work a flower. The stitch can be worked with the ribbon flat, or you can allow a little slack in the ribbon between where it comes up from the back and where the side stitch is placed. Both versions are shown on the same flower to add interest to the petals.

To keep the flower shape round, use chalk or quilter's gray pencil to draw a circle the desired size of the flower center on the fabric. Work the petals around this circle. Fill in the flower center last, using either ribbon or thread to stitch French or sloppy knots.

**Ways to use:** flowers, leaves

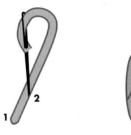

Piercing the ribbon

## JAPANESE RIBBON

This stitch is similar to the side stitch. The stitches can be placed in any direction. With a gentle hand, come up from the back, keeping the ribbon straight. Lay the length you want the stitch to be flat against the fabric. Bring the needle and ribbon straight down into the tip of the length of ribbon. Gently pull the ribbon through the fabric until the end of the flat ribbon curls. As soon as you see the curl start, stop pulling on the ribbon. If the ribbon has not curled enough, just pull a little more; too much and the curl will disappear. This is a stitch you might want to practice on a scrap of fabric before working on the project. When working around a flower or area, vary the size and curled effects of the stitches.

**Ways to use:** leaves, petals

  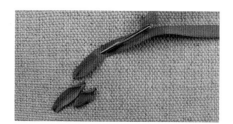

Piercing in the center

Pulling the ribbon through

## LACED RUNNING

This stitch travels right to left for both the running stitch and the lacing. It is a variation of the running stitch. Work the running stitch using a sewing motion; then weave the laced stitches over and under the running stitches.

Use a tapestry needle to work the laced ribbon to avoid picking up material or splitting the running stitch. Use the same loop height for each laced stitch. The example shows 4 mm silk ribbon, with stitches ¼" (6 mm) apart and ¼" (6 mm) long. Having the laced ribbon flat and smooth against the fabric adds beauty to the stitch.

Weaving ribbon under

**Ways to use:** bands, borders, corner bracket borders

## FLY

This versatile stitch can be worked diagonally, vertically, horizontally, circularly, side by side, or curved. Travel top to bottom. The tie-down stitch can be long or short depending on how you are using the stitch. It can be worked as a wide or narrow stitch, giving it a V or Y shape. When used for filling, it can have either type of tie-down. Placed in a circle with the tie-downs meeting in the center, it can be used as a motif. Use it as foliage around and among flowers, adding greenery to fill in the area. This stitch can be worked using thread that adds texture to a design. Use wool, wool blends, pearl cotton, velvet, or any of the threads shown in the other chapters.

**Ways to use:** bud and flower sepals, filling, grass, motifs, foliage

**Also known as:** tied, Y, open loop

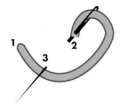 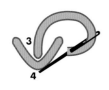 

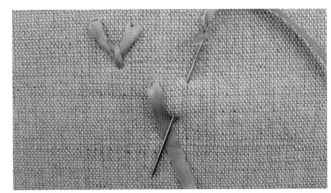

Keeping the ribbon under the needle

# Snippets

Save short pieces of silk ribbon to work small stitches on a project. If the ribbon is pierced with the needle and you change your mind, smooth the fibers back into place with your fingernail.

## FLY LEAF

This stitch travels top to bottom down the leaf shape. The stitches can be placed close together or slightly apart, depending on the look you prefer. Leaving the ribbon slightly loose creates a leaf with a fuller look. For added interest, do not straighten all the ribbon as you stitch the leaf. When working the tie-down stitch, leave it slightly loose rather than pulling it snug. Your eye will tell you how much to pull the ribbon by the way the ribbon underneath looks. As you work down the leaf, increase the size of the stitches to create the leaf shape.

This stitch can be worked using thread that adds texture to a design. Use wool, wool blends, pearl cotton, velvet, or any of the threads shown in the other chapters.

**Ways to use:** leaves, flower petals, bands

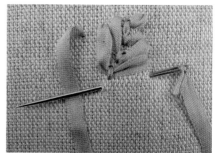

Increasing leaf width

## FERN

This stitch can travel in any direction. Work it from top to bottom following the numbers and arrows. It is an easy stitch and works well for foliage. As you work the stitch, the length of the stitches can be worked evenly or unevenly as required for the area. The stitch length may need to be adjusted for curves. A long wandering fern can be used for greenery in a floral design.

Any thread can be used for this stitch when used for foliage or veins of a leaf. Pearl cotton and hand-dyed or over-dyed single-strand work especially well.

**Ways to use:** borders, filling, foliage, motifs, veins of leaves

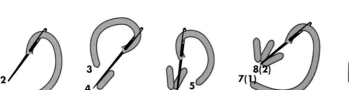

Working center stitch

# FEATHER

This stitch travels vertically, horizontally, circularly, or in a curved direction, working top to bottom. Keep both ends of the loop even in height, and keep the stitch size even or vary the size depending on the desired look. The rhythm of this stitch works well with the sewing method as you place the stitches on alternate sides. Use your finger to hold the ribbon in place while completing the stitch.

**Ways to use:** circular motifs, grass, ferns, leaves, foliage, embellishment on clothing, as an appliqué stitch to secure edges together

**Also known as:** single coral, briar, plumage

Working second stitch

 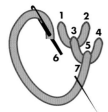 

# FLOWERED FEATHER

This stitch travels vertically, horizontally, circularly, or in a curved direction, working top to bottom in the same manner as the feather. Size 11/0 seed beads are used as an embellishment to create the look of flowers. You can place them either on the tip of each loop or randomly, as shown. This stitch can be worked in any type of thread when used as foliage among flowers.

**Ways to use:** borders, foliage, embellishment on clothing, as an appliqué stitch to secure edges together

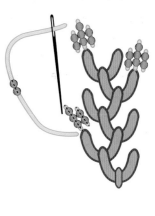

## BLANKET

This stitch travels left to right. Keep the vertical stitches straight and the same height, and keep the horizontal stitches the same distance apart. The bottom loop of the ribbon should be pulled at the same tension. The stitch height is determined by how the stitch is used. Decorative stitches can be slightly longer. If using the stitch to close two pieces of fabric or felt for a pillow, use a smaller stitch length. This stitch can be worked along an edge, flat against a seam, or to create a narrow decorative hem.

**Ways to use:** edgings, bands, outlines

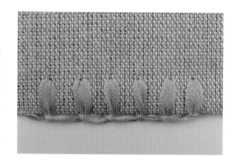

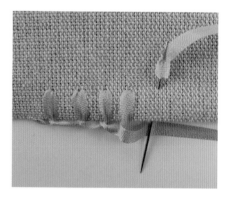

Keeping ribbon under needle

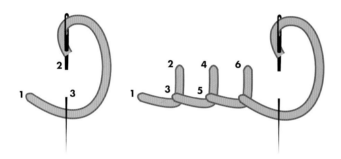

## CLOSED BUTTONHOLE

This stitch travels left to right and is worked similarly to the blanket stitch. Vertical pairs of stitches slant toward each other and share a hole without piercing the ribbon of the first stitch placed. As you work the stitch, always keep the ribbon under the needle on the downward stitch. The stitches look their best when stitched evenly. It may take practice to keep the stitches at the correct angle.

**Ways to use:** decorative hems, borders, bands, edgings

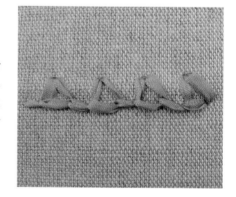

Slanting stitch

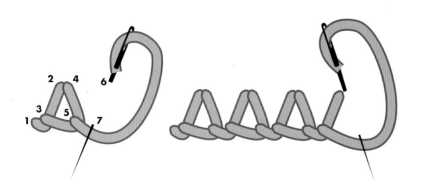

THE COMPLETE PHOTO GUIDE TO NEEDLEWORK

# FRENCH KNOT

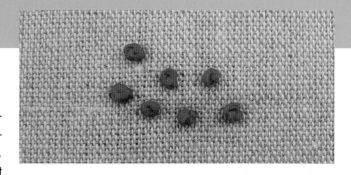

Place knots where desired. The size of the ribbon and number of wraps—one or two—determine the knot size produced. The example shows 4 mm ribbon with two wraps. Once the ribbon is wrapped on the needle, it is important to keep the needle straight and the ribbon taut as it enters the fabric. Use your other hand to hold the ribbon taut.

**Ways to use:** flower centers, filling, single row of knots spaced for outline of leaves or motifs

**Also known as:** French dot, knotted, twisted knot, wound

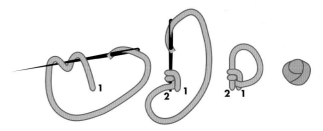

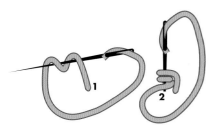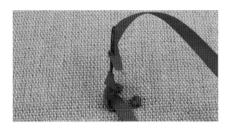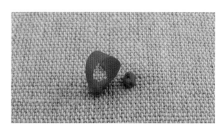

Placing the needle in fabric    Tightening the ribbon    Pulling knot into place

# SLOPPY KNOT

Place knots where desired. The sloppy knot is worked similarly to the French knot. To work this knot, leave the wrapped ribbon slightly loose as you pull it down into the fabric. You can adjust the size of the knot by adjusting the tension used when wrapping this knot. The French and sloppy knots can be combined in the center of a flower, adding texture to the center. Using a combination of ribbon work and knots worked in thread gives a nice texture to the finished project.

**Ways to use:** flower centers, filling

Keeping ribbon loose    Pulling knot into place

## ARROWHEAD

This stitch travels left to right in diagonal stitches. It is very effective when worked in a circle for a flower, but it is shown here in a straight line to emphasize an important point. It should be worked so the diagonal lines meet without the slight gap that you see between the first two stitches on the left. The last four stitches are correctly worked close together. The varying heights give the stitch a slightly different appearance. When working in a circle, draw the desired size of the circle on the fabric with chalk or quilter's gray pencil.

**Ways to use:** borders, bands, flowers, sun rays

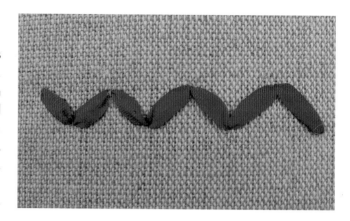

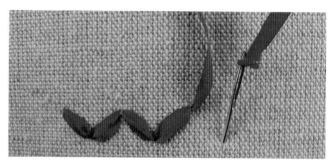

Placing diagonal stitch

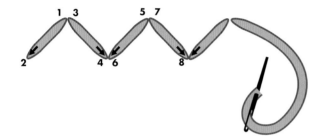

## CHAIN

Travel in any direction, working top to bottom. Keep the ends of the loop even and the ribbon smooth as it forms the loop. If your ribbon stitch has an opening in the center of the loop, either the ends were not even or the ribbon was twisted. Use your finger to hold the ribbon in place while completing the stitch. Watch the tension. The ribbon should lie flat against the fabric with no puckering of fabric.

**Ways to use:** borders, curved motifs, circular shapes, outline, stems, vines

**Also known as:** tambour, point de chainette

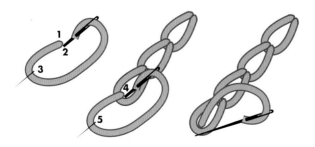

Completing a chain

# PISTIL

This stitch can be worked in any direction. It is a variation of a French knot with an added stem.

When working this stitch, you can use any length of stem that works for the application. When using on a curved line, as you take the needle down into the fabric have the ribbon for the stem slightly loose to conform to the area. For a straight pistil, keep the stem and wrapped ribbon taut as it enters the fabric. Pearl cotton pistil stitches are a nice texture contrast used as stamens for silk ribbon flowers.

**Ways to use:** flower stamens, flower petals, filling

Taking needle down into fabric

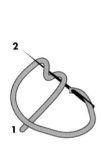   

# LAZY DAISY LEAF

This stitch can travel in any direction. It is worked like a lazy daisy flower except the tie-down is slightly off center, causing half the loop to fold over the edge of the other half. You can work the tie-down either slightly to the right or the left. This leaf complements flowers that are worked using a lazy daisy stitch.

**Ways to use:** leaves, filling

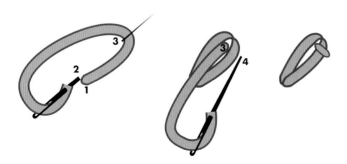

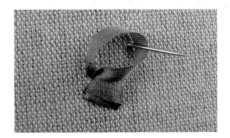

Placing tie down off center

## LAZY DAISY DETACHED

This stitch is worked across the area, traveling in any direction. Quick to work, this stitch is perfect for working in a cluster to fill in an area around floral work. In the same area of the fabric, adjust the leaf size and use different green colors to give the stitches a different appearance.

**Ways to use:** filling, leaves

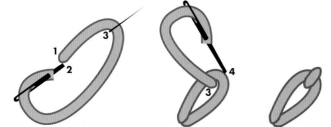

Working a detached daisy

## LAZY DAISY FLOWER

This stitch travels around in a circle to form a flower. It is worked the same as a chain or lazy daisy stitch. When working this stitch, keep the ends of the loop together (no space between) for a neat look and a flatter stitch. If you find your daises have an open space between the loops, add a straight stitch in the center. This versatile stitch can be used singly or grouped together for a bouquet of flowers. Work one or more French or sloppy knots in the center. The size of the center depends on the size of the flower created. Stems can be added using the stem or chain stitch.

**Ways to use:** flowers, filling, bands

Coming up through a loop

## LAZY DAISY FAN

This border travels left to right across the area. Two stitches and beads have been combined to create the border: lazy daisy and French knot. Each component of the border is stitched as discussed under the stitch name and description in this section. The bead work is a small bugle and a 11/0 seed bead sewn in place using bead thread. For an even line at the bottom of the fan, use a piece of quilter's tape placed straight on the fabric.

This fan shape can be made without the beads, using pistil stitches instead. Pistils with the French knot can be worked in a fan shape for a different looking border.

**Ways to use:** edging, individual motifs, filling, borders

## LAZY DAISY BORDER

This border travels left to right across the area. Three stitches are combined to create the border: lazy daisy, stab, and French knot. Each component of the border is stitched as discussed under the stitch name and description in this section.

The stab stitch can be replaced with a bugle bead and 11/0 seed bead, as shown for the fan lazy daisy above. Pistil stitches can be placed coming outward from the daisy motif. Short or longer pistils can be used depending on the desired look.

**Ways to use:** borders, individual motifs, filling

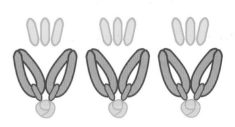

## FLOWER BORDER

This border travels left to right across the area. Three stitches have been combined to create the border: lazy daisy, long straight, and French knot. Each component of the border is stitched as discussed under the stitch name and description in this section.

**Ways to use:** edging, individual flowers, filling, borders

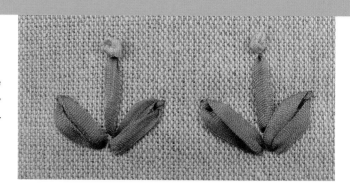

## CHAIN ROSE

This stitch travels in a circle. Work a French knot for the center of the rose using three to five strands of embroidery floss or 4 mm ribbon. Simply work chain stitches in a circle around the knot until you reach the desired rose size. To end, slide the ribbon under the chain stitches and secure on the back. Use this rose when you want to fill an area quickly. While it resembles the spiderweb rose (page 135), it is quicker and easier to make but not quite as beautiful.

**Ways to use:** filling, borders, gardens scenes, clothing embellishment

Working chain around knot

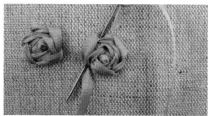

Adding another chain

Going into fabric under rose to end

## TULIP

This stitch is worked across the area, traveling in any direction. A lazy daisy and long straight stitch are used to create the tulip. Slide the straight stitch ribbon behind the tie-down, creating the tulip base. This stitch can be worked any size desired. It can be used to fill in around floral motifs. For a beautiful clothing embellishment, place a tulip between the buttonholes on a blouse or suit jacket.

**Ways to use:** edgings, motifs, clothing embellishment, group filling

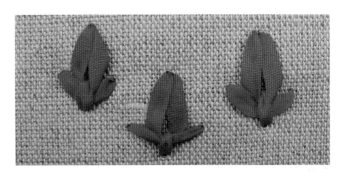

Completing the tie-down positioning for the straight stitch

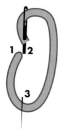 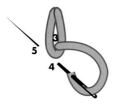  

## PETAL

This stitch is a combination of the daisy stitch and backstitch, traveling right to left. It works well with 4 mm ribbon on straight or curved lines. Start stitching a stitch distance away from the end of the starting point. Place the first stitch back toward the starting point. Come up halfway under the first stitch to make the daisy. Repeat this process across the area. You can end with the last daisy in the center or add another daisy at the tip of the last straight stitch when using as foliage.

**Ways to use:** stems of flowers, bands, foliage, circular or swirl motifs, lacy edging, stem of leaves

**Also known as:** pendant chain

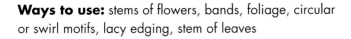

Completing daisy and positioning for next

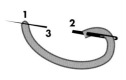   

## LOOP FLOWER

This type of flower is quick to make, adding more height to the silk ribbon than most other stitches. Decide the size of the loop you want for the flower. Bring the ribbon up from the back, smoothing the ribbon where it comes out of the fabric. Lay it flat against the fabric. Take the needle and ribbon back through the flat ribbon, 1/16" (1.6 mm) from where it exited the fabric. Pull gently on the ribbon until the desired loop height is reached. Making a tiny stitch in the flat ribbon will secure the two ribbons, keeping the loop from sliding back into the fabric. When the flower is complete, end the ribbon carefully on the back without disrupting the loops on the front. Make one to three sloppy knots for the center of the flower, depending on the size of the flower. These flowers can vary in both number and length of petals.

**Ways to use:** clothing embellishment, floral scenes, group filling

Ending stitch by piercing ribbon at start

Working in a circle

## LOOP BUD

This stitch is randomly placed. It is a quick stitch that can be used to fill in around other silk ribbon work. The loop can be made any size you desire. When making the loop, keep the ribbon straight and the fold-over flower will have a flat, smooth appearance. When the ribbon loop is in place, push the ribbon down onto the needle and bring the needle and ribbon up through the center of the ribbon loop. Place the French knot in the center of the ribbon to achieve the loop bud. Wider ribbon, 7 mm or 13 mm, works well for filling. If the surrounding silk work is smaller, use the 4 mm ribbon, as shown.

**Ways to use:** single flowers, group filling

**Also known as:** loop flower

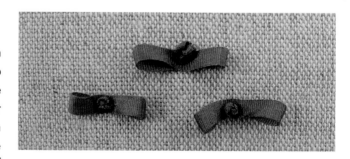

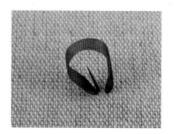
Bringing needle up to pierce ribbon

Working French knot

## SNOW DROP

This stitch is a combination of lazy daisies, stab, and pistil stitches. Work the three daises, then add the stab stitches, starting with the center daisy. Angle the two side stab stitches toward the center one. The pistil stitches can be one, two, or three per side. A stem and leaves can be added to each snow drop if desired. Work the stem and leaves in the same manner as the lily of the valley.

**Ways to use:** single flowers, clothing embellishment, floral scenes, group filling, motif centers

Placing a stab stitch

Working knot of pistil

## LILY OF THE VALLEY

This flower is a combination of the fly and lazy daisy stitches, with a straight stitch filling the center of the daisy. A stem stitch, long straight stitch, and twisted ribbon were used for the stem and leaves. Work the stem with three or four strands of embroidery floss or silk ribbon. Work the leaves with ribbon.

Work the flowers, starting with the fly. Add a lazy daisy with a straight stitch in the center of the daisy stitch. Although this daisy was closed, the straight stitch was added to the center to give fullness to the blossom. One, two, or three lilies can be placed on the stem. One leaf is worked using a long straight stitch. Place the long stitch, pierce the tip of the stitch, and angle a straight stitch out for the long one. For the other leaf, give the ribbon a twist before taking the ribbon to the back. I used the two different types of leaves to show how different leaves can be made for flowers.

**Ways to use:** single flowers, clothing embellishment, floral scenes, motif centers, group filling

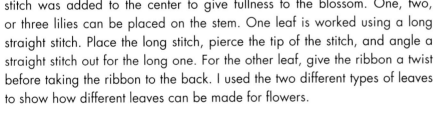

Working fly stitch

Working lazy daisy

Filling center of daisy

Working tip of leaf

## IRIS

This sweet iris is worked using a lazy daisy and twisted ribbons. Work the lazy daisy for the main part of the iris first. Then come up from the back, placing the left side petal. Twist the ribbon and carefully slide the ribbon through the bottom of the daisy for the right side petal, leaving the ribbon slightly loose on both sides. When placing the stem, come up directly under the daisy to avoid a gap. Twist the ribbon until it is tight, then allow it to loosen to the desired round size. Then, take the needle and ribbon down into the fabric. Secure the ribbon on the back. Work the leaves just under the stem. You can twist the ribbon to the left or right before taking it down into the fabric. The leaf ribbon sometimes requires a little more manipulation than just twisting the ribbon to get it to stay in place.

**Ways to use:** single flowers, clothing embellishment, floral scenes, motif centers, group filling

Sliding behind daisy stitch

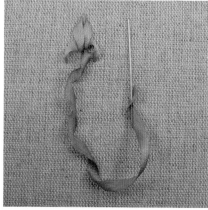

Twisting the stem ribbon

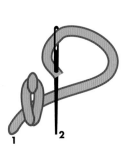

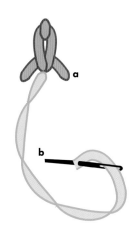

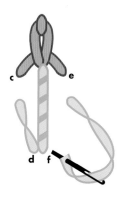

## SPIDERWEB ROSE

Using chalk or quilter's gray pencil, draw a circle on the fabric for the desired rose size. The stitched ribbon will go slightly farther out than the circle. Work five straight stitches for the base of the rose, using one or two strands of embroidery floss. With ribbon, begin in the center, going over and under the spokes. The first two rows of weaving will hide the center spokes; keep the ribbon snug for those. Loosen the ribbon to create a soft effect for the rest of the weaving. To end the ribbon, take the needle and ribbon down into the fabric under the rose.

The traditional spiderweb rose is worked keeping the ribbon smooth as you weave. However, a slight loose twist in the ribbon, as shown produces a more realistic looking rose.

You can start the rose with a very tiny stitch in the fabric between spokes to secure the tail of the ribbon on the back. The rose shown was not started in that manner. The ribbon was secured around the spokes on the back.

**Ways to use:** single flowers, clothing embellishment, floral scenes, group filling

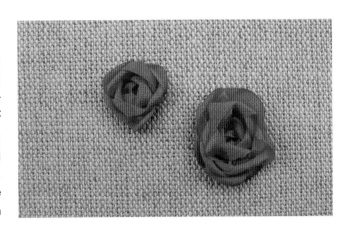

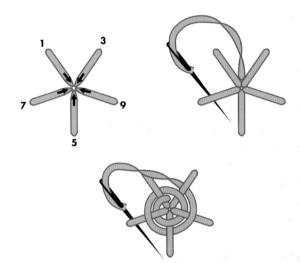

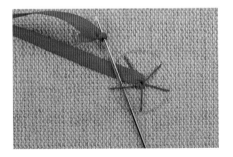

Starting to weave

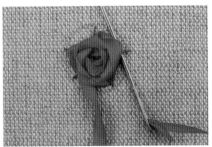

Weaving over and under

Going into fabric under rose to end

## PLUME

Place randomly over area, traveling top to bottom. The plume is quick to make and will add more height to the silk ribbon than most other stitches. Bring the ribbon up from the back, smoothing the ribbon where it comes out of the fabric. Take the needle down into the fabric ¼" (6 mm) in front of the other end of the ribbon. Pull the ribbon through to the back, leaving a ⅜" (1 cm) loop. As you pull the ribbon into the fabric, use your finger, another needle, or a laying tool to keep the ribbon smooth. It is very easy to pull too quickly and have the stitch disappear into a tiny stitch on the fabric. Use a gentle hand! To make the second loop, come up from the back, piercing the previous loop ⅛" (3 mm) from where the ribbon goes into the fabric. Work the desired number of loops in the same manner, except make the additional loops slightly shorter than the first loop. For the last loop, go between ⅛" and ¼" (3 and 6 mm) away and take the last loop down into the fabric, leaving this stitch slightly loose.

**Ways to use:** foliage, filling, embellishment

Placing first stitch

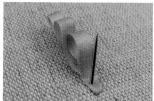

Piercing previous loop

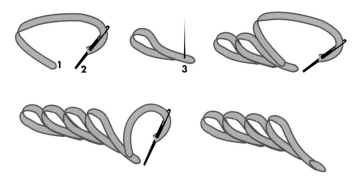

## FRENCH KNOT LOOP

This stitch is randomly placed. It is a quick stitch that can be used to fill in around other silk ribbon work. The loop can be made large as shown or any size desired. When making the loop, keep the ribbon straight for a flat, smooth appearance. Bring the ribbon up from the back and make a loop the desired size. Use a straight pin to hold the two pieces of ribbon in place while working the French knot. Wider ribbon—7 mm or 13 mm—works well for filling. If the surrounding silk work is smaller, use the 4 mm silk ribbon, as shown.

**Ways to use:** single flowers, group filling, embellishment, foliage

Piercing base of loop with knot

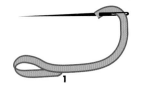

# CRETAN LEAF

This leaf is worked top to bottom. Work the stitches either close together or slightly apart. It is important to follow the numbers and arrows, keeping the ribbon under the needle. Using the sewing motion works best to create a more even appearance. As you work, take the same size stitch in the fabric in the center of the leaf, if possible. Slightly increase the size of the stitches as you work down the leaf. The rhythm of this stitch makes stitching it a pleasure.

**Ways to use:** flower leaves, leaf borders, filling

**Also known as:** long arm feather

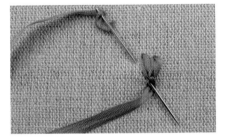
Starting second stitch

Keeping ribbon under needle

Ending with small stitch at base

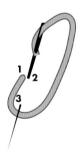

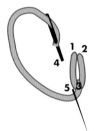

## LOOP DAISY

This stitch is simply a long piece of ribbon folded over. Using chalk or quilter's gray pencil, draw a small circle to work the petals around. When you bring the ribbon to the front of the fabric, fold it back over and take it down in front of the previous stitch. Use a gentle hand to pull the ribbon to the back of the fabric to avoid pulling it too far. For a smoother petal, carefully straighten the ribbon as it goes in and out of the fabric. Work the number of flower petals desired, keeping the petal length as even as possible.

Use one strand of embroidery floss to make a stitch on each petal to secure the loops in place. Bring the needle and thread up from the center circle, going approximately ⅜" (1 cm) up the petal, and taking the needle down in the center of the petal. Make silk French or sloppy knots in the center of the daisy. The small stitches will show on the finished flower. If you prefer they not show, add more knots in the center.

**Ways to use:** single flowers, clothing embellishment, floral scenes, group filling

Ending stitch next to starting point

Tying loop down

## ROSETTE

This is a sweet little bud flower that is easy to create. Bring the ribbon up in the area where the rosette is to be placed. Slide the needle into the fabric, picking up slightly less fabric than the size of the stitch to be worked. Wrap the ribbon around the needle twice. For the second wrap, keep the ribbon flat. It should be left a little loose so it will lie slightly away from the first wrap. Keep your thumb on one side of the wrapped ribbon and pull the needle through the fabric. Place tie-down stitch at the top of the rosette. Carefully bring the needle and ribbon up inside the open bottom area. At the edge of the wrapped ribbon, take a tie-down stitch to secure the bottom of the rosette. When the wrapped ribbon is tied down, the ribbon loops will be slightly curled. This gives the appearance of the ribbon being wrapped more than twice. A stem and leaves can be added for a stemmed flower.

**Ways to use:** single flowers, group filling, embellishment

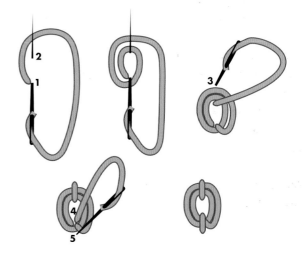

Wrapping ribbon under needle

Placing top tie down

Coming up for bottom tie down

# Rainbow of Ribbons Purse

The combination of silk ribbon and hand-dyed wool in this little pouch reminds me of a rainbow in the sky. The ribbon flowing across the fabric brings a soft sheen to the rough texture of the tulle and wool.

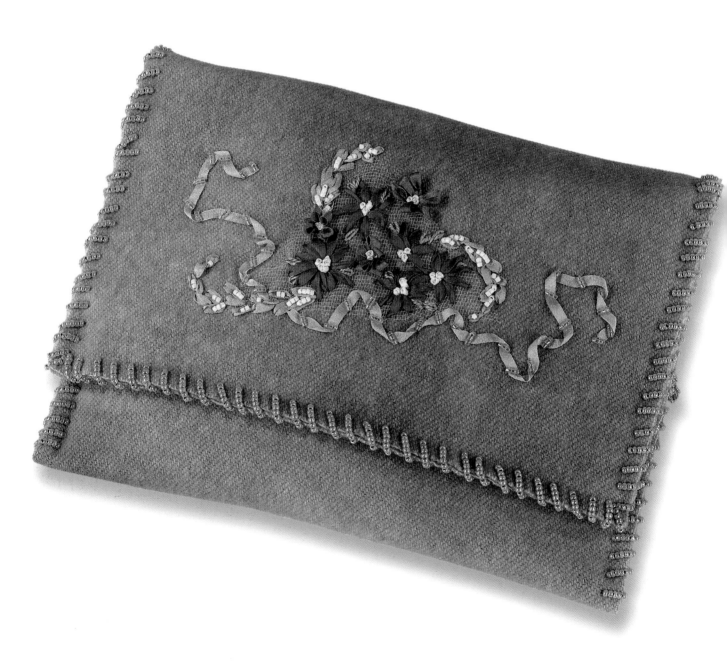

## YOU WILL NEED

- two pieces 8" × 16½" (20.3 × 41.9 cm) hand-dyed 100 percent wool fabric: iris
- 7¾" × 16" (19.7 × 40.6 cm) piece of flannel: white
- 4" × 4" (10.2 × 10.2 cm) piece of tulle: white
- 4 mm silk ribbon: medium lavender, medium French lavender, pinkish red, medium peachy pink, and off white
- Delica beads: opaque rainbow ivory, luster wisteria lavender
- three packages of 4.54 gm seed beads, size 11/0: ice lilac
- six-strand embroidery floss: very light topaz
- wool blend: olive green and blue purple
- Silamide bead thread: purple, light gray, and natural
- sewing thread: white
- beading, embroidery, and size 22 crewel needles
- general sewing supplies

## STITCHES USED

- side ribbon
- folded flower
- stab
- lazy daisy
- bead couching over ribbon
- beaded whipped edging
- sloppy knot
- French knot

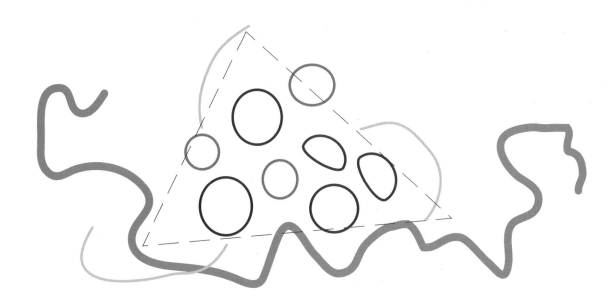

Design pattern (actual size). Use the pattern as a guide to work the silk stitches.

*(continued)*

## Stitching Instructions

**1** Center the flannel on the back of one piece of wool and baste the two fabrics together using the white sewing thread. Set the extra piece of wool aside for finishing. The flannel is used as a stabilizer for the beads and an interlining for the purse.

**2** Baste a line across the width of the wool/flannel, 5" (12.7 cm) up from the bottom edge for the purse pocket. Baste a line 5" (12.7 cm) down from the top edge of the wool for the front flap of the purse. Lay the front side of the fabric down; then fold the bottom of the wool over on the flannel until the basted line is along the bottom edge of what will be the pocket of the purse. To see how the front flap will fit, fold the top of the fabric over onto the flannel until the basted line is along the top edge. See photograph for front flap placement. Make adjustment to basted lines, if needed. Mark the front flap with a pin.

**3** Cut the piece of tulle into a triangle shape. Pin the tulle in place using the pattern as a guide and baste in place.

## Plan Ahead

Place the basting thread knot on the front of the wool for easy removal once the purse is complete.

**4** Optional step: Cut a circle the size of the flowers from tissue paper to use as a guide for working the flowers.

**5** Use peachy pink ribbon and a stab stitch to work the three curved shapes. Starting at the bottom of the curve, place one to three stitches together as you work upward. Use ivory beads with natural bead thread to attach the beads to the stitches. Use one to four per stitch, as desired. Place the beads from the bottom of the stitch upward.

**6** Use pinkish red ribbon and the side ribbon stitch to work the four red flowers. Notice that two of them are a half of a flower. Use the olive green wool blend and the lazy

daisy leaf to work a few leaves around the flowers. Use off-white ribbon and work sloppy and/or French knots in the center of each flower.

**7** Use French lavender ribbon and the folded loop flower to work the three lavender flowers. Use the topaz embroidery floss to work sloppy knots in the center of each flower.

**8** Use medium lavender ribbon and the bead couching over ribbon and lavender beads. Place the ribbon as desired over the area. I used two pieces, bringing the ribbon up from under the lower left swirl.

**9** Place the remaining piece of wool and the flannel interlining with backs together. Pin in place.

**10** Fold the pocket toward the center of the piece of plain wool until the basted line is along the bottom fold of the pocket. Pin in place. Baste the pieces of fabric together. Baste along the two sides and across the edge of the front flap.

**11** Use seed beads and the whipped edging stitch to finish the fabric edges. Start the beading stitch on one side of the bottom fold, working upward along the side, across the front flap edge, and down the other side. The bottom fold and top edge of the pocket are not beaded. Instructions for the whipped edge is in the Bead Embroidery chapter. On the corners, work three whipped stitches using a shared top hole for all three. Couch the stitch that goes across the corner of the fabric. The beginning and ending threads can be hidden between the layers of fabric. When ending the beading by the bottom folded edge, slide the needle between the layers of fabric to the inside of the pocket. Turn the pocket inside out and take three small stitches along the bottom folded edge to end the thread. If preferred, finish the edge of the purse with the blanket stitch and wool blend in blue purple instead of the beaded edge.

**12** Use the blue purple wool blend and the buttonhole stitch to secure the top edge of the pocket.

# Orientation

Rotate the fabric to make stitching easy. It may be helpful to turn the 5" (12.7 cm) top basted section toward you and work the front flap that way.

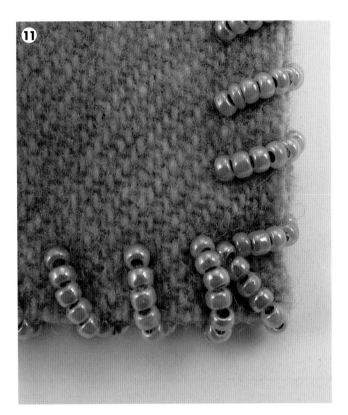

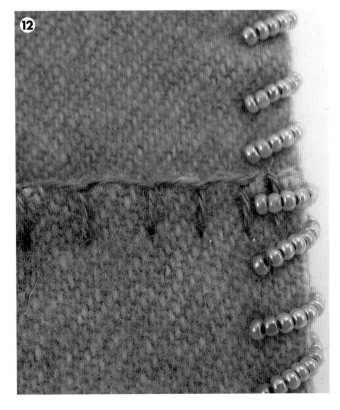

# Silk Magic Lamp Shade

This little lamp is the perfect size for an end table or bedroom. The design, stitched on the bronze shade in Mediterranean blue silk, will dance in the night when the lamp is used.

A fabric lamp shade with a fabric lining is the easiest to stitch. The needle will slide in and out of the fabric without leaving holes if the stitch direction is changed. If using a shade with a plastic backing, first punch holes through the shade where the needle will be inserted using an awl or large needle. Punch holes for a few inches (cm) and work that section, repeating this sequence until the shade is stitched.

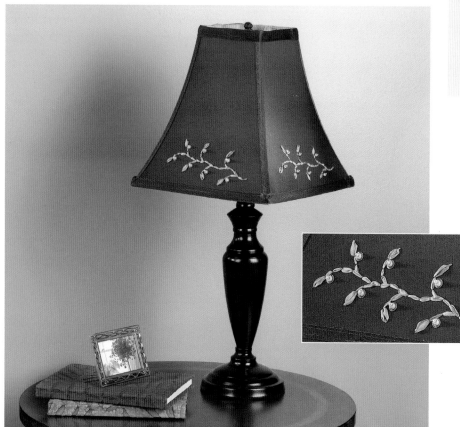

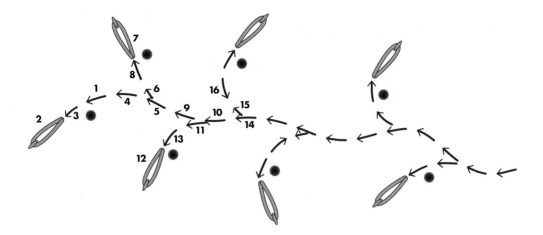

Pattern

The pattern is a guide only. The size and number of stitches will be determined by how you stitch them. The lazy daisy is indicated at the tips of the branches. The dashes indicate back stitches and straight stitches, and the arrows indicate the direction the stitches should be worked. Work these stitches close together so the shade fabric does not show between them. The ribbon needs to follow the same path on the back of the shade as it does on the front so that when the light is on, you don't see ribbon shadows outside the design stitches. As you work, periodically hold the shade up to the light and check for shadows. Working from the back with blue sewing thread, carefully take a stitch in any errant ribbon, and gently secure it in line with the other stitches.

The pattern can be sized to fit most lamp shades. If using a round shade, leave space between the motifs or trace the branch in a continuous border.

Use the tissue paper method for tracing and stitching through the paper (page 22). For information on how to work the stitches used in this design, refer to the Stitch section of this chapter and the Bead Embroidery chapter.

# Bolder Design

If you prefer a bolder design, use 7 mm ribbon.

## Stitching Instructions

**1** Use blue silk ribbon to work the stitches as shown on the pattern. When starting to work a small limb, the first stitch (6) should come up from under stitch 5 on the branch. Before working the last stitch on the limb (8), from the back, slide the needle/ribbon through the ribbon of stitch 6 and into the ribbon of 5 on the branch. This should keep the ribbon on the wrong side behind the ribbon on the front. Continue to work the branch with 9. When working each limb, use this process for best results.

**2** Bead locations are indicated on the chart by dots. Use the bead thread to attach a sequin and a Rondelle bead using a seed bead to hold them in place. Work this combination to place the berries on the branch and limbs. Place them close to the silk so the thread will not show when the light is turned on.

**3** Trim ribbon and thread close to work to be sure they do not show. Place the shade on a lamp and test. If necessary, adjust the threads.

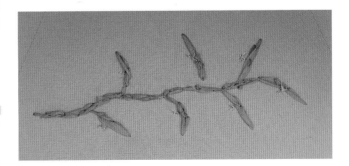

Ribbon on the back stays in line with the design.

# BEAD EMBROIDERY

Needle artists have been applying beads to fabric for centuries. Beads continue to be popular with needleworkers today, and they can be combined with any technique in this book. Beads and sequins can be used to embellish clothing and home décor items from pillows to towels. It's fun to see a little sparkle in projects, and beads give life to items being created or embellished.

# Fabric

Any surface that the beading needle can slide through easily can be used, except for very stretchy fabrics. These fabrics make it difficult to maintain the tension required for a smoothly beaded project.

In the Creative Embroidery (page 31), Crewel (page 78), and Silk Ribbon (page 113) sections, some of these same fabrics have been discussed. Be sure to read about them in each of those chapters. For bead embroidery, most types of fabric can be used. Play around with the different types to see how they look with your favorite stitches.

Iron the fabric to remove the wrinkles, and keep the fabric as wrinkle free as possible when attaching the beads. If it is necessary to press the fabric after beading, place the work upside down on a fluffy terry bath towel and press with a low-temperature iron.

## ULTRASUEDE

This is a wonderful surface for bracelets, clutch purses, headbands, belts, vests, or other clothing items. It is easy to work through the surface of the synthetic suede. For small projects the edges can be left raw, making it easy to finish.

Ultrasuede comes in many colors. Black is an elegant color that shows off the sparkle of the beads and sequins. This fabric is available in many fabric stores and on the Internet.

A much thinner imitation suede is also available. If you use this fabric for projects, you'll need to finish the edges.

## FLORAL AND GEOMETRIC PRINTS

The right size print is needed for beading. Some floral fabrics lend themselves to beads better than others. If a flower has one or two layers of larger petals, the beads will leave enough room for the fabric of the petal to show after the beading.

If the petals are too close, the beads will hide the fabric. It is best to stay away from flowers that have multiple layers of small petals. The beads will change the shape, and the beauty of the pattern will disappear.

The geometric prints that work best contain sections within the pattern that are large enough to accommodate beads; such patterns are enhanced when beads are added. Stripes or plaids work well. Choose certain colors within the pattern to bead, allowing space between the beaded areas to create a dimensional appearance.

When using a floral or geometric pattern, you need to decide how much fabric to purchase for the project. Choose a print that will work with the size of the project. For example, if a fabric has flowers that are 5" (12.7 cm) across from petal to petal and you plan to make a small 8" (20.3 cm) clutch purse, this floral is too large for the area and would not be a good choice for the project. A smaller print would be better.

Look at the available fabric and chose the one you like. Decide where the focal point would be on the fabric. Ask the sales person how often the floral pattern repeats. Check to see where the fabric was previously cut within the pattern repeat. Taking all of this into consideration will help you decide how much fabric will need to be purchased for the project. Purchase a little extra to use for the lining or another project.

## SHEER FABRIC

Place sheer fabric over other types of fabric to give a shimmery appearance to the surface. Simply baste the fabrics together and bead through all the layers.

## LACE

Lace can be placed over satin, taffeta, silk, synthetic, wool, cotton, or whatever fabric strikes your fancy.

## OTHER FABRICS

Refer to the Creative Embroidery and Crewel chapters for information on quilter's cotton, dupioni, velvet, felt, synthetic, and wool.

# Fabric to Avoid

Do not use fabric manufactured for outdoor use for beading projects. Although outdoor fabrics now feature beautiful floral patterns that will be tempting to use, the fabric is too thick and the hand needle does not slide easily through this fabric.

# Thread

The most important tip for beading on fabric using beading thread is to always pull the thread through the beads securely.

Beading thread likes to tangle and catch on the rough insides of the beads. You'll need to give it a gentle tug, being sure all the thread is snug against the fabric, without causing the fabric to pucker or the stop bead to curl. Sewing with a looser tension does not work with beading. Beads like to be secure against the fabric. As you learn fabric beading, remember to check that the bead is pulled snug with no thread showing.

### SILAMIDE

This thread comes on a card or spool. It is a waxed nylon twisted thread that is very strong and does not fray as you bead. For fabric beading or as a couching thread, use size A.

To smooth out the wrapping marks on carded threads, simply run your nail down the thread to straighten it. It will fray slightly at the tip if a sharp scissors is not used to cut it. It threads easily in the beading needles. Use two strands of this thread and a size 10 milliner needle. For fringes, beaded flowers, bead rows, etc., use a two yard (1.8 m) length, doubling the thread to give you two strands.

### NYMO

This thread is a waxed nylon twisted thread that comes on small spools. For fabric beading, size B is used. It comes in many colors and sizes. Use short lengths of this thread because every once in a while the strands will separate. It does have the advantage of being available in a larger color range than Silamide. Try both types of thread to find out which one you prefer.

The larger sizes in this thread are used for weaving.

## SOFT TOUCH

This very fine stainless steel, nylon coated wire comes on a spool. It is 50 percent softer than other wires of this type and is flexible enough to use with a needle for sewing beads to fabric. You can place a knot in the end of the wire for sewing on the beads and to tie off. It is used for beaded items that will have a lot of heavy use.

## ECONOFLEX

This is a very fine stainless steel, nylon-coated wire. It can be used for beading 4 mm size beads or larger for embellishing baskets, straw hats, lamp shades, and other items of this kind. You can place a knot in the end of the wire for sewing beads to fabric and to tie off.

## SEWING THREAD

Polyester sewing thread, available in a wide range of colors, comes on a spool and is found in fabric stores. It should be waxed with beeswax before using, as discussed in the ABC section. (Some stitchers do not wax their thread and use only sewing thread for bead embroidery.)

Sewing thread without beeswax can be used to stitch on sequins and to work a sequin row. Match the thread to the sequin.

## HAND-DYED OR SOLID COLORED SINGLE STRAND

This thread, which comes in a skein and is used for other techniques in this book, works well for the bead embroidery stitches. You don't need to wax this thread when it is used to work the beaded embroidery stitches. If it is used for a bead row or fringes, then it should be waxed before using.

## SIX STRAND EMBROIDERY FLOSS

This thread, which comes in a skein and is used for other techniques in this book, works well for the beaded embroidery stitches. Like the hand-dyed single-strand thread, it doesn't need to be waxed when used with the bead embroidery stitches or for attaching sequins using the lazy daisy or couching techniques. Embroidery floss is not recommended for sewing bead rows. It is not as strong as the other threads discussed in this section.

## PEARL COTTON (COTON PERLÉ)

This thread gives a nice shine to the bead embroidery stitches. Sizes 8, 12, and 16 can be used depending on the size of the bead. For the beaded stitch samples that begin on page 156, size 8 pearl cotton and a size 10 Crewel Thomas needle were used. It is difficult to find a needle that works both with the beads and the slightly larger pearl cotton. Size 12 and 16 do not work as well for the bead embroidery stitches like the stem, blanket, and lazy daisy. They are thinner threads and will not reveal the beauty of combining the embroidery stitch with the added bead.

# Beads and Sequins

Fabric beading isn't difficult once you learn the rhythm of the stitch and the amount of space to leave between beads. If you find it difficult, measure the bead and mark on a piece of quilter's tape the desired space between beads. When beads are worked this way several times, your eye will begin to judge the correct distance for you.

Any bead that the fabric can support and that has a hole running through the length or width of the bead can be used. Beads that have a small hole in the top can also be used. You can randomly attach these on clothing or embroidery projects for a little sparkle.

When embellishing floral or geometric prints with a bead row stitch, use Delica or 11/0 beads. These beads come in a wide range of colors and types. There are opaque, metallic, galvanized, matte, silver-lined matte, silver lined, and opaque rainbow to name a few. You can also use flat, disk, or barrel beads on these prints to accent certain areas on the fabric. Use bead colors that are slightly darker or lighter than the fabric area to be covered, so they will stand out instead of blending into the fabric color. Use bead thread the color of the beads. If that color is not available, use a neutral color like natural or silver. When using a bead that does not have matching beading thread, use a light gray thread. Sewing thread can be used but should be strengthened by coating it with beeswax several times. When attaching beads, be sure to pull the thread securely so the beads do not move. Begin by knotting the end of the thread. End thread by taking two small stitches on the back of the fabric and tie off.

If you enjoy the fabric beading projects in this book, continue to play around with the beads and experiment with different types of beads. Have fun exploring the world of beads.

It's helpful to have a foam bead mat or divided dish to keep the beads from rolling around. The foam bead mat makes it easier to pick up the beads. The foam can be cut to fit within a small box top lid, recycled metal mint box, or glass dish. The advantage of a box over a dish is that you can carry it around with you if you like to bead while watching TV or sitting outside in the sun.

Foam bead mat in tin box lid

## DELICA

This type of Japanese 11/0 glass seed bead is more consistent in size than other seed beads. These beads give fringes and bead row stitches a more even look. When stitching with this type of bead, they average nineteen beads per inch (2.5 cm). They come in a wide range of colors and finishes.

Although Delica is considered an 11/0 bead, it is slightly smaller than the 11/0 seed bead.

*(continued)*

## SEED BEADS

These beads come in various sizes. The 11/0 (smallest) to 8/0 (largest) are the most commonly used for fabric beading. The 8/0 will require a heavier stabilizer to support the fabric for  their weight. If you use the 8/0 bead, use flannel for the stabilizer, as discussed in the ABC section of the book. When stitching with these beads, 11/0 average eighteen to nineteen bead per inch (2.5 cm) and 8/0 average eleven to twelve beads per inch (2.5 cm). They come in a wide range of colors and types of finishes.

## BUGLES

These thin tube-shaped beads come in various sizes. They can be labeled large, medium, or small or ½" to 2" (1.3 to 5.1 cm). The colors range from transparent to metallic to rainbow to shiny.

# Rough Edges

Bugles that are not cut straight or that have a rough edge can cut the thread over time. For items that receive heavy use, place a Delica or seed bead on each end.

## ROUND MILLIMETER BEADS

These beads come in sizes ranging from small to large. The 4 mm and 6 mm work well for flower centers. They can be beaded as you would a seed bead or by using a stop bead.  When looking through the stitch diagram section, you will see this type of bead used for the stop bead stitch.

## BEAD MIX

Some companies sell a bead mix that contains several types of beads in color families that complement each other and in shades of the various colors. When working a project that calls  for seeding, these mixes give an interesting look. You can also pick out the various types of beads to use for different stitches or beading areas on a patterned print. The mix usually includes bugles, 11/0, 8/0, and cube beads. They may also include other types of beads in the mix.

## FACETED

These beads contain flat surfaces that reflect the light. They come in a wide range of shapes and sizes. You can find faceted beads in crystals to ordinary glass.

## CUBE

This square bead can look similar to a faceted bead. Some cubes have facets cut on the edges. It can add sparkle and height to a seeding project or floral design.

## FLAT, DISK, BARREL, AND OTHER SHAPES

There is a wide range of beads that fall into this category. These beads add more interest to those beaded projects where a little more zing is wanted. Any shape found in a small bead can be used for fabric beading. Beads with a hole in the top create interest by

grouping three together for a flower bud. Let your imagination run wild in the beading shop and choose beads that appeal to you.

## CRYSTAL PEARLS

Pearls come in all sizes and a nice range of colors. These are fun to use on purses, pillows, or anything that you want to have a stylish look.

## BEADS ON A STRING

When working with beads on fabric, you often want a bead color or shape that goes with the fabric and is slightly larger in size. The pillow shown on page 6 falls into this category. The beads that resemble wisteria blossoms came on a string. Although these are used mainly for jewelry work, they often work well for beading on fabric. Check out this type of bead on your next visit to the bead store.

## SEQUINS

Sequins have a hole in the middle for sewing to fabric and come in sizes ranging from 2.5 mm to 10 mm. They are available in a wide range of colors. They can be cupped, flat, round, or square. Finishes include metallic, transparent, iridescent, opaque iridescent, iris, and silky. Paillettes are larger sequins that have a hole in the top rather than the center. The most common sizes are 20 mm and 30 mm.

Sequins also come in various sizes and shapes like flowers, leaves, stars, and crescent moons to name a few.

The best source for sequins is on the Internet, though some bead shops do carry sequins and a few types and colors can be found in craft shops, often in the scrapbook section.

# Spooning

Use a small demitasse spoon or baby spoon to scoop up extra beads. Keep one with your beading supplies.

# Stitches

Work these stitches following the numbers and arrows. If more stitching information is needed about one of the beaded embroidery basic stitches, refer to Creative Embroidery (page 37) or Crewel (page 79). For more information, refer to Special Stitching Information (page 24).

When beading on fabric, use two strands of bead or sewing thread for all beading. When beading large areas, thread the beading needle with 2 yards (1.85 m) of thread; then double and knot the end for a 1-yard (0.92 m) length. For smaller areas, use a 1-yard (0.92 m) length, doubled. Use a frame—especially for large projects—to keep the project from losing its shape and to keep the tension more even. Beads should lie flat against the fabric. When attaching the beads, be sure to pull the thread securely so the beads do not move.

End the thread by taking two small stitches on the back of the fabric, one on top of the other, and tie off. Always use a stabilizer behind the fabric to support the beads; flannel or fusible fleece work best.

Beads enhance stitches and designs. These sample stitches will give you an idea of how a stitch looks with beads added. When working these beaded stitches, you can use fewer beads or add more beads than shown. Experiment and have fun as you bead!

## STRAIGHT

These single stitches can travel in any direction. Stitches should range from ¼" (6 mm) to 1" (2.5 cm) or slightly longer. Working this stitch longer than 1" (2.5 cm) creates a leggy stitch that will not support the bead. You can couch each bead in place on a longer stitch. Use one, two, or three beads per stitch. You will find many uses for these small, versatile stitches.

You can use Delica or 11/0 seed beads with any thread that will work with the bead and needle.

**Ways to use:** grass, leaves for small flowers, field flowers, insect antennae

**Also known as:** stroke, single satin

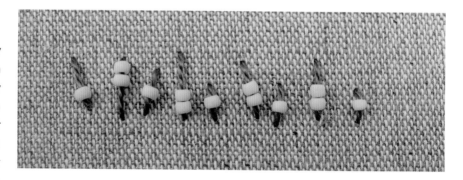

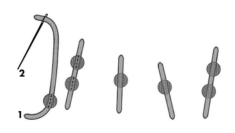

Using a single bead

## SEED

This filling stitch works up quickly. Place bead stitches randomly in different directions, without a given pattern. Seeding creates a light beaded effect in the desired shape.

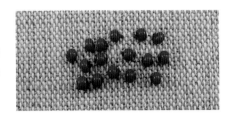

Two beads can be used for a longer length seed stitch, or place two beads side by side for a double-seed stitch.

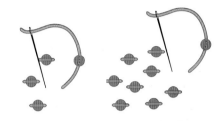

This wonderful stitch will add interest to an embroidered outline flower or leaf or any shape. Fill the petal or leaf with seeding using bead thread.

Delica, 11/0 seed beads, or bugles can be used with any thread that will work with the bead and needle. If you prefer that the thread not show, use bead thread. Gray Silamide works well with all light to medium fabric colors.

**Ways to use:** filling for flower petals or leaves, backgrounds, shapes, geometric areas, embellishment on clothing

**Also known as:** seed filling, speckling, rice grain, dot stitch

Placing a random bead

## SINGLE BACKSTITCH BEAD

A single backstitch bead can travel in any direction. When working a backstitch to hold the bead in place, always have the needle/thread come up on the right side where the bead is to be placed. Take the thread through the bead, going down into the fabric on the left side of the bead. Turn the fabric a quarter turn to keep the thread going in the correct direction when attaching beads randomly. Using a backstitch to secure a single bead will hold the bead more securely and it will sit straighter on the fabric. Although the photo shows a row of these beads, they can be randomly placed over an area. Single beads randomly spaced give a background area a stunning appearance.

This stitch is similar to a seed stitch. The single backstitch beads are placed farther apart from each other than when you are seeding.

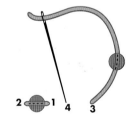

You can use any small bead with bead thread.

**Ways to use:** backgrounds, filling, motifs

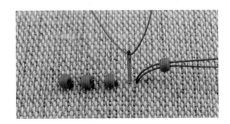

Working bead backstitch

## SINGLE BEAD WITH STOP BEAD

This bead technique is used to hold larger beads down in the center of a flower. It is also used to hold a bead in place when reversing directions for fringes and bead strings. The uses are endless and the bead sizes vary from bugles to 10 mm beads. This technique works well for beads with a top hole instead of a center hole. Many patterns call for a stop bead.

You can use any round or square bead that will work for the desired effect with bead thread. The thread that holds the stop bead should blend in with the bead or be the same color in order not to detract from the beading.

**Ways to use:** fringes, flowers, leaves, anything requiring the bead to dangle

Going into large bead

Pulling thread loop to secure stop bead

## BACKSTITCH BUGLE

Travel in any direction. Using a backstitch to secure a single bugle holds the bead securely against the fabric. Bugles can be worked singly or use a Delica or seed bead on each end. If using a bugle on an item that will receive heavy use, place a small bead on each end. Bugles are sometimes cut unevenly or have rough edges that can cut the thread.

You can use any size bugle that works with the stitch length, thread, and needle. If you prefer that the thread not show, use bead thread.

**Ways to use:** randomly placing beads over an area

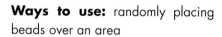

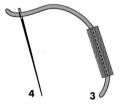

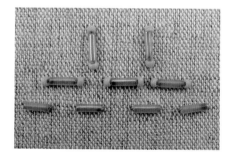

Positioning stitch

THE COMPLETE PHOTO GUIDE TO NEEDLEWORK

## COUCHED BUGLE

This stitch can travel left to right or right to left as you couch down the bugles. A couching stitch is a straight stitch placed over the laid bugle. If possible when working the couching, stitch up and go down in the same hole or area under the bugle. Any size bugle can be used. The size used will depend on how the stitch is being used. For a swirl, smaller bugles work best.

Metallic braids add a touch of sparkle to the couching. To give the large bugles a fancy couching effect, use a small cross-stitch (page 81), zigzag back (page 47), or lazy daisy (page 58) to hold the bugle in place.

You can use all sizes of bugles with any type of thread that will work with the bugle and needle. For the decorative fancy stitches, a 1" (2.5 cm) or longer bugle works best.

**Ways to use:** decorative swirls, filling shapes, securing lacing threads and decorative braids

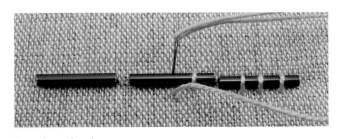

Couching bugle

## RUNNING

This stitch travels right to left by sliding the needle/thread in and out of the fabric. As the stitch is worked, slide on the beads before completing each single stitch. One, two, or three beads can be used, depending on the size of the stitch. This is a great stitch to use for outlining motifs.

You can use Delica, 11/0 seed beads, or any small bead that works with the stitch length, thread, and needle.

**Ways to use:** outlining, borders, straight lines, curved lines

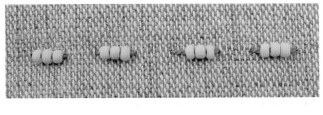

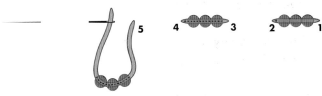

Keeping row straight

## STEM

This stitch travels left to right. As you work the stitch, keep the thread below the needle at all times. A single bead is used with each stitch. A rope effect can be seen between the stitches. The longer the stitch, the more you see this effect. When you slide on the bead, be sure the thread is below the needle before finishing the stitch. For a change, use a deeper bead color than thread or vice versa.

You can use Delica, 11/0 seed beads, or any small bead that works with the stitch length, thread, and needle.

**Ways to use:** branches, flower stems, outlines, filling, lettering, embellishment on clothing

**Also known as:** crewel, stalk

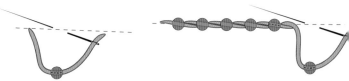

Keeping thread below needle

## SATIN

Work this stitch diagonally, vertically, or horizontally, traveling left to right. Place the bead stitches close together, keeping them snug and smooth against the fabric. Use three, five, seven, or nine beads per stitch. They can be placed in a straight row or unevenly across the area. Beads should be kept snug against each other and the needle/thread should go down into the fabric straight in front of the row. If you would like a slight curve to the stitch, place the needle/thread slightly to the left or right, depending on the way the curve will go.

You can use Delica or 11/0 seed beads with beading thread.

**Ways to use:** monogrammed initials, small borders, filling flower petals and leaves, accent areas on jewelry or home décor items

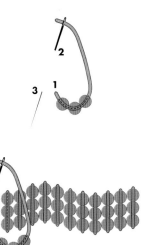

Working a wave pattern

## BEAD ROW

This stitch can travel in any direction, including circular. It is widely used for working beaded designs or for embellishing floral fabric. It is a very secure method for using on items that will have heavy use.

When working the bead row, keep the needle straight and in the center of the row as you come up between the first and second bead in the row. Go back through these two beads and add three more beads on the needle. Pull the beads snug against the previously placed beads, and use your opposite thumb to hold the beads snug against each other when taking the needle/thread straight down into the fabric right in center front of the beads. Repeat until the area is completed. Three important things to remember: (1) If the needle is not kept straight going up and down into the fabric, the row will not be straight. (2) Keep the beads snug against each other. (3) The fabric should remain flat and not puckered. Pull the bead thread securely through the beads after each step, checking the back of the fabric to be sure the thread is flat against the fabric.

You can use Delica, 11/0 seed beads, bugles, or any small bead that works with the stitch length, thread, and needle. Bead thread like Silamide or Nymo works best.

**Ways to use:** embellishing floral and geometric prints, motifs, outlines

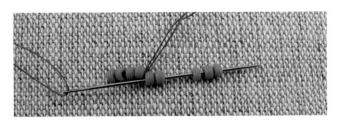

Going back through two and adding three

## DOUBLE-THREADED BACKSTITCH

First work the row of backstitches, traveling left to right. Begin these stitches a stitch length from the starting point, and keep the stitches snug against each other. Start the threaded stitch on the right side under the first backstitch. Thread on a bead and weave it under the next stitch. Repeat this to the end of the backstitch row. End the threading thread under the last stitch in the row. Start the new thread on the right side under the first stitch. Keep the loops of thread as even as possible.

When used on items that will have heavy use, you may want to couch the bead in place, as shown in the couched bead stitch in this section.

You can use Delica, 11/0 seed beads, or any small bead that works with the stitch length, thread, and needle.

**Ways to use:** borders, bands, outlines, embellishment on clothing

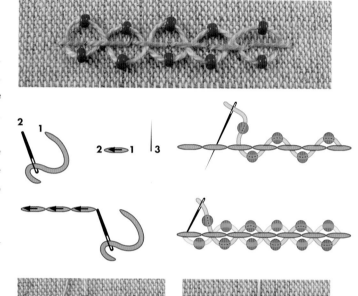

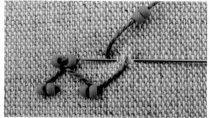
Weaving under backstitch          Weaving under both threads

## CHEVRON

This stitch travels left to right. It can be worked at different heights. The thickness of the thread will determine the height, but keep in mind the needle has to go through the bead. The sample was stitched with size 8 pearl cotton and seed beads which did not want to stay together as they should have. A small bugle could be used in place of the seed bead. As the horizontal stitches on the top and bottom are worked with the beads, try to make the stitch slightly longer than the beads. Using a single-strand thread or size 12 pearl cotton would give a smoother look.

You can use Delica, 11/0 seed beads, or bugles with any thread that will work with the bead and needle.

**Ways to use:** borders, bands, filling, embellishment for clothing

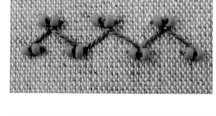

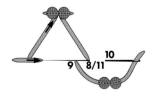
Placing second top stitch

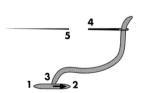 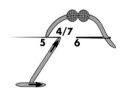 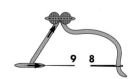

# BLANKET

This stitch travels left to right. The beads are added as you work the stitch. The horizontal thread should be pulled at the same tension. The stitch height is determined by how the stitch is used. Keep the thread under the needle on the downward vertical stitch. Have the stitches the same distance apart to accommodate the beads.

If desired, you can compensate so the beginning of the blanket stitch looks like all the other stitches. When stitching is completed, place a vertical stitch above the first horizontal stitch, sliding the needle/thread down behind the beginning tip of the horizontal stitch.

If using the stitch to close two pieces of fabric or felt for a pillow, a smaller stitch length will be necessary. Use one or two beads, depending on the horizontal stitch length.

You can use Delica or 11/0 seed beads with any thread that will work with the bead and needle.

**Ways to use:** edgings, filling for flowers and leaves, bands, outlines

Keeping thread under needle

# LONG AND SHORT BLANKET

This stitch travels left to right. The stitches are worked just like the blanket stitch, except every other vertical stitch is a shorter length. The beads are added as you work each vertical stitch. Keep the thread under the needle on the downward stitch. Have the stitches the same distance apart to accommodate the beads.

You can use one or two beads, depending on the length of the stitch. Two colors work well, but one is stunning.

You can use Delica or 11/0 seed beads with any thread that will work with the bead and needle.

**Ways to use:** edgings, filling for flowers and leaves, bands, outlines

Keeping thread under needle

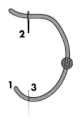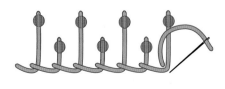

## CLOSED BLANKET

This stitch travels left to right. The beads are added to the horizontal stitch. When starting the stitch, the thread will slant slightly to the right. The two vertical threads come together at the top, with the right thread slanting to the left to complete the stitch. Notice that the threads on the worked stitches meet at the top of each stitch unit. Keep the thread under the needle on the downward stitch. One or two beads can be used.

You can use Delica or 11/0 seed beads with any thread that will work with the bead and needle.

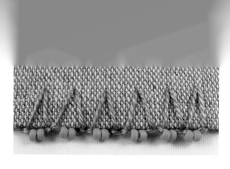

Starting a new stitch unit

**Ways to use:** decorative hems, borders, bands, edgings

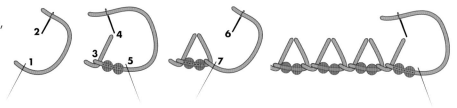

## BUTTONHOLE WHEEL

This stitch travels in a circle. It is worked the same as the blanket stitch, except the stitches are much closer together. The wheel can be worked as a complete circle or a half circle, as shown. Use a chalk pencil or quilter's grey pencil to draw the half or whole circle on the fabric. For the half circle, baste the bottom straight edge of the stitch. If a line is drawn on the bottom, it may show when stitching is completed. As you work the stitches, bring the needle up from the back, pick up a bead with your needle, and slide the bead down next to the previous stitch. This helps to keep the smooth rhythm of the stitch flowing. Two colors can be used, if desired.

For the half circle, you'll need to add a compensating stitch at the end to complete the right side of the half circle, as the right side will be slightly up from the basted line of the bottom edge. When the last stitch on the left is placed, come up in the center area on the right side and work a long straight stitch over to the first stitch placed. Tuck the needle/thread under the start of the first stitch, sliding the needle behind and down into the fabric. Work a smaller half circle, and add a stem and leaves for a small flower. You can use Delica or 11/0 seed beads with any thread that will work with the bead and needle.

**Ways to use:** bands, borders, flowers

**Also known as:** buttonhole circle, wheel, pinwheels, buttonhole ochka

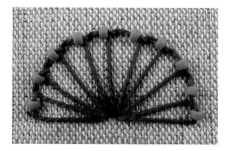

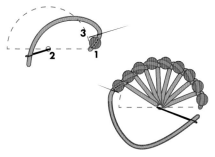

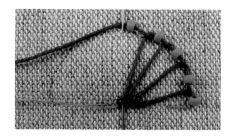

Keeping spokes uniform

## ALTERNATING PEKINESE

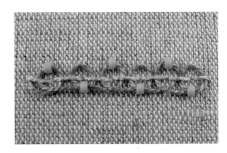

This stitch travels left to right for the backstitches and the lacing. The Pekinese is worked first, then the lacing with the beads. Use a tapestry needle for the lacing. Be careful not to pierce the fabric or thread as you weave the laced stitches. Keep the loop circles as even as possible. Notice that the thread goes through the bottom bead twice. This helps to control the loop circles and keep them from shifting. This is a beautiful stitch, especially when two or three colors are used.

You can use Delica or 11/0 seed beads with any thread that will work with the bead and needle.

**Ways to use:** bands, outlines, corner borders, filling floral work, embellishment for clothing

**Also known as:** Chinese, forbidden, blind

Weaving under backstitch and over beading thread

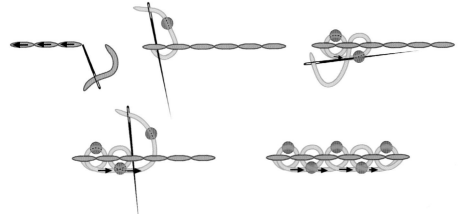

Going through bead second time

# Laced Corners

· · · · · · · · · · · · · · · · · · · · · · · · · · · · · · · · · · · · · · · · · · · · · ·

My favorite way to use the laced or threaded stitches is as corner (L-shaped) borders on a square or rectangular pillow. I work the stitch in the four corners after the center design is completed.

· · · · · · · · · · · · · · · · · · · · · · · · · · · · · · · · · · · · · · · · · · · · · ·

# FEATHER

This stitch can travel in a vertical, horizontal, circular, or curved direction. It is worked top to bottom. The most important step when working this stitch is to keep both ends of the loop (1 and 2) even in height. The rhythm of this stitch works well with the sewing method, as you slide on the bead and place the stitches on alternate sides. Use your finger to hold the thread in place while completing the stitch. You can use one, two, or three beads depending on the size of the loops used.

You can use Delica, 11/0 seed beads, or any small bead that works with the stitch length, thread, and needle.

**Ways to use:** circular motifs, borders, outlines, light filling, grass, ferns, leaves, embellishment on clothing, as an appliqué stitch

**Also known as:** single coral, briar, plumage

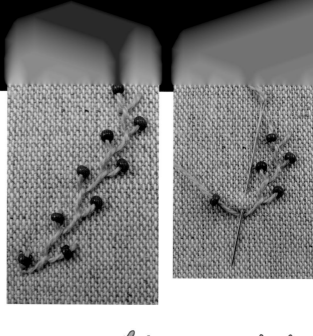

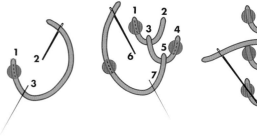

# DOUBLE FEATHER

This stitch can travel in a vertical, horizontal, circular, or curved direction. It is worked like the feather stitch, except two stitches are placed on each side before alternating sides. The beads are added as you work the stitch. One or two beads can be used, depending on the desired look.

You can use Delica, 11/0 seed beads, or any small bead that works with the stitch length, thread, and needle.

**Ways to use:** circular motifs, borders, outlines, light filling, grass, ferns, leaves, embellishment on clothing, as an appliqué stitch

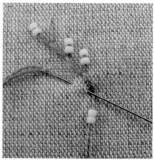

Switching sides

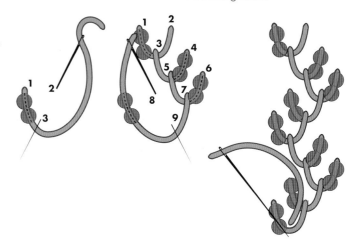

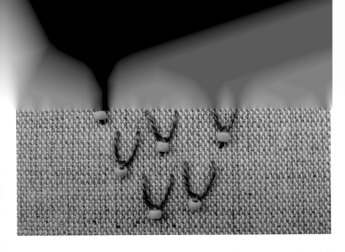

## FLY

This stitch travels in any direction. It is a simple and very effective little stitch. The tie-down stitch with the added bead can be long or short in length, depending on how you are using the stitch. With a longer tie-down stitch, use the number of beads needed to cover the tie-down thread. The fly can be worked as a wide or narrow stitch, giving it a V or Y shape.

You can use Delica or 11/0 seed beads with any thread that will work with the bead and needle.

**Ways to use:** bud and flower sepals, filling, borders, leaf veins, grass

**Also known as:** tied, Y, open loop

Placing tie-down bead

## FERN

You can travel in any direction, working the stitch from top to bottom. Using the stab method makes adding the beading a faster process. One, two, or three beads can be used, depending on the size of the side stitches. This is a beautiful edging stitch for home décor or clothing items.

You can use Delica or 11/0 seed beads with any thread that will work with the bead and needle.

**Ways to use:** edgings, borders, filling, foliage, motifs, scrolling background patterns, veins of leaves

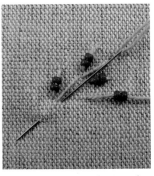

Completing side stitch, positioning for next stitch

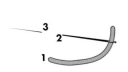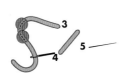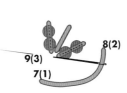

# CHAIN

Travel in any direction, working top to bottom and adding beads as you work the stitch. Keep the ends of the loop even, or share the same hole. Use your finger to hold the thread in place while completing the stitch. Watch the tension. The stitch should lie flat against the fabric with no puckering of fabric.

When working this stitch, the beads can be placed as shown or the entire loop of the chain can be filled with beads. You can also place only one bead on a side, allowing it to slide down in the middle of the thread. Notice that a single bead is placed on the tie-down stitch to end the chain. Match the bead color to the thread for a chain that is simply stunning.

You can use Delica or 11/0 seed beads with any thread that will work with the bead and needle.

**Ways to use:** borders, curved motifs, circular shapes, filling, outlines, embellishment on clothing

**Also known as:** tambour, point de chainette

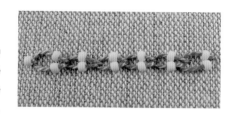

Keeping a bead on each side of the needle

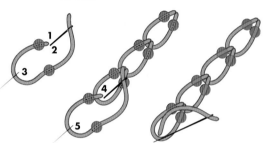

# CHAIN LACED

Travel in any direction, working top to bottom. A bead is added as you work over each stitch. This stitch is worked the same as the chain stitch with a lacing thread added. Work the chain stitch first; then place the lacing. Slide the lacing up from the back on the right side, slide on a bead, and take the thread across the chain. Use a tapestry needle for the lacing. For added interest and to fully show the features of this stitch, use a different color thread or type of thread for the lacing and another color for the bead.

You can use Delica or 11/0 seed beads with any thread that will work with the bead and needle.

**Ways to use:** bands, outlines, embellishment on clothing, edging on pillows

Weaving under chain

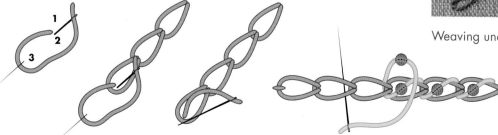

# WHEATEAR CHAIN

This stitch can travel in any direction. Although it looks similar to the chain, it is worked very differently. Add a bead and place an "ear" on each side. Work the chain, sliding the thread behind the "ears" and complete the chain.

You can use Delica, 11/0 seed beads, or any small bead that works with the stitch length, thread, and needle.

**Ways to use:** blooming shrubs, borders, bands, geometric filling

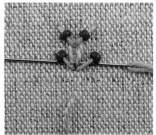

Weaving under previous ear

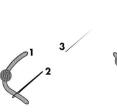
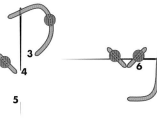
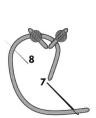
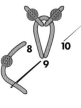

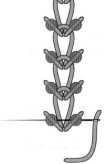

# BACKSTITCH CHAIN

Travel in any direction, working top to bottom. This stitch is worked like the chain stitch, except a backstitch and bead have been added. Work the chain first; then place the backstitch and bead, being careful not to pull too snug. The backstitch can be longer than the bead or approximately the same length. It was used for a project in this chapter.

You can use Delica or 11/0 seed beads with any thread that will work with the bead and needle.

**Ways to use:** bands, outlines, embellishment on clothing, circles, flower stems

Working backstitch over chain

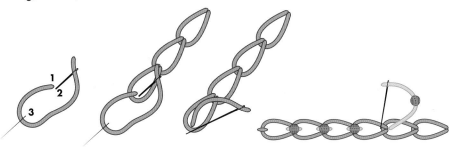

# CROSS

This stitch can be worked horizontally, vertically, or diagonally. For plain weave fabric, use quilter's tape to mark the placement of the crosses. You'll need to place tape below and above the area to be beaded. The distance between the tapes should be slightly over ¼" (6 mm), allowing room to work the stitch. Line up the marks on the top and bottom so the crosses are as even as possible. If working crosses on clothing, baste two straight parallel lines to bead between. Notice that three beads are placed on the thread for the first diagonal stitch. For the second stitch, place one bead on the thread and go through the center bead of the first stitch. Place another bead on the thread to complete the stitch. You can use Delica or 11/0 seed beads with bead thread.

**Ways to use:** filling geometric patterns, borders, small flowers, cross-stitch or needlepoint designs

**Also known as:** sampler stitch

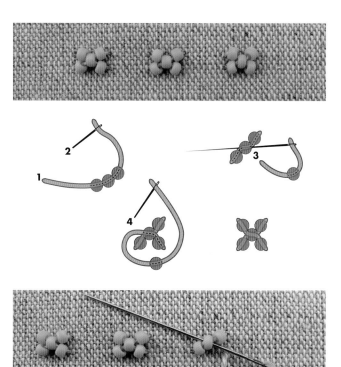

Going through center bead

# HERRINGBONE

Travel left to right in a straight row. The beads are added as you work the stitch and are held in place as the threads cross over each other. This stitch lends itself to having beads added. It is great for clothing embellishment.

You can use Delica or 11/0 seed beads with embroidery floss or single-strand thread or pearl cotton.

**Ways to use:** borders, bands, filling, embellishment, trim on Christmas trees

**Also known as:** plaited, witch, catch, Mossoul, fishnet, Persian, Russian, Russian cross

Positioning the next stitch

Keeping thread above bottom bead

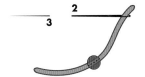

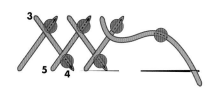

# HERRINGBONE AND BLOSSOMS

This stitch travels left to right, with the beaded blossoms and lazy daisy stitches added after the herringbone is in place. The beaded blossom should be pulled straight up, keeping the beads snug together for the tie-down stitch. Use your finger to hold the beads in place as you take the fifth bead across to tie down the stitch. I found that my small lazy daisy stitches varied slightly in size. This stitch can be worked in one or two colors. I find that Delica beads work best because of their size.

You can use Delica or 11/0 beads with embroidery floss or single-strand thread or pearl cotton.

**Ways to use:** borders, bands, filling, embellishment, trim on Christmas decorations

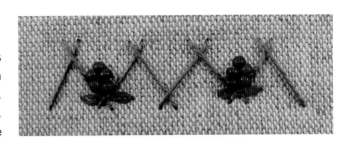

Creating bead loop using stab stitch instead of sewing stitch

Tying down bead loop

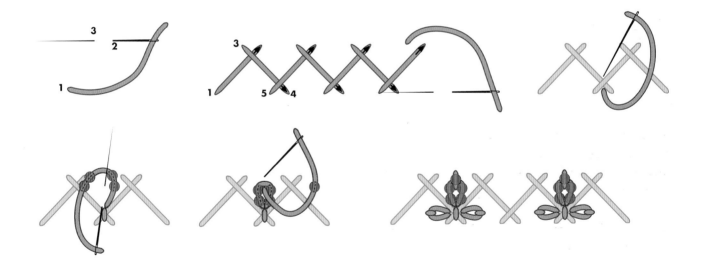

## LAZY DAISY

This stitch is worked in any direction. It is worked like a chain stitch and is anchored with a small vertical tie-down stitch where the beads are added. The number of beads you use with this stitch will depend on the look you desire. To add interest to the stitch, use a straight stitch in the middle of the loop and add two to three beads to fill the center of the lazy daisy. It can be stitched using beads to make the loop and on the tie-down. This versatile stitch can be used singly or grouped together.

You can use Delica or 11/0 seed beads with any thread that will work with the bead and needle.

**Ways to use:** filling, flower petals, buds, leaves, bands

**Also known as:** detached chain, tail chain, knotted knot, daisy, loop, picot, tied loop

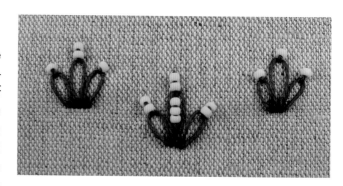

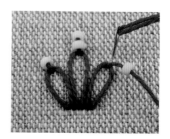

Tying down daisy with bead

Placing filling stitch with three beads

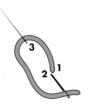

## COUCHING BEADS

The laid thread strung with beads can travel in any direction, including circular. This stitch looks similar to a bead row stitch when beads are placed close together. The couching method works up faster.

The laid thread can show between the beads or the beads can be closer together, as shown here. The laid thread should be one long continuous thread. Use two needles when couching beads. Use a crewel needle for the laid thread and a beading needle with bead thread to work the couching stitch. If laying a long thread, you'll need to work small areas at a time. Thread on six or nine beads, using the beading needle and thread. Place the couching stitch between the beads every two or three beads. The same type thread can be used for the laid thread and couching thread using two needles. When using beaded stitches on items that will have heavy use, use a couching stitch to ensure that they will stay in place.

You can use Delica, 11/0 seed beads, or any small bead that works with the stitch length, thread, and needle. If you prefer that the couching thread not show, use bead thread.

**Ways to use:** decorative swirls, filling shapes, outlines, borders, securing lacing threads and decorative braids

Couching single bead in place

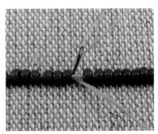

Couching between beads

# LOOP FLOWER PETALS

The flower petals are detached from the fabric, and the flower center is held down with a stop bead. Notice that two beads are placed at the tip of each flower petal, with one used as a stop bead in order to reverse the direction. This flower can be worked any size desired. Use an uneven number of beads, keeping the second side of the petal two beads less than the first side. The sample flower was nine beads for the first side of the petal, with two of the beads being used for the tip of the petal. Seven beads were used for the second side of the petal.

You can use Delica, 11/0 seed beads, or small beads with bead thread.

**Ways to use:** embellishment

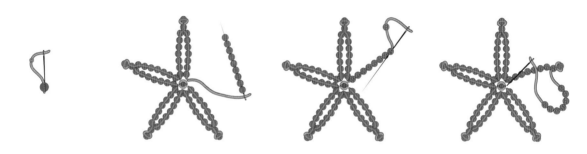

Adding the stop bead

Placing stop bead at end of petal

Pulling beads into place to complete petal

## SIMPLE PICOT

This fringe travels left to right. It is important to keep the beads snug against each other. String on three beads, move a bead distance away, and take a small stitch into the back of the fabric, coming out just above the last bead placed. Come down through this last bead and add two more beads, repeating the process. This edging can be worked using three or five beads. You can use Delica or 11/0 seed beads with bead thread.

**Ways to use:** edging on clothing, pillows, towels, pillowcases, window treatments, edge of fabric bracelet

**Also known as:** classic edge

Taking small stitch through back of fabric

Going back through last bead placed

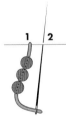  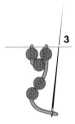 

## SPACED PICO

This fringe travels left to right and is worked on the edge of fabric. When working this stitch, keep the beads close to each other. String on the first five beads, move ¼" (6 mm) away, and take a small stitch into the back of the fabric, coming out just above the last bead placed. Come down through this last bead and add four more beads, repeating the process. This fringe can be worked using more beads, different types of beads, or using more than one color of bead. You can use any type of small bead with bead thread.

**Ways to use:** fringe on clothing, pillows, window treatments, edge of fabric bracelet

**Also known as:** classic spaced variation

Taking small stitch through back of fabric

Going back through last bead placed

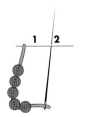  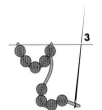 

## BUGLE WITH SINGLE BEAD PICOT

This fringe travels left to right. It is important to keep the beads snug against each other. It is worked with a size 8 seed bead, ½" (1.3 cm) bugle, size 8 seed bead, and three 11/0 seed beads. String on the first six beads, use the three 11/0 beads as the stop bead, and go back through the size 8 seed bead. Slide on a bugle, size 8 seed bead and go ¼" (6 mm) over, taking a small stitch into the back of the fabric and coming down through the size 8 bead. Repeat the process. Notice you start the second stitch with the bugle. This fringe can be worked using more beads, different types of beads, or using more than one color of beads.

You can use Delica or 11/0 seed beads, ½" (1.3 cm) bugles and size 8 seed beads with beading thread.

**Ways to use:** fringe on clothing, accessories, purses, towels, pillowcases, window treatments

**Also known as:** classic picot bugle bead variation

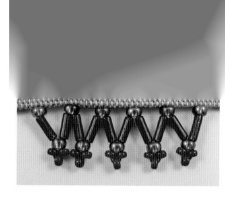

Placing three stop beads

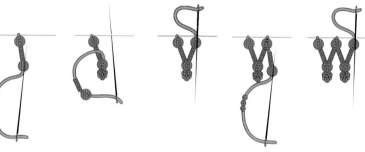

## DANGLE FRINGE

This fringe travels left to right. I used a 4 mm bead, ½" (1.3 cm) bugle, and three seed beads. Each fringe was placed a bead distance away. The three stop beads on the tip of the fringe form a small triangle. The fringe should hang straight, with all the beads snug against each other. Fewer beads or smaller beads without a bugle can be used, or all seed beads can be used.

**Ways to use:** fringe on purses, pillows, towels, window treatments, accessories

**Also known as:** classic dangle fringe

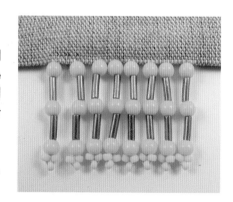

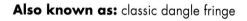

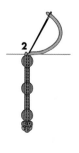

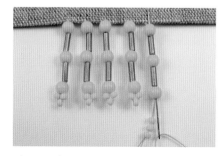

Placing three stop beads

# ONE-ROW NETTING

This netting travels left to right. It is important to keep the beads snug against each other. String on the first nine beads, move ⅜" (1 cm) away, and take a small stitch into the back of the fabric, coming out just above the last bead placed. Go down through this last bead, and add eight more beads, repeating the process. You can easily alter the appearance of the netting by using a different amount, type, or color of beads. You can use any type of small bead with bead thread.

**Ways to use:** fringe on clothing, pillows, towels, window treatments

**Also know as:** shallow loops

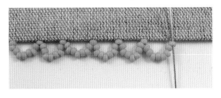

Going through last bead placed

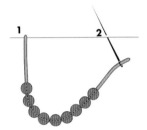

# TWO-ROW NETTING

This netting travels left to right. It is important to keep the beads snug against each other. The stitch is worked the same as the one-row netting. Notice that when first row is complete, a second row of the netting is worked right to left. Follow the bead graph to place the first and second rows.

You can easily alter the appearance of the netting by using a different amount, type, or color of beads.

You can use any type of small bead with bead thread.

**Ways to use:** fringe on clothing, pillows, window treatments

**Also known as:** two-row tapered horizontal netting

Going through center bead of first row loop

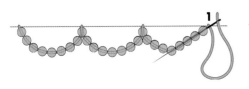

## OVERLAPPING NETTING

This netting travels left to right with the overlapping row traveling right to left. It is important to keep the beads snug against each other. The first row is worked the same as the one-row netting. Then the second row is worked right to left, weaving over and under the first row. Follow the bead graph to place the first and second rows.

You can easily alter the appearance of the netting by using a different amount, type, or color of beads. Use any type of small bead with bead thread.

**Ways to use:** fringe on clothing, pillows, towels, window treatments

Going over first loop and under second loop

## WHIPPED EDGING

This edging travels left to right. It is a simple edging, adding elegance to items. For best results, place stitches an even distance apart and keep the beads snug. The sample stitches are spaced ½" (1.3 cm) apart. If used to close a pillow, the edging beads should be placed closer together so the pillow insert does not show.

To achieve an even distance, use quilter's tape or a chalk pencil to mark the distance on the fabric.

You can use Delica or 11/0 seed beads with bead thread.

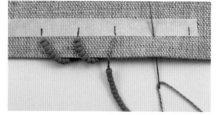
Taking needle through back of fabric

Pulling edging into place

**Ways to use:** edging on clothing, pillows, towels, pillowcases, fabric bracelets, simple projects

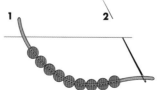

# ROSETTE

This small rosette is simple to make. For a nice round rosette, use an odd number of beads on each side of the needle. String the beads onto the thread and wrap them around the needle, being sure you have the same number of beads on each side of the needle. The beads should be snug on either side of the needle before the tie-down stitch is placed. A flower can be created from this rosette by adding a stem and leaves. You can use Delica or 11/0 seed bead with bead thread.

**Ways to use:** filling, motifs, flowers

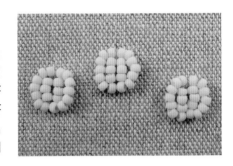

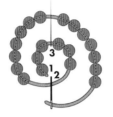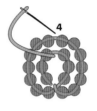

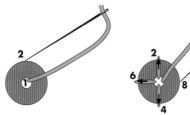

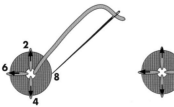

Wrapping first beads around needle   Adding second row   Placing tie down

# SINGLE SEQUIN ATTACHMENT

These sequins are quick to work and add interest to a project. For the straightest lines, the sequins should be attached following the stitch graph. You will notice that the securing threads for the middle and left sequins are not as straight as the one on the right. When the numbers are not followed, the thread is pushed in the wrong direction as you add stitches. You can use any size sequin with single-strand, fine braid, pearl cotton, or embroidery floss.

**Ways to use:** embellishment for clothing, backgrounds, flower centers, embellishing floral or geometric prints

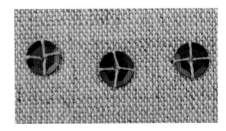

Place side stitch

## SINGLE SEQUIN WITH STOP BEAD

This sequin technique is used to hold a sequin or paillette in place. A sequin has a hole in the middle and the paillettes have a hole at the top rather than in the center.

You can use any size sequin, or use size 20 or 30 paillettes. Use a Delica or 11/0 or larger seed bead for the stop bead with bead thread. The bead size will depend on the sequin or paillette size.

**Ways to use:** embellishment for clothing, backgrounds, flower centers, embellishing floral or geometric prints

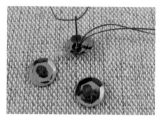

Adding stop bead

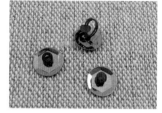

Pulling stop bead into place

## SEQUIN ROW

These sequins travel from left to right. After the first sequin is in place, move a half-sequin distance away to work the next sequin. The row is quick to work. The thread should match or complement the color of the sequin.

If working a sequin row that should be straight, baste a straight line on the fabric or use marked quilter's tape.

You can use any size sequin with single-strand, fine braid, pearl cotton, embroidery floss, or bead thread.

**Ways to use:** embellishment for clothing, backgrounds, borders, bands, filling, embellishing floral or geometric prints

Moving a half-sequin distance away

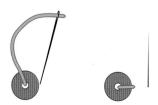

## LAZY DAISY SEQUIN

This decorative sequin technique is used to hold a sequin in place. Sequins can add interest to handwork and beaded prints. This lazy daisy stitch is quick to work and gives a sequin a completely different appearance. Use threads the same color as the sequin or complement the sequin color. You can use any size sequin with single-strand, fine braid, pearl cotton, or embroidery floss.

**Ways to use:** embellishment for clothing, backgrounds, flower centers, embellishing floral or geometric prints

Coming up through daisy

## SEQUIN FLOWER

When working these flowers, it is difficult to get them round unless you draw a circle on the fabric. Decide what size you would like the flower to be, then use a chalk pencil or quilter's gray pencil to draw a circle. Notice that a portion of the sequin hole does show. Use thread that matches or complements the sequin color. Sew on the first sequin, bringing the needle/thread up on the drawn line. Take the needle through the front of the sequin down into the fabric. Place the next sequin on the thread, and take a tiny stitch on the line just below the first sequin. As you pull the thread, the sequin will slide into place under the first sequin. Adjust placement of the small stitch if needed. Continue to attach the sequins in this manner. Once the sequins are in place around the circle, complete the flower by attaching a 4 mm bead or several 11/0 seed beads in the center. Use beading thread for the center beads. You can use any size sequin with single-strand, fine braid, pearl cotton, embroidery floss, or bead thread.

Taking small stitch

**Ways to use:** embellishment for clothing, backgrounds, embellishing floral or geometric prints

     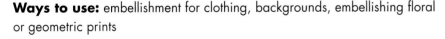

# Beaded Bliss Checkbook Cover

The dark background and soft floral design of the checkbook fabric is the perfect setting for bead embroidery embellishment. Working on a premade item eliminates the finishing process of the project. Beading a few key areas enhances the design.

## YOU WILL NEED

- premade checkbook cover or other item
- several tubes of Delica beads: the colors of the floral design
- Silamide, size A: color to match beads

## STITCHES USED

- seed stitch
- bead row
- backstitched chain

## General Information

Use fabric or a premade garment or other item with a floral design that beading would enhance. If using a premade item, make sure you can access the front from the back or inside of the item and that you will be able to hide threads.

Use Delica, 11/0 seed, or bugle beads that will enhance the floral fabric. Notice on this project only a portion of the floral design is embellished to give a softer look to the finished piece. See page 152, for information on how to choose the beads that complement your fabric.

Use bead thread for the bead stitches and embroidery floss or hand-dyed or a solid color single-strand thread to work the project. A combination of threads and stitches adds more interest to the finished project.

**1** The seed bead stitch was used to fill in an area of the flower petals.

**2** The bead-row bead stitch was used around the large petal, the inner petal, and several highlight lines.

**3** The backstitch chain embroidery stitch was used for the stem of the large flower. Using this stitch gave the stem a textured appearance.

You can use any of the bead embroidery and bead stitches to complete your design. For the jewelry roll on page 146, several bead embroidery stitches were used to cover the seams of a crazy quilt fabric. These same stitches can be used to enhance the fabric you have chosen. On a scrap of the fabric, play around with different stitches, beads, and threads. Relax and bead, keeping in mind there are no rules on what to use, and just have fun! You may surprise yourself.

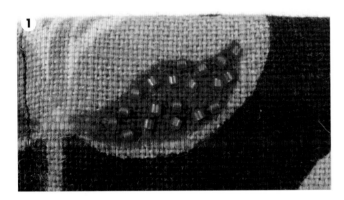

# Sub Sequins

Substitute small sequins for all or some of the beads in the checkbook cover project.

# Midnight Shimmer Bracelet

The shimmering colors of the rainbow beads worked across black Ultrasuede set the mood of this quick-to-stitch bracelet. Customize the colors of the Ultrasuede and beads to go with your wardrobe.

## YOU WILL NEED

- Ultrasuede: black
- Delica beads in silver-lined light purple and purple
- seed beads 11/0 in silver-lined diamond rainbow and turquoise frosted
- fine braid, size 4: turquoise
- sequins 6 mm in iridescent turquoise
- Silamide bead thread in light gray

- fabric adhesive
- ribbon clamps in 1" (2.5 cm)
- 1½" (3.8 cm) piece of extension chain in silver finish
- two jump rings in silver finish
- lobster clasp
- needle-nose pliers, small
- nylon-jaw or flat-nose (smooth inside) pliers

## STITCHES USED

- satin
- lazy daisy

- sequin
- seed

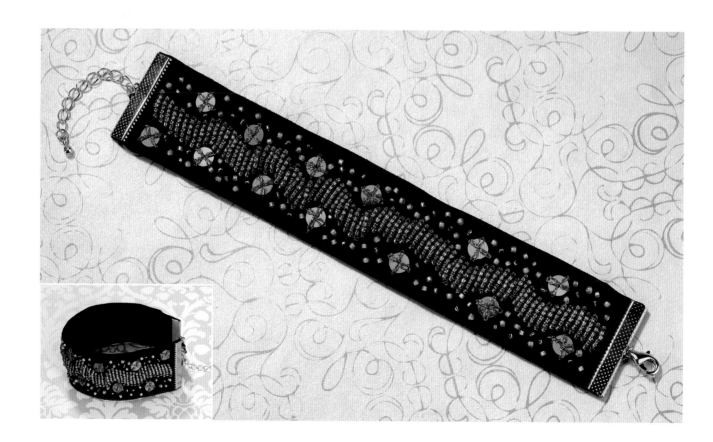

## Instructions

**1** Cut one piece of Ultrasuede 1¼" (3.2 cm) wide and long enough to wrap around your wrist. Cut another piece ¹⁄₁₆" (1.6 mm) narrower and a little longer than the first cut piece. This piece will be used during finishing and will be trimmed to length at that time. Use a rotary cutter and mat to ensure a clean edge on the bracelet.

**2** Use gray bead thread and the satin stitch to work a random wave pattern along the length of the bracelet. Be sure to leave enough room at ends for the clamps.

**3** Use gray bead thread and the lazy daisy sequin stitch to randomly place sequins above and below the satin stitch along the length of the bracelet. Keep the sequins near the satin stitch.

**4** Use gray bead thread and the seed stitch to randomly place the Delica and 11/0 seed beads between the sequins. Keep these beads approximately ⅛" (3 mm) from the outer edge of the fabric.

**5** Run two thin lines of fabric adhesive along the back outer edges of the 1" (2.5 cm) wide strip of Ultra suede and secure it over the back of the beaded bracelet. Press the two pieces together and allow to completely dry before working the next step.

**6** Trim the back piece of Ultrasuede to match the front of the bracelet.

**7** Center a ribbon clamp over one end of the bracelet (trim the fabric to fit, if necessary). Using nylon-jaw jewelry pliers, press the center of the clamp halfway; repeat on each side. Then press down firmly in the center and sides, closing the clamp completely. Repeat on the opposite end with the other ribbon clamp. If using other pliers, wrap the jaws with masking tape to avoid scratching the metal.

**8** Use the needle-nose pliers to gently open and attach a jump ring to one clamp. Attach the piece of extension chain to the jump ring and gently close.

**9** Attach the other jump ring to other clamp. Attach the lobster clasp to the jump ring with the catch side facing the front of the bracelet. Gently close the jump ring.

# Snap Closure

Small snaps can be used as closures for the bracelet instead of the ribbon clamps and clasp. Cut the fabric long enough to overlap the ends and accommodate the snaps.

**2 - 3 - 4**

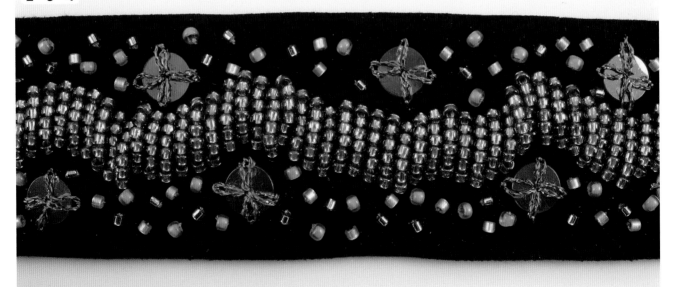

CROSS-STITCH

Cross-stitch is counted embroidery following a charted pattern, most often worked with the basic cross-stitch that is an X shaped stitch. This technique is worked on even-weave fabric, counting each stitch and working uniform cross-stitches across the area to create the design. It is easy to learn and will give you hours of pleasure creating all types of projects for family and friends.

# Fabric

This section provides information about some of the fabrics that can be used for cross-stitch. Once you try stitching on various types of fabric, you will find the type you prefer. There are stitchers who will only work on Aida and others who prefer linen. If you have a needlework shop close by, stop in and look at all the fabric.

There is an endless range of colorful fabrics for cross-stitch. You can also purchase premade items, including bath towels, kitchen towels, aprons, and baby bibs, that come with inserts of cross-stitch fabric. Create a quick gift by cross-stitching a design on the insert of a premade item.

Before purchasing fabric for a pattern, choose the type of fabric and count size to determine the amount of fabric needed. Extra fabric is needed for finishing the project. Allow two to three inches (5 to 7.5 cm) on all sides for finishing. I always use a larger piece than is necessary in case I change my mind on how I am going to finish the project. Allowing extra fabric allows you to use a frame or hoop when working the project. For information on hoops and frames, refer to page 14. Before you start cross-stitching a project, finish the fabric edges by zigzag or serging or apply masking tape to the fabric edges to keep them from raveling.

## Washing

If it is necessary to clean a finished cross-stitch project, hand-wash in cool water using a mild soap or shampoo (dye free). Rinse well. Do not wring the fabric. Roll it in a towel to remove excess water. Smooth out on a flat surface to dry. While the fabric is still slightly damp, you can press the needlework by placing it face-down on a clean terry towel and using a pressing cloth.

## AIDA AND AIDA BLENDS

Aida is available in count sizes from 8 to 18. It comes in 100 percent cotton and cotton blends. The 100 percent cotton is a stiff fabric, making it easier to stitch. After stitching, Aida fabric can be washed and pressed (see tip) and it becomes much softer. The most popular size is 14 count, which is currently available in over five dozen colors. The color wheel is represented well with all the available colors.

There are different kinds of Aida—the metallic collection, country, homespun, and vintage to name a few. These are made from 100 percent cotton or cotton blended with rayon, polyester, or linen.

## LINEN

Linen comes in many colors, in 18 to 40 count. There are many colors available including natural linens in natural colors such as Belfast, Cashel, and Pearl Linen. Some blends fall under the heading of linen. The different kinds have a slightly different look and feel. Some are very stiff and others are extremely soft.

## SPECIALTY WEAVE FABRICS

These blended fabrics are manufactured using a combination of two of the following types of threads: cotton, rayon, linen, and metallic. The count ranges from 7 to 28. Two higher count fabrics that are easy to work on are Tula (rayon and cotton) in 10 count and Klostern (rayon and cotton) in 7 count. Jute (100 percent Jute) in 12 count is wonderful for country-style projects. Cross-

# Initials

Monogramming is very popular and with the help of waste canvas (page 190), you can use plain weave fabric to create monogrammed gifts.

stitch metallic fabric has flecks of gold or silver sprinkled over the cloth. These flecks of gold and silver add interest to certain types of designs.

## OVER-DYED FABRIC

Aida, linen, metallic, and specialty-weave fabrics all come in over-dyed varieties. There is a large range of counts and colors in these fabrics. Aida comes in 11 to 20 count. Linen comes in 28 to 40 count and the Specialty-Weave 10 count Tula. More colors and types of over-dyed fabric are becoming available all the time, as cross-stitchers love working on them.

## PERFORATED PAPER

This paper has greatly improved since it was introduced in the nineteenth century. It is available in several solid colors and hand-painted sheets with a tone-on-tone design. One stunning color is the antique brown that gives the effect of old world gold. It comes in 14 count, in packages of two 9" × 13" (22.9 x 33.0 cm) sheets. Perforated paper is perfect for holiday ornaments, bookmarks, gift tags, embellishments for cards, 3-D projects, and other small designs. The design on the journal (page 208) is done on perforated paper.

This paper resembles Aida fabric. When stitching on paper, use less complicated patterns and stitch with a gentle touch. Be careful not to bend the paper as you work the stitches. Watch your tension; pulling the thread too snug will tear the paper. When cutting the paper to the desired size or shape, cut close to the solid area of the paper or down the middle of the open holes for a scalloped effect.

When working on this paper, use an away waste knot to begin stitching. To end threads, weave the ending thread carefully under previously worked stitches; avoid crossing over an area without stitches, as the thread will show on the front side. The hardest part of using perforated paper is the lack of places to secure the thread without it showing.

*(continued)*

## STITCH BANDS

These bands have a plain or decorative edge. The edging can be the same color as the band, slightly lighter, or different in color. They come in Aida and linen in counts ranging from 14 to 30. Width sizes range from ¾" to 7¾" (1.9 to 19.7 cm). The bands can be used as candle bands (as shown on page 206), pillow bands, camera or guitar straps, basket bands, chatelaines, and flower vase bands. The ends of the bands can be turned to the wrong side and glued using Fabri-Tac or slip stitched in place.

## WASTE CANVAS (BLUE LINE)

Waste canvas is designed to be removed after it is stitched. This allows you to do counted cross-stitch on plain weave fabric. You can embellish clothing, home décor items, linens, or whatever a needle and thread will stitch through. Mesh sizes are available in 6.5 to 16.

Use the directions at right to work waste canvas projects. Try a few stitches on a piece of plain fabric using the canvas to see how the waste canvas works. This will let you know if you have made any stitching mistakes before working on the real project. Remember to keep an even tension.

Waste Canvas Example

## Cross-stitching with Waste Canvas

**1** Cut the piece of canvas larger than the finished design.

**2** Find the center of the canvas and mark it with a permanent marker.

**3** Find the center of the fabric and mark it with a straight pin. Place the marked canvas center over the fabric center, keeping the lines of the canvas straight across the fabric. Pin in place. Readjust as needed so the canvas lines are straight.

**4** Baste the canvas to the fabric along the outer edges.

**5** If using a lightweight fabric, use a nonfusible stabilizer (page 23) on the back of the fabric, basting it through the fabric and waste canvas. When the project is complete, trim away the excess stabilizer.

**6** Work the design, centering it on the waste canvas. Work each stitch by going down and coming up into the middle of the corners that surround the square. Work each stitch so the thread touches the previously placed stitch or stitches in that corner. If the threads do not touch, you will end up with a small gap, showing the fabric between stitches. Take your time and place each stitch carefully.

**7** When all stitching is completed, remove basting. Use a lightly dampened clean, lint-free cloth to gently sponge over the canvas. You can also use a clean spray bottle with a fine mist to lightly spray the area. Work carefully, barely dampening the threads. A word of caution: if the canvas becomes too moist, the threads will be more difficult to remove. Use a tweezers or your fingers to pull each thread up out of the stitching area.

# Thread

New threads for cross-stitch are being continually introduced. You can use a variety of threads, depending on the desired look for your finished project. This section includes information on some of the threads that are available. When purchasing your threads, purchase enough to complete the project. Dye lots can change and it will be noticeable on the project. For more information, refer to Special Stitching Information (page 24). Many of the cross-stitch threads are interchangeable between techniques. In the Creative Embroidery section (page 34), you will find more information on several of the threads that are listed on the following pages.

*(continued)*

## Red

If using red thread or embroidery floss with waste canvas, rinse the thread and let dry thoroughly before using. Red is such a strong color and the dye is not always permanent. It could bleed onto the fabric or other threads.

## SIX STRAND EMBROIDERY FLOSS

This 100 percent cotton thread is available in solid and variegated colors. It has a slight sheen. Several companies make these threads. They are all very similar in texture and colors available. If you have a chance, test the different brands to determine your favorite.

## TWISTED HAND-DYED COTTON

This three-ply pima cotton thread comes in beautiful variegated hand-dyed colors. The variegated colors of this twisted thread give your stitches beautiful color flowing across the fabric. You'll need to separate the plies of thread (page 25) before using for cross-stitch. One ply can be used on 11–20 count depending on your choice of fabric. For some linen fabric, two-ply thread may be necessary. Dye lots vary so it's best to purchase the amount needed.

## PEARL COTTON (COTTON PERLÉ)

Pearl cotton threads come in several sizes from 16 (smallest in diameter) to 3 (largest in diameter). Sizes 12, 8, and 5 can be used for cross-stitch on Aida and linen. This twisted, single-strand thread has a slight sheen. When working with pearl cotton, the section of thread that is in the eye of the needle loses its sheen and becomes dull. Avoid using this section for working stitches.

## COTTON HAND-DYED AND OVER-DYED

These threads come in a single-strand or six-strand embroidery floss. Single-strand cotton threads come in many colors, solid, and variegated shades. The variegated colors provide a flow of several colors and shades when stitched. For the best color flow, use the thread as it comes from the skein. Dye lots vary, so it's best to purchase the amount needed.

The six-strand embroidery floss has been hand-dyed or over-dyed. Some brands come in only the variegated, while others come in solid colors. The solid colors give you different colors than the regular stranded floss. The variegated threads come in a variety of colors.

## STRANDED METALLIC

Stranded metallic can be used as a single strand or in combination with floss. If you would like a little sparkle but not the full effect of metallic, you can use one strand of floss and one strand of metallic.

# Conversion Charts

If you like the colors in a pattern but would like to change the thread type, there are conversion charts available to assist you. Thread companies provide conversion charts so you can reference a six-stranded floss color and find out which single-strand thread is closest in color. There are also conversion charts for silk to floss. Look for these and other conversion charts on the Internet. Most thread companies allow you to print their conversion charts.

## BRAIDS (METALLIC)

This flexible braid can be used to highlight areas of a design or to work a complete motif. Size 4, 8, and 12 work best for even-weave fabric. This braid should have a little space in the corner it comes up and goes down in. Using a braid that is too large for the thread count will take away from the beauty of the braid. It should lie flat against the fabric.

## LINEN

There are several 100 percent linen threads available. These textured threads come in six strand and a single strand. The strands vary in width along the strand. There is a wide range of colors. Dye lots vary, so it's best to purchase the amount needed.

## SILK

Silk thread provides sheen to the stitches that no other thread can match. It adds a soft, shiny, smooth appearance to the work. Once you become familiar with this thread, you will know when you are viewing silk work. There is a silk lamé that has flecks of sparkle to add a little bling to your stitches. Silk comes on spools, half skeins, and full skeins. Most silk thread is stranded. The information on the package will tell you the number of plies.

## SPECIALTY THREAD

Bamboo is becoming popular to use in making both thread and fabrics. Bamboo thread gives the appearance of wool and feels like soft velvety cotton. It can be used as it comes from the card or separated into six strands. This thread has a nice soft sheen.

Velvet thread looks like tiny round strips of velvet. It is wonderful for Christmas ornaments, stockings, and other festive items. It adds more texture than most threads and is easy to use.

## MEMORY THREAD

This wired thread adds a dimensional appearance to a design. It is a flexible copper wire that is wrapped with a soft fiber. It comes in eighteen vibrant colors. Memory thread can be used for basket handles, flower stems, butterfly wings, and coiled for flower centers. It is handy to use for dimensional embellishment on all needlework, not just cross-stitch.

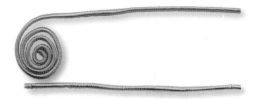

# Stitches

This chapter begins with the five basic stitches: the cross, quarter cross, half cross, three-quarter cross, and backstitch. The following eighteen stitches are counted decorative stitches or specialty stitches that will give you many new options.

## HOW TO WORK CROSS-STITCH

Cross-stitch is worked following a pattern. The pattern is shown on a chart that is divided into squares. The key to cross-stitch charts is in understanding the cross-stitch square. A cross-stitch square represents the portion of the fabric to be covered by a cross-stitch. If you look at Aida even-weave fabric, you can easily see the fabric squares. The photo of a cross-stitch square (right) shows a simple cross-stitch worked over one square on Aida fabric. If working on linen, each cross-stitch would go over two threads unless indicated otherwise on the pattern. Symbols on the chart indicate where a cross-stitch is to be placed. Each unique symbol specifies a type and color of thread to use. Study the chart example and stitched example to understand how stitches are represented on the chart.

Design size is determined by the number of stitches and the fabric thread count (stitches per inch [cm]). You need to determine the count, both horizontal and vertical,

to obtain the height and width of the fabric needed. To determine size, divide the number of stitches by the thread count. A design 32 stitches wide would be 2" (5.1 cm) wide on 16-count fabric and 4" (10.2 cm) wide on 8-count fabric.

Cross-stitch square

When centering the design and stitching the project, counting correctly is the most important concern. If you do not count up, down, or over correctly when starting to stitch or while stitching the design, it will not be worked correctly. Count and mark the spot with a straight pin, then count again to be sure it is correct. Patterns are marked with darker lines that run through the center area, or they have marks on the edge of the chart on all four sides to indicate the center. You may find it helpful to mark the horizontal and vertical center lines on the pattern with a highlighter.

Find the center of the fabric by using a ruler or carefully folding the fabric in half vertically, making sure the edges meet. Then, using your fingers, gently pinch the center folded area so it leaves a slight mark. Open the fabric and fold it in half horizontally, repeating the marking process. Open the fabric and you should have a marked center. Baste along each of the creases, creating a marked center line on the fabric. If you are working on perforated paper, count both horizontally and vertically to find the center line of your paper. Baste the center lines with a light color sewing thread. A darker thread could bleed onto the paper.

Chart example                    Stitched example

For ease of counting, start stitching in the middle of the design. When working the stitches, don't carry the thread on the back for more than a stitch or two; rather, end the thread and start anew. Avoid using knots to begin or end your thread. Begin with a waste knot or away waste knot (page 28). Otherwise, leave a short tail on the back as you take the first stitch, and catch the tail under the next few stitches on the back of the fabric, securely burying the tail. End the thread by running it under the last few stitches worked.

For clarity, all of the stitches that follow are shown on an 8-count Aida. Decorative stitches work best on 14-count or higher linen fabric or Aida. When you are stitching on linen fabric, work over two threads for each square shown on the pattern.

The colored grid lines on the stitch graphs represent the threads in cross-stitch fabric; the white blocks represent the openings that the needle slides through to work the stitch.

## CROSS

This stitch is worked from left to right as a single unit or in horizontal rows. Use the stab stitch or sewing method. Work the cross so all the top stitches slant in the same direction and use even tension. Avoid catching the thread of the previously placed stitch as you work the next cross.

You can use any type of thread for this stitch. Embroidery floss and over-dyed or hand-dyed floss work especially well.

**Ways to use:** home décor items, embellishment for clothing, monograms, pictorial scenes, filling

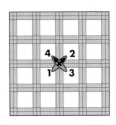

**Also known as:** Berlin, counted cross, point de marque cross-stitch

## QUARTER CROSS

This partial stitch can be worked in any corner of the square. It is used to give the design a more realistic appearance. When working the quarter cross, it comes up at the corner of the square and goes down in the center fabric of the square. Use the stab stitch method, following the numbers and arrows on the graph.

You can use any type of thread for this stitch.

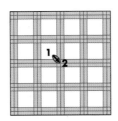

**Ways to use:** to add detail, round out outer edges of shapes

**Also known as:** partial cross

Going down into the center of the square

## HALF CROSS

The half cross can be worked in either direction. It is always worked on the diagonal. These stitches are indicated on patterns by a colored diagonal line shown in the direction they are to be stitched. The color key will also indicate the color to use. Use the stab stitch method or sewing method.

The half cross can also be used to work a border around the pattern. Work one row with the diagonals going to the right and the next row with the diagonals going to the left. Repeat the row of diagonals going to the right to create a border of three rows. Each of these rows can be stitched in a different color, or work all the rows in the same color.

You can use any type of thread for this stitch. Twisted or hand-dyed single-strands threads work especially well.

**Ways to use:** lacy affects, background, bands

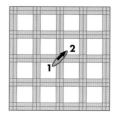

## THREE-QUARTER CROSS

The three-quarter stitch can be worked in any direction. Work the first half of the cross-stitch; then come up as if you were placing the second half, but take the thread under the previous half stitch and down into the center of the square.

These stitches are usually indicated on the pattern by colored diagonal lines with the short stitches going in the direction they are to be stitched. The color key will list them in the color to be used. Use the stab stitch method, following the numbers and arrows on the graph.

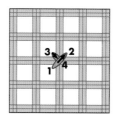

Stranded threads or single-strand threads work best.

**Ways to use:** add rounded appearance, detail

**Also known as:** partial cross

Going down into the center of the square under half cross

## HORIZONTAL CROSS

Place all the diagonal half stitches in one direction, working left to right and going horizontally across the area to be stitched. To complete the stitch, work back across the row. Use the stab stitch or sewing method, being sure to work the cross so all the top stitches slant in the same direction.

You can use any type of thread for this stitch.

**Ways to use:** bands, borders, large areas of same color stitches, home décor items, embellishment for clothing, monograms, pictorial scenes, filling

**Also known as:** cross, cross-stitch

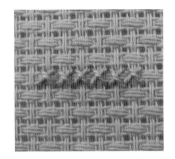

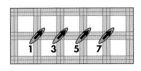

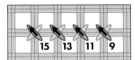

## VERTICAL CROSS

This cross can be worked by placing all the diagonal half stitches in one direction, going vertically and then working back up to complete the cross. Use the stab stitch method or sewing method, working as the numbers and arrows indicate on the graph. Work the stitch so all the top stitches slant in the same direction.

You can use any type of thread for this stitch.

**Ways to use:** backgrounds, filling, bands, borders

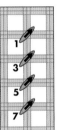

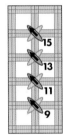

## DIAGONAL CROSS

This cross can be worked individually. It can also be worked by placing all the diagonal half stitches in one direction, going diagonally over the area, then working back up the area to complete the cross. Use the stab stitch method or sewing method, following the numbers and arrows so all the top stitches slant in the same direction.

You can use any type of thread for this stitch.

**Ways to use:** diagonal bands, filling, backgrounds

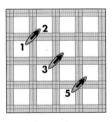

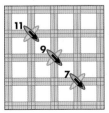

# BACKSTITCH

This stitch can be worked in any direction. The backstitch will be indicated by a straight colored line on the pattern where it is to be stitched. The color key will show the color to be used. Use the stab stitch method, following the numbers and arrows on the graph. Backstitches add depth to areas in the design. The pattern will indicate the number of strands to use.

Backstitch is often used to achieve the desired effect rather than half or quarter stitches.

You can use any type of thread for this stitch.

**Ways to use:** outline shapes, define areas, borders

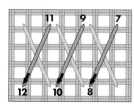

# OBLONG

Work this stitch horizontally left to right and then back across the area to complete the stitch. It is a quick and easy stitch to work using the stab stitch method. Follow the graph to work the stitch and count carefully. Although the rhythm of this stitch is similar to the cross-stitch, the top cross is slanted in a different direction.

You can use any type of thread for this stitch.

**Ways to use:** borders, bands, lacy backgrounds

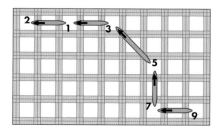

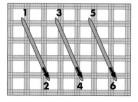

# HERRINGBONE

This stitch is worked from left to right. Watch your tension, being sure the fabric lies flat and smooth as you work the crosses. Use the stab stitch or sewing method, following the numbers and arrows on the graph to work the stitch.

You can use any type of thread for this stitch.

**Ways to use:** bands and borders

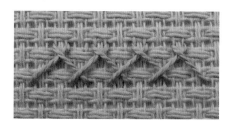

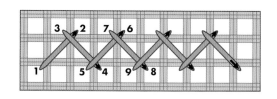

## LACED HERRINGBONE

This stitch is worked from left to right. Use the stab stitch or sewing method. Work the herringbone base stitch across the area. Use a tapestry needle to work the laced thread. For a striking look to this stitch, use two colors in different types of thread and different thread weights. Notice on the stitch graph that the laced thread starts from the base of the first herringbone stitch own the left side of the area. Leave the laced thread slightly loose but pulled into place next to the base stitch.

You can use any type of thread for this stitch.

**Ways to use:** borders, bands

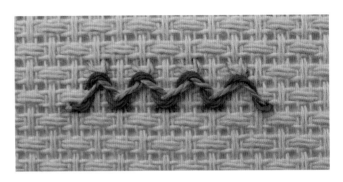

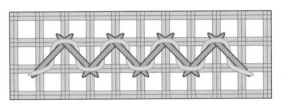

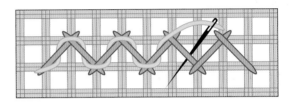

## LONG-ARM CROSS

This stitch is worked from the left to right. Notice on the graph that there are two compensating stitches in green at the beginning and end of the row of stitches. The compensating stitch on the left is worked first with the stitch pattern starting at 3. The longest arm of the stitch is worked over six squares. Counting is very important in working this stitch correctly. It is a beautiful border stitch.

You can use any type of thread for this stitch. Pearl cotton and hand-dyed twisted threads work especially well.

**Ways to use:** bands, borders

**Also known as:** long-leg cross, twist, plaited Slav, Portuguese twist

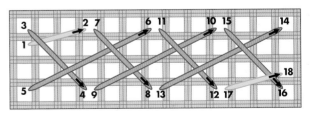

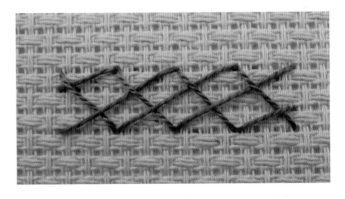

## UPRIGHT CROSS

This simple stitch is quick and easy to work. It can be worked from left to right or on the diagonal using the stab method. Working three rows of this stitch close together creates a very nice frame effect around an area. Add some interest using Delica beads or French knots between the crosses.

You can use any type of thread for this stitch.

**Ways to use:** borders, bands, filling, petals, large leaves

**Also known as:** St. George, straight

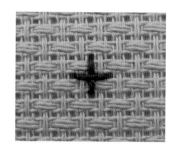
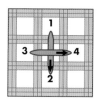

## SMYRNA CROSS

This stitch is worked from left to right, right to left or vertically. This versatile stitch is a combination of two cross-stitches. The size of the stitch can be changed to fit the area. It is shown stitched over four threads. It can also be stitched over two, six, or eight threads. For a border area, alternate the over two threads and over four threads sizes of this stitch across the area.

You can use any type of thread. Hand-dyed single strand threads work well for this stitch.

**Ways to use:** borders, bands, filling

**Also known as:** Leviathan, railway, double cross, straight cross

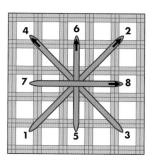

## DOUBLE STRAIGHT CROSS

This mainly decorative stitch can be worked in any direction. It does not work as well if compensating is required. Keep all the top crosses going in the same direction. This is a beautiful stitch and can be worked in two colors. Work the larger upright cross first; then go back with another color of thread to make the center cross. You can use two textures of thread for this stitch. Metallic thread or braids are beautiful when used for the center cross.

You can use any type of thread for this stitch. Pearl cotton and single strand threads work best.

**Ways to use:** borders, bands

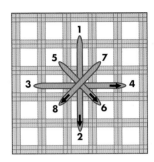

## RICE

Work this stitch from left to right or vertically. It can be worked in two colors of thread. If using two colors, work the large cross-stitches in the darker color. Work the half crosses to complete the stitch. Shades of one color are lovely when used for this stitch. This stitch can be a little tricky until you learn the rhythm. Follow the numbers and arrows on the graph. This stitch is wonderful for working block letters.

You can use any type of thread for this stitch.

**Ways to use:** borders, bands, alphabets, filling

**Also known as:** crossed corners, William and Mary

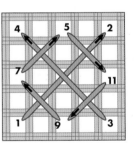

## ALGERIAN EYELET

This stitch is worked from right to left. It is a versatile stitch that can be stitched over multiple threads. It can be worked over two, four, or six threads. For best results, work the stitches as the arrows indicate on the graph so you will be going down into a dirty hole, not coming up through a dirty hole. If working a band or border, hand-dyed floss or single-strand thread show this best.

You can use any type of thread for this stitch. Pearl cotton and single strand threads work best.

**Ways to use:** bands, borders, alphabets

**Also known as:** star

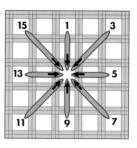

## DIAMOND EYELET

This stitch is worked from right to left. For best results, work the stitches as shown on the graph so you will be going down into a dirty hole, not coming up through a dirty hole. This stitch gives a lacy look when worked over a large area or worked as a border stitch.

You can use any type of thread for this stitch. Hand-dyed single strand thread or metallic braid work especially well.

**Ways to use:** stars, bands

**Also known as:** star eyelet

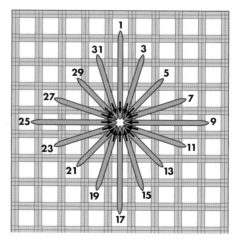

## HALF-DIAMOND EYELET

This stitch is worked from left to right. For best results, work the stitches as shown on the graph so you will be going down into a dirty hole, not coming up through a dirty hole. This stitch gives a lacy look when worked over a large area. For an interesting border, use this stitch in a variegated embroidery floss or hand-dyed single-strand thread.

You can use any type of thread for this stitch.

**Ways to use:** borders, bands

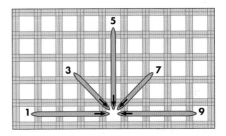

## DAISY MOTIF

This sweet motif is a variation of a lazy daisy. This stitch can we worked in any direction. As you work the stitch, you'll need to use your finger to hold the left side of the loop in place while you complete the tie-down stitch. Watch the tension on this stitch, as it is easy to pull it too snug. When the motif is complete, check to be sure it lies flat against the fabric with no puckering of the fabric.

You can use any type of thread for this stitch.

**Ways to use:** bands, borders, filling

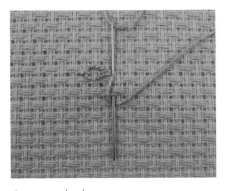

Creating the loop

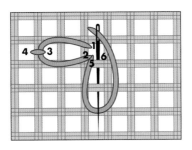

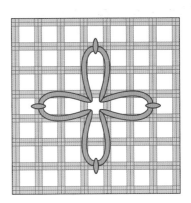

## MOSAIC

This stitch is worked from left to right or diagonally from left to right. It is an easy small stitch and works well for flower petals or other small shapes. Hand-dyed or over-dyed threads gives the flower petals a shaded look. When choosing a thread, use fewer strands rather than more so the slanted stitches aren't crowded in the area. If using floss, lay each stitch so it spreads out over the fabric.

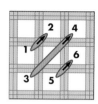

You can use any type of thread for this stitch. Stranded threads show off the pattern of this stitch.

**Ways to use:** filling, borders, block alphabets, stems, trunks, bands

**Also known as:** diagonal Hungarian

## BLANKET

Work this stitch from left to right. Keep the vertical stitches the same height and the horizontal stitches the same distance apart. When working the stitch, the thread should always be under the needle when it comes out of the fabric for the vertical part of the stitch. Keep the bottom loop of the thread pulled at the same tension. The tension for this stitch is very important. If pulled too snug, it will cause the fabric edge to curl up. This can be a tricky stitch to work on Aida, but with the right tension it is beautiful.

This is a great finish for pillows backed with felt and finished on the edges by joining the two fabrics together.

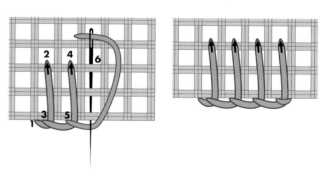

Twisted hand-dyed, hand-dyed single strand, and pearl cotton work best for this stitch.

**Ways to use:** edgings

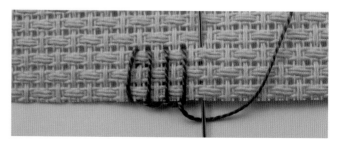

Looping thread under needle

## FRENCH KNOT

The size of thread and number of wraps will determine the knot size produced. Use one, two, or three wraps, depending on the desired size. Once the thread is wrapped on the needle, it is important to keep the needle straight and the thread taut as it goes down into the hole. Use your other hand to hold the thread taut. Pull the thread gently to complete the knot.

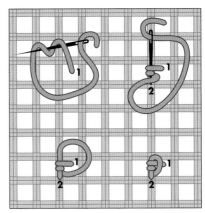

You can use any type of thread for this stitch.

**Ways to use:** flower centers, filling, peppered for backgrounds

**Also known as:** French dot, knotted, twisted knot, wound

Placing needle through center of square

Holding thread firmly

Pulling thread through

# Violet Blossoms Candle Band

Fields of wild violets blooming are a wonder to behold. These stitched violets will add a touch of beauty to your home for guests and family to enjoy.

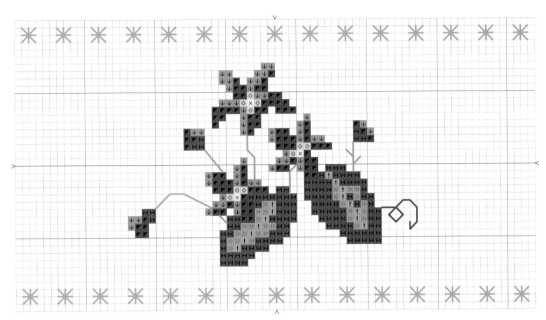

Violet Blossoms Chart

| | | |
|---|---|---|
| H | 987 | dark forest green |
| >> | 989 | forest green |
| ↓ | 341 | light blue violet |
| ◤ | 3807 | cornflower blue |
| ◇ | 307 | lemon |
| ! | 164 | light forest green |
| × | 3078 | very light golden yellow |
| ▬ | 470 | light avocado gree (stem) |
| ▬ | 3051 | dark grey green (tendril) |
| ▬ | 907 | light parrot green (smyrna) |

Color Key

Smyrna stitch: 2 strands
Cross-stitch: 2 strands
Backstitch stem and tendril: 1 strand

**Stitch count (excludes border):** 41 w x 28 h
Stitch design centered on band. Baste the center lines.

**Approximate finished size:** will depend on candle size

## Stitching Instructions

**1** Baste center line on Stitchband.

**2** Stitch design using center line as a guide.

**3** Remove center basting thread.

**4** Trim ends of band as needed for a straight edge.

**5** Fold under one end of the Stitchband ¼" (0.6 cm). Use ecru sewing thread to sew raw edge to the back of the band. Stitches should not go through the fabric to the front.

**6** Measure the circumference of the candle. Create a circle the size of the circumference by overlapping the sewn edge of the Stitchband on the outside of the circle until measurement is reached. Pin layers together. Sew the two pieces together along the folded edge of the top piece.

**7** Trim loose band as needed and slide band on candle. The band can be positioned in the center of the candle or placed at the bottom of the candle.

*Never leave burning candles unattended.*

# Springtime Journal

Spring brings beautiful color with sweet smells from all the blooming flowers. This posy will call forth thoughts of spring as you write in your "Go Green" journal with its handmade paper and hemp cover.

## YOU WILL NEED

- 5" × 7¼" (12.7 × 18.4 cm) natural hemp handmade journal

- 4½" × 6" (11.4 × 15.2 cm) piece of 14-count perforated paper: pale gray green

- six-strand embroidery floss: medium light moss green, black, dark coral, coral, avocado green, very light topaz, and black avocado green

- tapestry needle, size 24

- rotary cutter and cutting board

- cardstock paper: dark mocha brown and bright orange red

- permanent adhesive

## STITCHES USED

- cross

- backstitch

## Stitching Information

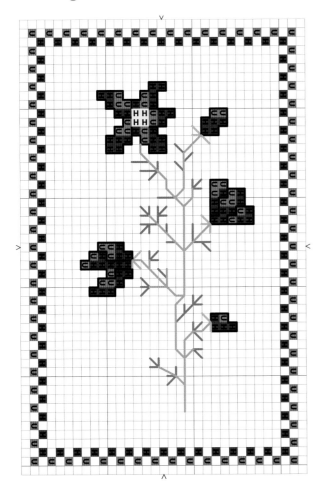

Springtime Journal Chart

**Stitch count:** 31 w x 49 h
Stitch design centered on paper. Baste the center lines.

**Approximate finished size (perforated paper):**
2¼" × 3½" (5.7 x 8.9 cm)

**1** Baste center line on paper.

**2** Stitch design using center line as a guide.

**3** Remove center basting thread.

**4** Trim the perforated paper to within one row of the stitching.

**5** Use ine rotary cutter and cutting board to cut a piece of the brown cardstock ⅛" (3 mm) larger on all four sides than the stitched work. Cut the red cardstock ⅛" (3 mm) larger on all four sides than the brown cardstock.

**6** Use the permanent adhesive to glue the needlework to the brown cardstock. Using a toothpick, place permanent adhesive on the back of the stitched work along the back of the cross-stitches and on each flower. Glue to the center of the front of the brown cardstock.

**7** Place permanent adhesive on the front side of the red cardstock and glue it the back of the brown cardstock. Glue the back of the red cardstock to the front of the journal. Refer to the photograph for placement, or chose your own location on the journal front.

| | | |
|---|---|---|
| ▉H | 34 | coral dark |
| C | 35 | coral |
| H | 72 | topaz very light |
| ▬ | 310 | black |
| ▬ | 934 | black avocado green |
| ▬ | 166 | moss green medium light |
| ▬ | 469 | avocado green |

Color Key

Cross-stitch: 3 strands
Backstitch flowers and petals: 1 strand
Backstitch main stem, branches, and leaves: 3 strands

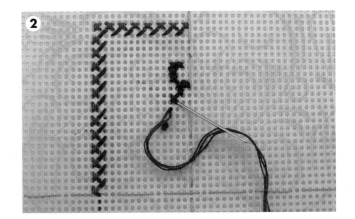

# NEEDLEPOINT

Needlepoint, sometimes referred to as canvas embroidery, is a counted-work technique stitched on stiff mesh canvas. It is easy to learn and fun to work, giving hours of pleasure while creating projects that will last for generations. Stitchers who try needlepoint soon discover that they cannot put it down because it is so intriguing. Many actors and surgical doctors do needlepoint—actors to fill their downtime on the set, and doctors to help keep their fingers flexible. Regardless of occupation, many stitchers find needlepoint relaxing and calming. You can become so involved in stitching that you forget all the worries of the world. It's like reading a good book. Time flies by.

# Needlepoint Canvas

All types of canvas are referred to by the number of threads per inch in the canvas mesh.

Canvas ranges in size from the largest, 3.5 (rug canvas), to the smallest, 24 count (congress cloth). Designs are worked using a wide range of threads and yarns. History tells us that hundreds of years ago canvas embroidery was worked with 100 percent wool using the tent stitch. We have come a long way from there—with hundreds of threads made from different types of materials and a wide range of canvas, including colored canvas. At first, the only color choices were white or tan canvas. Today you can choose lavender or black or aqua or any of the other colors available. Although there are still mesh counts that only come in white or tan, they are usually the larger counts.

## INTERLOCK CANVAS

The threads for this very flexible canvas are woven evenly. The threads are intertwined at the intersection where the horizontal and vertical threads come together. Be sure your interlock canvas is a high-quality canvas made of 100 percent combed cotton yarns. If possible, check the canvas to be sure that the canvas threads are straight and that there are no flaws within the piece you plan to use. Keep in mind that interlock does not block easily. Therefore, when you attach the interlock canvas to the stretcher bars, you must be sure the canvas threads are straight so it will not be necessary to block your work.

When preparing the canvas (page 214) put your thumbtacks every inch (1.3 cm) to ensure the canvas remains firm to the touch as you stitch. The flexibility and strong intersections make this the perfect choice for projects that are being trimmed close to the canvas thread. Some projects that work well on this type of canvas are ornaments, bookmarks, checkbook covers, eyeglass cases, and small handbags.

Interlock is available in 5 to 18 count in white. There is a large range of colors in the 14 count. In the 14 count, a white with silver or gold metallic fleck on the canvas is available. For the metallic-flecked canvas, lacy stitches are used so the metallic flecks show. It works well for ornaments and Christmas stockings.

## INTERLOCK RUG CANVAS

This canvas is available in 3.5 count white.

## MONO DELUXE ORANGE LINE CANVAS

This is a tightly woven canvas and much stiffer than interlock. The 100 percent cotton mesh has slightly rounded threads that are woven over and under each other. One of the threads is woven horizontally and the other vertically. One very important difference between mono and interlock is that mono can ravel if cut close to your work. You will need to stabilize the edges of the canvas threads before you trim the canvas around your needlework. You can do this by either stitching several close rows of machine stitches or using a stabilizer like Fray Check or Fabri-Tac fabric adhesive that dries clear. Always leave several canvas threads between the stabilized edge and the needlepoint stitching. The round, stiff canvas threads tend to ravel.

Mono Deluxe is available in 10 to 18 counts. There is a large range of colors in 18 count.

## CONGRESS CLOTH

This is a fine, flexible mesh canvas that has twenty-four threads to the inch (1.3 cm). It is used for small delicate designs stitched with single strands of silk, embroidery floss, very fine braid, or any type of thread that will work for the fine count.

## DOUBLE MESH (PENELOPE) CANVAS

This is a 100 percent cotton polished, twisted mesh canvas. This canvas has two canvas mesh threads, side by side, allowing an extra stitch to be taken by using the needle to open the space between the two threads for an added stitch. When these additional stitches are used on the double mesh canvas, it becomes a petit point canvas. For example, if the double mesh canvas is a 14 count, adding the additional stitches to the canvas increases the mesh count to a 28.

To work a piece of petit point, work across the canvas by splitting the two canvas threads and placing a stitch over one of the threads. Then work a stitch over the other canvas thread.

## DOUBLE MESH QUICK POINT

Double mesh is a 5-count canvas that is available in white and brown. It is used to work quick projects that do not have detail. Geometric patterns work well for this type of canvas.

## HAND PAINTED CANVAS

If you prefer not to follow a needlepoint chart, use a needlepoint-painted canvas. These canvases have the design already painted on them. They come in a wide variety of subjects and can be found in needlepoint shops or online. The best type of painted canvas is one that is stitch painted. This simply means that the paint is placed over the canvas thread where you will work the stitch of that color. With stamped canvases it's more difficult to know where to place the stitch.

Painted canvases allow the stitcher to decide which stitches to use. In years past, they were worked using the

(continued)

basketweave stitch. However, using decorative stitches on a painted canvas adds interest and life to the finished canvas. Some painted canvases come with a stitch guide that suggests threads and stitches that work well on the canvas. The shop clerk can tell you if a stitch guide is available for a canvas.

On the other hand, it is always fun to play around with the stitches and decide for yourself which stitch to use. The stitches in this chapter will give you an idea of other stitches that can be used (page 220).

## PRE-WORKED CANVAS

These canvases come with the center area worked. You work the background around the preworked center. The main use for this type canvas is for dining room chairs, pillows, and other home décor items. The basketweave stitch is usually used to complete the background, because it is the strongest stitch with the woven pattern it creates on the back. Look for this type of canvas on the Internet, or ask your favorite needlework shop if they have a catalog you can order from. Most shops do not stock this type of canvas.

## PREPARING THE CANVAS

To begin, either tape or serge the edges of the canvas to keep it from raveling. Secure the canvas to the stretcher frame with tacks or staples spaced approximately one inch (1.3 cm) apart. For best results, place the tacks following the framing diagram. When tacked to the stretcher bars, the canvas should be firm to the touch with the threads straight. This will ensure that the finished canvas is straight when removed from the frame. If you follow the stitching instructions, you should not have to block your finished piece.

A taut canvas ensures even tension on all stitches from the first to the last. If canvas becomes loose when stitching, carefully remove one tack or staple at a time, pull canvas to tighten, and replace tack or staple. Continue working around the canvas in this manner until the canvas is again taut and square.

Use a permanent pen or paint to mark on a canvas. This will prevent the ink or paint from bleeding down the canvas threads should the canvas become damp or wet.

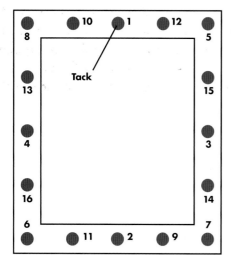

Framing Diagram

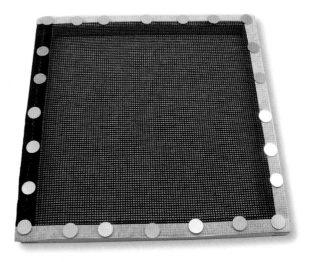

Stretched Canvas

Hand-Painted Canvas GERBER SURPRISE, a Julie Mar Design

## BLOCKING THE CANVAS

It will not be necessary to block your work if you used the stretcher frames and secured the canvas in the manner described. If your hands were clean each time you stitched, your piece should have remained clean.

However, if blocking is necessary, I recommend using the dry block method. You will need stainless steel straight pins and a triangle ruler. The triangle ruler will help ensure that your corners are square before you begin the blocking process.

Use a padded ironing board or a quilter's padded board as a blocking board. Using the stainless steel pins and the triangle ruler, start in the upper right corner and work around the piece. Stretch your canvas flat and straight by placing a stainless steel pin every 1" to 1½" (2.5 to 3.8 cm) as you work around the area. Insert the pin through a canvas hole into the ironing board. Use the triangle to be sure the edge of the canvas is straight. When you are sure the canvas is taut and straight, leave it for seventy-two hours.

# Blocking

Needlepoint shops often have blocking services.

# Thread

The threads listed in this section are a sampling of what's available in needlepoint shops. The colors and types of threads and wools are vast. Each year at the needlework market, companies are showing new types of threads and yarns. It is exciting to know we have new choices in the shops.

In the Creative Embroidery (page 34), Crewel (page 76), and Cross-Stitch (page 191) sections, some of these same threads have been discussed. For needlepoint, most any type of thread can be used. Play around with the different types to see how they look with different stitches. For more information, refer to Special Stitching Information (page 24).

When looking for supplies for a new project, it is best to choose the pattern first and the size you want the project to be when it is finished. Knowing your project size will help you determine the count of the canvas you need.

Needlepoint shop owners are very knowledgeable about what they are selling and can help you determine how much thread you will need for your project. Be sure to

make a list before you go shopping. If you want to match the color of an item within your home, bring a small sample if possible. Thread colors should be pleasing to the eye and complement each other. If you're using a pattern, it will indicate the stitches and colors to use. If using a painted canvas, you will decide what threads, colors, and stitches to use. Choosing the stitches to use for the design can be done once you return home. If you prefer help, ask the shop owner for suggestions.

When choosing threads for your project, keep in mind that straight stitches require a thicker thread or more strands than diagonal stitches. Larger stitch units work well with flat synthetic ribbons or silk ribbon to reveal the beauty of the stitch. The larger the canvas count, the more thread it will take to fill the mesh hole.

## 100% WOOL

This thread comes in single strands of very fine wool made in England. It comes in many colors. When working with the fine thread, you will need to use several strands to cover the canvas thread. The number of strands needed will depend on the count of the mesh. One hundred percent merino wool is a thicker single strand of twisted soft wool thread. It comes in beautiful colors.

## PERSIAN YARN

This 100 percent virgin wool yarn is a three-ply yarn. It can be purchased in a skein, hanks, or by the pound. Some needlework shops also sell it by the strand. It comes in 230 shaded colors.

## TAPESTRY WOOL

This 100 percent virgin wool yarn is a four-ply, inseparable, twisted yarn. It is a heavy yarn used with the larger mesh, 12 count and up. It works well for chair seats and pillows—items that will be used for years. It comes in a skein or by the hank.

## WOOL BLENDS

The wool and silk blends come in single-strand skeins and three-ply skeins. The cotton, wool, and acrylic blends are a single-strand thicker thread that comes on a card. All of these threads come in many beautiful colors. They work well for projects that will be used regularly.

## SILK

Silk threads work up with a special sheen that is not found in other threads. There are many different kinds of silk thread. It comes on spools, in half skeins, and in full skeins. The stranded thread comes in three, six, or twelve strands. The number of stands is indicated on the package. Single-strand silk comes in a skein with either thick or thin strands. Over-dyed silk is available in single-strand, six-strand, or twelve-strand skeins. Sparkle has been added to silk. It comes single strand on a card or three-ply in a skein. These silks with added bling give just a touch of sparkle to your stitches.

## SILK RIBBON

Use only 100 percent silk ribbon that is woven individually, not cut from cloth. It has a woven selvage on both sides and is a high thread count, making it durable enough to use for needlepoint. Before purchasing silk ribbon for this technique, be sure it is durable enough to stitch with on canvas. If the ribbon doesn't have the selvage edges and high thread count, it will fray and ravel. Using silk will give a beautiful sheen to the finished design. It comes

*(continued)*

in solid or variegated hand-dyed colors. It is a pleasure to work with. The Market Basket project (page 246) was stitched using some silk.

## HAND-DYED AND OVER-DYED EMBROIDERY FLOSS

This 100 percent cotton thread comes in a six-strand embroidery floss thread that is available in solid and variegated colors. It also comes in a hand over-dyed thread that is six-strand embroidery floss. The over-dyed colors give the stitches a shaded look. All of these threads add a slight sheen to the stitch.

## TWISTED HAND-DYED COTTON

This thread comes in a three-ply pima cotton and a single-strand skein. The variegated colors of these twisted threads create stunning gradual changes of color as they are stitched across the canvas. These hand-dyed threads add beauty to any of the stitches in this chapter.

## PEARL COTTON (COTON PERLÉ)

This slightly twisted, single-strand thread has a slight sheen. For needlepoint, sizes 12, 8, 5, and 3 can be used. These threads come in a skein or on a ball, depending on the brand. It is also available in a variegated size 5. If you want to use a certain color that only comes in size 5, you can use more than one strand so it covers the canvas thread.

## HAND-DYED AND SOLID COLORED SINGLE STRAND COTTON

These threads come in a single-strand skein. They are available in many colors in solid and hand-dyed variegated shades. When stitching with this thread, the color flow is very gradual.

## SIX STRAND EMBROIDERY FLOSS

This 100 percent cotton thread is available in solid and variegated colors. There is a large range of solid colors to choose from and many of these colors come in a range of shaded tones.

## BRAIDS (METALLIC)

These braids can be used for all techniques. They are discussed in other chapters of this book. For needlepoint, the round sizes 4, 8, 12, 16, and 32 can be used. This braid also comes in a flat braid in 1/16" (1.6 mm) and 1/8" (3 mm). The flat braid works well for many of the needlepoint stitches, especially stitches worked straight across the canvas. For a tip on how to work with the braid, see the Cross-Stitch chapter (page 193).

## LINEN

There are several 100 percent linen threads available. These textured threads come in a single-strand thread on a card and a six-strand skein. The strands may vary in width along the strand. There is a wide range of colors. Dye lots vary, so it's best to purchase the amount needed.

## SYNTHETIC RIBBON

This flat ribbon comes on a plastic bobbin in metallic, sparkly, and solid colors. They add shine while giving the work a flat, smooth appearance. Square, multi-layered stitches are smooth and flat when stitched with these beautiful synthetics.

## TUBULAR THREAD

Tubular thread is made from nylon. It will add a shiny wet look to the stitches. It is easy to work with.

## SPECIALTY THREAD

Furry threads are usually made from rayon and/or nylon. This thread comes in several different types—check them out at the needlework shop. They are great for stitching hair and animals.

## POLYESTER

This thread comes in a single-strand skein. It is a polyester filament thread that has a slight twist and a metallic fleck, which adds sparkle to projects. This is a beautiful thread that works well for Christmas ornaments and stockings.

## FLAT RAYON RIBBON

This flat ribbon comes on a card and is available in solid, frosty, or sparkly colors. Multi-layered stitches are smooth and flat when stitched with this type of thread.

# Stitches

Needlepoint stitches are worked following numbers and arrows. You count the needlepoint canvas threads to determine the placement of stitches.

As you work, the threads completely cover the canvas. However, stitches cover the canvas in different ways. On lacy stitches, the canvas threads will show if the stitch pattern isn't followed. Stitch tension will also affect the look of the stitches. Tension that is too snug will pull the thread tight against the canvas, letting too much canvas show. As you work these stitches, keep that in mind.

When working certain types of designs, it is often hard to know where the top of the canvas is. It is a good idea to mark the top of your canvas on the taped edge with a T, using a permanent pen. This will give you the reference needed to know which way to turn the canvas when a new stitch is started.

When working a geometric design, it is sometimes helpful to rotate the canvas a quarter turn as you stitch, so you can maintain the direction of travel.

The stitched needlepoint examples have a single contrasting stitch to show how the stitch unit fits within the area. To help you see how the stitch is worked, the stitch unit is indicated by a yellow stitch or, if the pattern was stitched in yellow, it is indicated by red. The stitch examples also show how to compensate the stitch on the left side and bottom of each example. The top and right side show how the stitches look without having the compensating stitches worked on the edges.

## Tip

When working needlepoint vertical straight stitches, you may need to use more strands of thread or a larger size of pearl cotton for the vertical stitches than the horizontal.

## BACKSTITCH

The backstitch can be worked in any direction over any number of threads. In the graph below, it is worked over two threads. When stitching, watch your tension, as a snug tension can cause the stitches to pull the canvas threads too close together. When worked over one thread, keep the tension looser so the stitch will show. It is very easy to pull the small stitch too taut.

When working around a curved area or around a corner, it may be necessary to reverse the direction of a single stitch. This will keep the back thread from showing on the front of the canvas, should there be any open canvas weave in that area. You can use any type of thread for this stitch.

**Ways to use:** outlines, single-row coverage

**Also known as:** Point de Sable, back

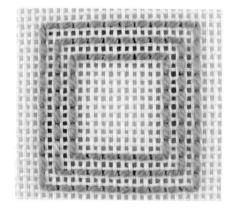

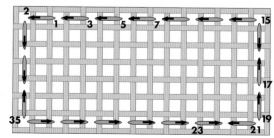

# BRICK

This stitch travels left to right, then reverses for the next row going right to left. Repeat until the area is filled. The pattern of the stitch alternates up and down as it is worked across the area. It will be necessary to fill in the compensating stitching on the top and bottom rows to complete the pattern.

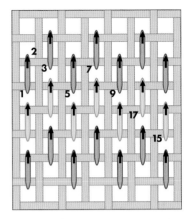

This stitch can be worked over two or four threads. On the graph, it is shown over two threads. The thread or yarn used to work this stitch should completely cover the canvas threads. If necessary, increase the amount of thread or yarn being used.

This is a quick stitch to use for backgrounds. It has a soft textured look and it blends well with other stitches. Pearl cotton, Persian yarn, synthetic tubular, and wool blends work best.

**Ways to use:** backgrounds, roofs, tree bark, chimneys or fireplaces

**Also known as:** alternating

# DOUBLE BRICK

This stitch travels left to right, then reverses for the next row going right to left. Repeat until the area is filled. Notice that the pattern of the stitch alternates up and down as it is worked across the area. It will be necessary to fill in the compensating stitching on the top and bottom rows to complete the pattern.

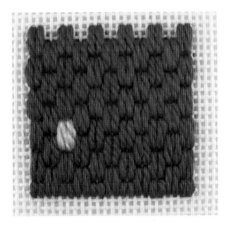

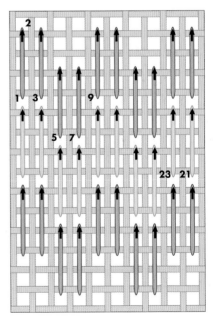

This stitch can be worked over two or four threads. On the graph it is shown over four threads. The thread or yarn used to work this stitch should completely cover the canvas threads. If necessary, increase the amount of thread or yarn being used. Pearl cotton, Persian yarn, synthetic tubular, and wool blends work best.

**Ways to use:** backgrounds, geometric patterns

## HORIZONTAL BRICK

This stitch travels in the direction indicated by the numbers and arrows. It can be worked over two or four threads. On the graph it is shown over four threads. The thread or yarn used to work this stitch should completely cover the canvas threads. If necessary, increase the amount of thread or yarn being used.

Pearl cotton, Persian yarn, and wool blends work best.

**Ways to use:** backgrounds, geometric patterns

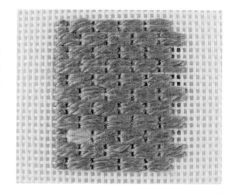

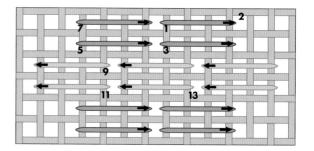

## HUNGARIAN

This stitch travels in the direction indicated by the numbers and arrows. There is a space between each stitch unit, and as the rows are worked it forms a staggered diamond pattern across the area. It will be necessary to fill in the compensating stitching on the top and bottom rows to complete the pattern. Keep an even tension on these straight stitches.

Pearl cotton, Persian yarn, synthetic tubular, and wool blends work best.

**Ways to use:** borders, geometric patterns, light texture

**Also known as:** Point d'Hongrie

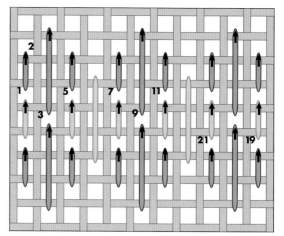

## PARISIAN STRIPE

This stitch travels left to right, then reverses for the next row going right to left. Repeat until the area is filled. Follow the numbers and arrows. It will be necessary to fill in the compensating stitching on the top and bottom rows to complete the pattern.

Work the short straight stitches between the rows, as indicated in green on the graph. Follow the letters and arrows. The stripe stitch is most effective if a second color is used for these short stitches.

Pearl cotton, Persian yarn, synthetic tubular, and wool blends work best.

**Ways to use:** borders, geometric patterns

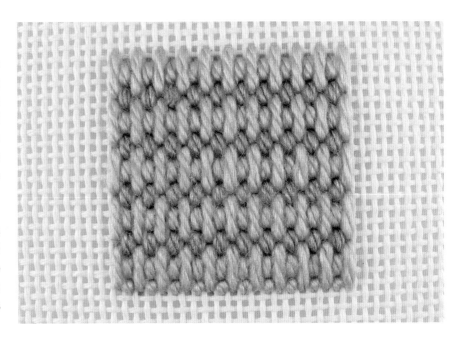

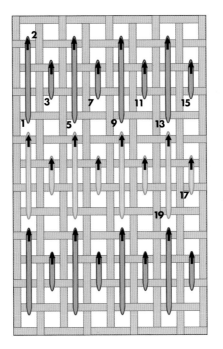

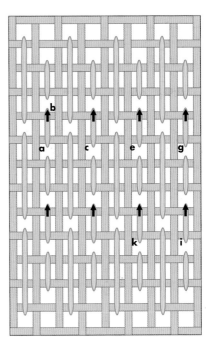

## PAVILLION

This stitch travels left to right, then right to left. Follow the numbers and arrows.

Diamonds are formed by the alternating rows. You can work this stitch in one color or use two colors giving a checkered look. It will be necessary to fill in the compensating stitching on the top and bottom rows to complete the pattern.

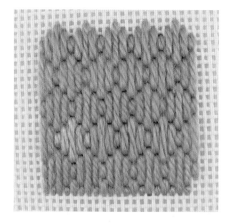

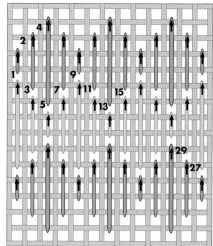

This stitch is similar to the Hungarian, as they share a pattern formation.

Pearl cotton, Persian yarn, synthetic tubular, and wool blends work best.

**Ways to use:** borders, geometric patterns

**Also known as:** pavillion diamonds, Hungarian diamonds

## STRAIGHT DIAMOND MOTIF

This stitch should travel as shown following the numbers and arrows. It can be used as shown or worked as a background stitch by continuing to fit the diamonds together across the area. You can also stitch individual diamonds in a horizontal or vertical line.

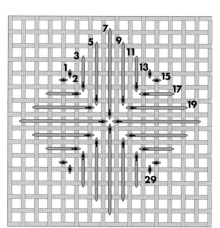

This stitch pattern is often used in the center of a design, as in the Iris Lace jewelry box on page 250.

You can use any type of thread or yarn for this stitch.

**Ways to use:** bands, borders, background, geometric patterns

## SLANTED GOBELIN

This stitch travels left to right as you work a border or rows. It can be worked over one to six threads. The stitch graph shows how to work around the corners when using this stitch as a frame or border stitch. It is shown here worked over three threads.

This stitch works well as a frame or border stitch. Because of the consistent diagonal direction of the stitches, it will distort the canvas if not worked on stretcher bars.

The slanted Gobelin over one thread is often used as a border stitch to cover an extra thread in a pattern between stitches of different thread counts.

You can use any type of thread or yarn for this stitch.

**Ways to use:** borders, frames, bands

**Also known as:** Gobelin oblique, slanting Gobelin

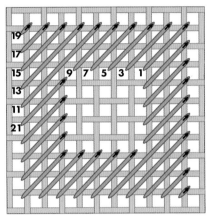

## INTERLOCKING SLANTED GOBELIN

This stitch travels left to right, then reverses for the next row going right to left. Repeat until the area is filled. It works up fast, completely covering the canvas with an interwoven look to the stitch.

It does have a tendency to pull the canvas threads out of shape, so watch the tension as you work the stitch. For best results, use stretcher bars when working this stitch.

You can use any type of thread or yarn for this stitch.

**Ways to use:** background, filling

**Also known as:** encroaching slanted Gobelin, encroaching slanted Gobelin

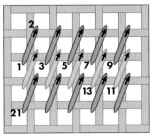

## TWO-WAY DARNING

This running stitch should travel top to bottom following the numbers and arrows on the graph. This is a lacy stitch and the back threads will show if the pattern is not worked correctly. The threads need to fill the area without leaving space between the thread being used and the canvas threads. Use a loose tension,

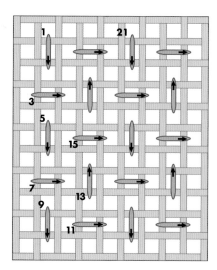

keeping the thread flat again the canvas. If pulled too snug, the beauty of the stitch will disappear within the canvas threads.

This stitch works up quickly and is used in the Market Basket design on page 246.

You can use any type of thread or yarn for this stitch.

**Ways to use:** borders, bands, filling, geometric patterns


## ALGERIAN EYE

This stitch travels left to right, then reverses for the next row going right to left. Repeat until the area is filled. Each individual stitch is worked clockwise following the numbers and arrows. The stitches come up on the outer edge and go down into the center hole. It may be necessary to slightly enlarge the center hole. Use the needle to gently push the canvas threads apart.

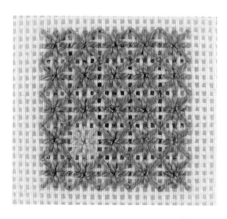

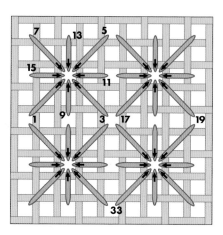

When a single strand or twisted thread is used, this stitch has a lacy look. It is a beautiful stitch to use, especially when working letters or borders. You can use any type of thread or yarn for this stitch.

**Ways to use:** alphabets, borders, bands, background, geometric patterns

**Also known as:** Algerian eyelet, square eyelet

## ZIGZAG BACKSTITCH

This stitch was created to add interest to open canvas areas for geometric patterns. When the stitch travels as shown on the stitch graph, long slanted lines are created on the back. No thread from the back shows.

Use metallic braid, single-strand, pearl cotton, or twisted thread for this stitch.

**Ways to use:** borders, bands

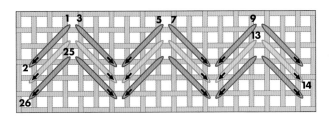

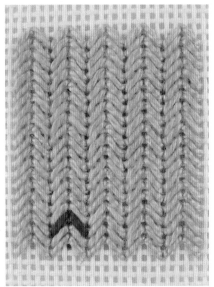

## DARNING PATTERN HEART

This darning pattern is worked horizontally across the area following the numbers and arrows. The thread from the back will show through, giving a shaded look to the work. For a delicate look, use a single-strand thread or silk thread, matching the color of thread to the color of canvas being used.

This stitch gives a very different look to canvas work.

You can use any type of thread for this stitch.

**Ways to use:** backgrounds, borders, filling, geometric patterns

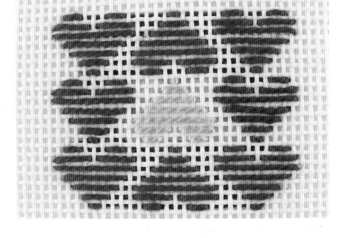

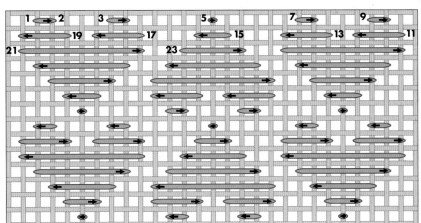

## DARNING PATTERN CHRISTMAS TREE

This darning pattern is worked horizontally across the area following the numbers and arrows. It is worked like the darning heart. The thread from the back will show through, giving a shaded look to the work. For a delicate look, use a single-strand thread or silk thread, matching the color of thread to the color of canvas being used. This is a beautiful stitch to use for ornaments or Christmas stockings.

You can use any type of thread for this stitch.

**Ways to use:** borders, backgrounds, geometric patterns, filling

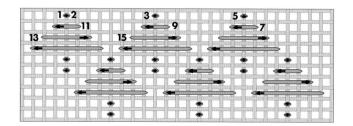

## CASHMERE

This stitch can travel horizontally, vertically, or diagonally. It is a rectangular stitch covering four canvas threads. It is often referred to as being in the Mosaic family. When worked, it gives the appearance of fabric. The pattern created by this stitch is rectangular boxes. You can stitch the "boxes" in different colors. It can be used to work individual boxes with an added bow on top for presents under Christmas trees.

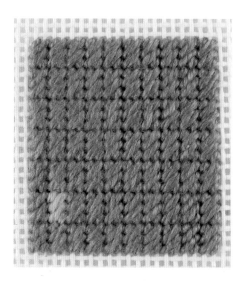

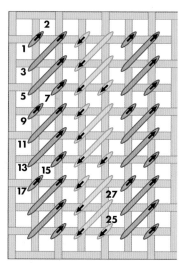

Work this stitch a little loose but keep the stitches even on top, watching the tension. It will distort the canvas if pulled too snug. For best results, use stretcher bars.

You can use any type of thread or yarn for this stitch.

**Ways to use:** borders, backgrounds, geometric patterns

# CONTINENTAL

Travel either horizontally or vertically following the numbers and arrows. This stitch is often referred to as a tent stitch. It is one of the most widely used stitches in needlepoint because it creates a beautiful smooth background. It distorts the canvas, pulling it out of shape if too snug a tension is used. If using a snug tension, you may need to block your work when the project is finished, even if stretcher bars are used.

Work this stitch a little loose, but keep the stitches even on top and watch the tension. For best results, use stretcher bars. Check the back of your canvas to be sure you are working it correctly. The stitches on the back should be slanted. If they are vertical, you might want to remove those stitches and stitch the area again. This is a stitch that will create an uneven appearance on the front if not worked correctly. It may not show until the project has been removed from the stretcher bars.

You can use any type of thread or yarn for this stitch.

**Ways to use:** backgrounds, filling

**Also known as:** continental tent

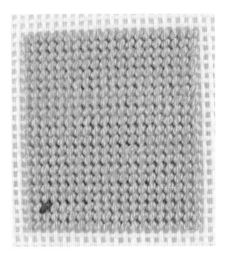

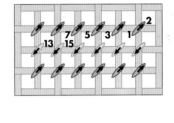

# FLY

This stitch travels top to bottom. Start at the top for each row and end the thread at the bottom. It can be stitched vertically or horizontally. This stitch can be worked so all canvas threads are covered or so some of the canvas thread shows. The amount of thread or yarn used depends on the desired look. Be careful not to pull the center stitch too snug or the stitch will disappear. For a striped effect, leave one canvas thread between rows.

You can use any type of thread or yarn for this stitch.

**Ways to use:** backgrounds, borders, stripes, plants

**Also known as:** open loop, Y

## BASKETWEAVE

This stitch travels diagonally across the canvas and should be worked exactly as the arrows and numbers indicate on the stitch graph. When it is stitched correctly, it looks like a woven basket on the back. Start stitching in the upper right corner, placing the diagonal stitches. Notice that the first stitch is placed, then one beside it and below it. The needle is placed through the canvas in a different direction, depending on how you are traveling. This is not an easy stitch, but if you study the chart and practice how to work it, the rhythm will come easily. Some stitchers love this stitch so much that it is the only one they want to use. It does give you a firm, smooth background. To avoid ridges on the front of the canvas, always end the thread by running it under previously stitched work, either vertically or horizontally. Never end diagonally.

You can use any type of thread or yarn for this stitch.

**Ways to use:** backgrounds, filling

**Also known as:** diagonal tent

Back of stitches

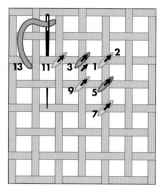

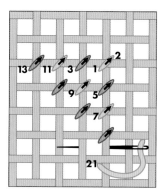

# Beads

Beads can be used on the needlepoint canvas, especially if stitching a painted canvas. Stitch them using a continental stitch and be sure to pull each bead snug so they sit straight up on the canvas. After two or three beads are placed, turn the canvas over and take a stitch on the back of a previous stitch to secure the bead.

## MOSAIC

This stitch travels right to left. It is made up of three stitches: a short stitch, a long stitch, and a short stitch that forms a square stitch unit. It is the smallest of the box stitches. When working this stitch, keep it neat in appearance by using an even tension. The three threads should lie flat and smooth against the canvas at the same height. The long center stitch will need to be pulled slightly snug to achieve this look. If the smaller stitches are pulled too snug, they will disappear into the canvas threads. The rhythm of working the stitch will become second nature. It's always a good idea to check the canvas to be sure you are keeping the stitch at the same height. It will distort the canvas if pulled too snug. For best results, use stretcher bars.

For a striking effect with the mosaic, use two colors to create stripes or shading. You can use any type of thread or yarn for this stitch.

**Ways to use:** backgrounds, filling, geometric patterns, filling in flower petals, leaves, and architectural shapes

**Also known as:** diagonal Hungarian

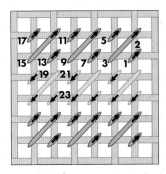

## DIAMOND RAY

This stitch travels left to right, then reverses for the next row going right to left. Repeat until the area is filled. This simple stitch works up quickly, covering the area. The threads should lie flat and smooth against the canvas.

If using as a background stitch, use a single-strand thread for a lacy look. As you work, you'll need to check that the back thread is not showing on the front.

This stitch is used as a border stitch in the Market Basket project (page 246).

You can use any type of thread or yarn for this stitch.

**Ways to use:** backgrounds, borders, geometric patterns, flowers or leaves

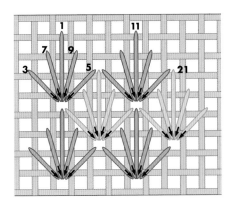

## DIAGONAL KNITTING

This stitch travels diagonally, following the travel path of the numbers and arrows. Once the rhythm is achieved, it works up quickly. For a smooth look, keep threads even in height.

It works well for areas on sweaters or clothing to give a knitted appearance. Using wool or wool blends gives a very realistic appearance of knit wear.

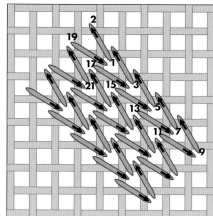

It is used as a small circular motif in the Market Basket project (page 246).

You can use any type of thread or yarn for this stitch.

**Ways to use:** clothing, circular motifs, knitted look for backgrounds

## SCOTCH

This box stitch travels right to left, then reverses for the next row going left to right. Repeat until the area is filled. Notice that you start the first row on the right with the top thread and the second row at the bottom thread of the stitch. This stitch can distort the canvas. For best results, use stretcher bars.

Scotch works well as a border stitch and is used in the Iris Lace project (page 258). This is a beautiful stitch when worked using over-dyed or hand-dyed twisted or single-strand thread.

You can use any type of thread or yarn for this stitch.

**Ways to use:** borders, backgrounds, geometric patterns

**Also known as:** flat, diagonal satin

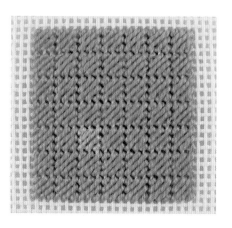
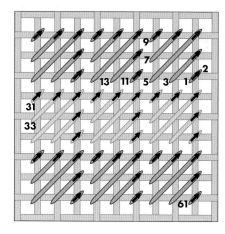

## REVERSE SCOTCH

This box stitch travels right to left, then reverses for the next row going left to right. Repeat until the area is filled. Notice that you start the first row on the right with the top thread and the second row at the bottom of the stitch. As you work the stitch, keep the tension even so the stitches will be at an even height across the top. This stitch can distort the canvas. For best results, use stretcher bars.

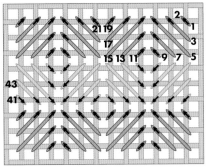

To add interest to this stitch, work it in two colors, alternating colors across the canvas. Count carefully so the second color of stitches will fit in between the previously placed stitches.

You can use any type of thread or yarn for this stitch.

**Ways to use:** backgrounds, filling, borders of two or more rows, clothing, geometric patterns

## T-SQUARE

This stitch travels diagonally, starting in the upper right corner of the area. It is a lacy stitch and should be worked following the numbers and arrows so the back threads do not show on the front of the canvas. As you work the stitch, hold the canvas up to the light. There should be no threads showing in the open weave of the canvas between stitches.

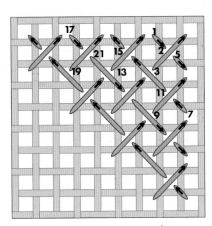

The T-square creates a beautiful lacy stitch that will quickly become a favorite.

Use hand-dyed single-strand thread, fine braids, pearl cotton, twisted thread, silk threads, silk ribbon, or ribbon floss.

**Ways to use:** backgrounds, borders, filling open areas in motifs

## SMYRNA

This stitch travels left to right, then reverses for the next row going right to left. Repeat until the area is filled. Notice that when working right to left you place the top horizontal stitch in the same direction as you did working left to right. You can work this stitch over two or four canvas threads. It is shown worked over two canvas threads.

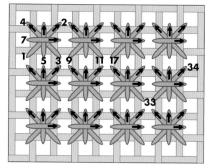

This is a wonderful border stitch as shown in the Iris Lace design (page 250). When worked with over-dyed or hand-dyed thread, it increases the beauty of the stitch. Metallic thread or fine braids make wonderful stars. You can use any type of thread or yarn for this stitch.

**Ways to use:** backgrounds, bands, filling, outline, borders

**Also known as:** railway, double cross

## LEAF

This stitch travels in diagonal rows when working a cluster of leaves. Start in the bottom right area, working diagonally upward toward the upper left corner. Once the cluster of leaves is in place, you will need to compensate on the edges of the area.

For two or more border rows, work in the same manner as a cluster. For single-leaf rows in borders or bands, place each leaf in from the other with the tip touching the end of the previous leaf. For a pretty leaf, keep the tension even so all the leaves are worked at the same height. This stitch can be compensated on the sides. On the top and bottom, it would be necessary to change the pattern slightly if you want to compensate to fill in along these rows. The sample does not show compensating stitches along the bottom edge.

You can use any type of thread or yarn for this stitch.

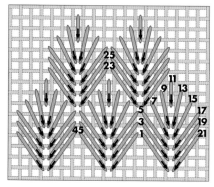

**Ways to use:** borders, bands, bushes, leaves, small trees

## LEAF MOTIF

This stitch travels around the motif, starting with the top leaf. Turn the canvas one quarter turn for each additional leaf. This stitch is similar to the leaf stitch, but it is wider. Notice in the center of the motif, there is blank canvas where other stitches can be worked—a Smyrna cross, straight, or upright cross to name a few. The motif can be placed on the corners of a project or in the center. A single leaf can be used for background or floral work. This motif is used for the Market Basket project (page 246).

 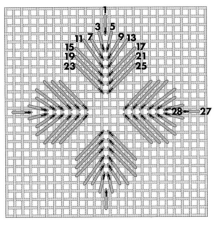

**Ways to use:** motifs, leaves

## SINGLE CROSS

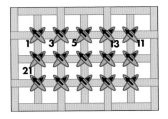

This stitch can travel horizontally, vertically, or diagonally. It is a small stitch that has many uses. It can be used as a border stitch to cover an extra thread in a pattern between stitches of different thread counts. Several rows can be worked together for an interesting border or band stitch. It can be used in combination with other stitches and works up quickly.

Work this stitch a little loose but keep the stitches even on top, watching the tension. Since it is over one thread, it can disappear within the canvas threads. For best results, use stretcher bars.

You can use any type of thread or yarn for this stitch.

**Ways to use:** borders, bands, filling

# SINGLE DOUBLE CROSS

This stitch travels across the canvas left to right. Work across the row, stitching the first slanted stitch of the crosses. Reverse direction, working right to left on the same row to complete the larger single crosses. Complete all the larger crosses in this manner before working the small single crosses between them. Work the small crosses in the same manner as the larger crosses, starting on the left.

When this stitch is worked using a single-strand thread, it gives a lacy appearance, making it a great background stitch. When the rhythm is established, it works up quickly.

You can use any type of thread or yarn for this stitch.

**Ways to use:** backgrounds, borders, bushes, tree trunks

**Also known as:** double stitch

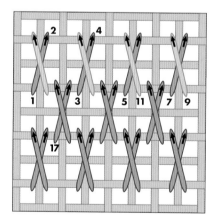

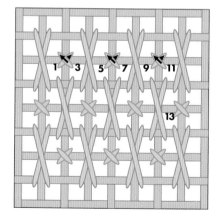

## LARGE LACY CROSS

This large cross-stitch travels across the canvas left to right to work the first half of the cross, then reverses direction working right to left back across the same row to complete the crosses. The size of this cross gives it a lacy look and will need to be worked as the numbers and arrows indicate to keep the back thread from showing on the front side of the canvas.

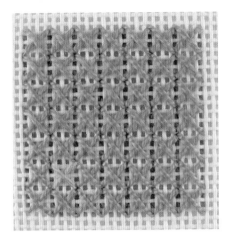

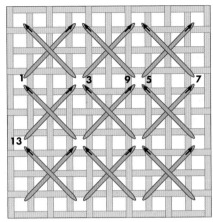

When using longer threads to complete a stitch like this one, maintaining an even tension can be more difficult. Watch the tension as you complete the crosses. This stitch was used as a background stitch for the Iris Lace project (page 250).

You can use any type of thread or yarn for this stitch.

**Ways to use:** backgrounds, borders, bands

**Also known as:** cross

## LONG UPRIGHT CROSS

This stitch travels left to right, then reverses for the next row going right to left. Repeat until the area is filled. It creates a woven textured effect, making it perfect for backgrounds. When this stitch is worked in wool blends or silk, it creates a beautiful texture. Linen thread creates a realistic looking basket effect.

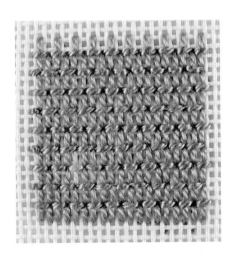

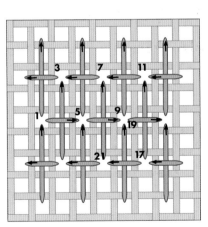

You can use any type of thread or yarn for this stitch.

**Ways to use:** backgrounds, baskets, Santa's bag, geometric patterns

## UPRIGHT CROSS

This stitch can travel horizontally or diagonally; many prefer to work it horizontally, starting on the left side. As you work this stitch, you will notice it creates the perfect resting place for a bead to nestle down between the rows of the crosses. It was used this way in the Iris Lace project (page 250).

When not adding beads to this little stitch, it will have a pineapple textured appearance that enhances a pattern. This pineapple texture shows to its fullest when the upright is worked with a twisted thread.

With the new furry threads, this is the perfect stitch to use for fur trims on clothing.

You can use any type of thread or yarn for this stitch.

**Ways to use:** backgrounds, tree bark, base for beads, flower centers, clothing

**Also known as:** St. George cross, straight cross

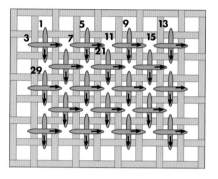

## DOUBLE STRAIGHT CROSS

This stitch travels diagonally when worked in a cluster. For a single-border row, work top to bottom with the tips of the longer center thread sharing holes.

For added interest, you can work the straight cross in one color. Then use a second color to work the cross-stitch over the straight cross. When used as a background, use a single-strand thread to give a lacy appearance to the area. When a fine thread is used, check to be sure the back threads aren't showing through on the front side.

You can use any type of thread or yarn for this stitch.

**Ways to use:** backgrounds, borders, stars, filling for a lacy look

**Also known as:** double cross-stitch

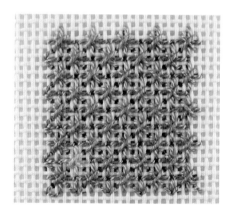

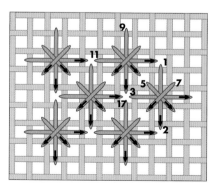

# CHECKERBOARD CROSS

This stitch can travel horizontally, as shown, or diagonally. The crosses are worked first. As you work the crosses horizontally, leave two threads between each cross to work an upright cross. Work one half of the cross left to right to the end of the area and the reverse, working right to left back across the area to complete the crosses. Work all the crosses in the area. Then fill in the upright crosses. You may find once the crosses are in place that working the upright crosses diagonally is easier.

You can use any type of thread or yarn for this stitch.

**Ways to use:** backgrounds, borders, filling

**Also known as:** St. George cross and St. Andrew cross-stitch

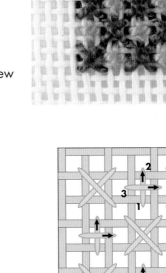

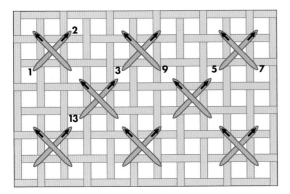

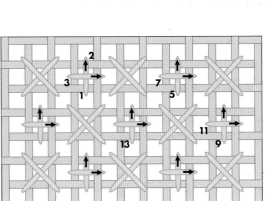

## FISHBONE TIED

This stitch travels vertically, top to bottom. It is worked in rows, left to right, producing a striped effect. Follow the numbers and arrows or it will be a difficult to find where to place the needle. It can be stitched over any number of threads to fit a given area. To completely fill an area, you'll need to compensate at the top and bottom of each row.

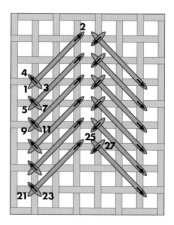

You can use any type of thread or yarn for this stitch. Wool blends and Persian yarn give a nice textured look to this stitch.

**Ways to use:** borders, backgrounds

## VAN DYKE

This stitch travels top to bottom, working a single row at a time. Work the rows from left to right across the area. It will be necessary to end each row, starting over at the top of the next row.

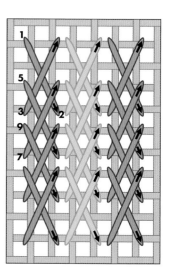

It is worked over two canvas threads wide but can be worked vertically over any number of threads needed to fit within an area. This stitch works best in single columns or as a striped effect using two or more colors.

You can use any type of thread or yarn for this stitch.

**Ways to use:** narrow borders, vertical stripes, knitted effects

# RAYS AND CROSSES

This border stitch travels vertically or horizontally following the numbers and arrows. It is a combination of a diamond ray stitch and double straight cross-stitch. The stitched example shows how it will look when used as a corner border. It can also be worked as a background stitch by traveling left to right across the canvas, working in rows. Keep the tension even on all the stitches, especially the longer ones. It may be necessary to pull the long stitch snug to keep the threads even. When working this stitch as a border, it is better not to compensate the stitch, giving it more of an open canvas effect.

This combination stitch is beautiful when worked using a single-strand thread or one strand of hand-dyed twisted thread. You can use any type of thread or yarn for this stitch.

**Ways to use:** borders, backgrounds

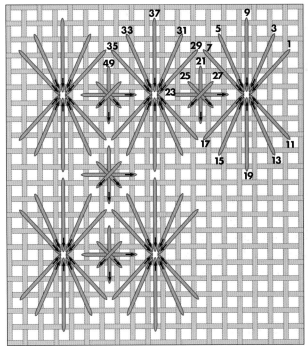

## ITALIAN CROSS

This stitch travels left to right, then reverses right to left to complete each row. The rhythm of this stitch is slightly tricky at first, until you remember the numbering sequence. Once you understand the rhythm, the stitching will go quickly. When used as a border or band, add a horizontal stitch across the top row to finish the edge of those stitches.

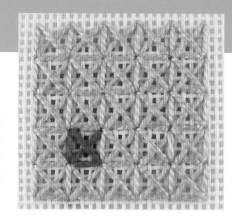

This stitch works up beautiful, giving the area a lacy appearance.

You can use any type of thread or yarn for this stitch.

**Ways to use:** borders, backgrounds, bands, geometric patterns, clothing, architectural

**Also known as:** two-sided cross, arrowhead cross

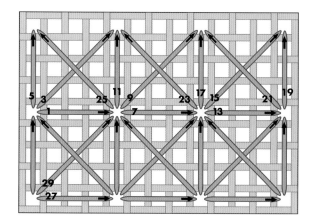

## RICE

This stitch travels left to right. In order to keep the tie-down stitches going in the correct direction, each row should start on the left. Work the crosses first across the area. Once they are in place, work the tie-down stitch over the four legs of each cross. Complete each row before working the next row. This stitch can be worked over two, three, or four threads.

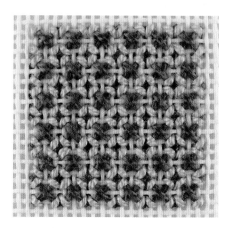

This stitch is very effective when the crosses are worked in one color of thread and a second color is used to tie down the stitch. For more texture, use different types of thread, one for the crosses and another for the tie-downs.

You can use any type of thread or yarn for this stitch.

**Ways to use:** borders, bands, backgrounds, architectural brick, geometric patterns

**Also known as:** William and Mary, cross corners

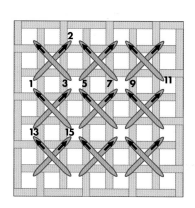

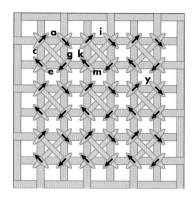

THE COMPLETE PHOTO GUIDE TO NEEDLEWORK

## RHODES

This stitch travels counterclockwise to create a single square stitch unit. It can be worked over any number of canvas threads greater than three. It is shown here over six canvas threads, with twelve thread passes creating the stitch. Pull each thread using the same tension for a smooth, even stitch.

It will add a dimensional look to any design. It can be used in Christmas pictures, stockings, ornaments, items that are not handled often, or needlework that will be admired but not used. The outer threads have a tendency to snag, giving the Rhodes a shorter life span than other stitches.

A little bit of history: This stitch was named for Mary Rhodes, a British needlework designer.

You can use any type of thread or yarn for this stitch. Metallic flat braids and flat threads like ribbon floss or silk ribbon work quite well.

**Ways to use:** borders, Christmas packages, door panels, corners

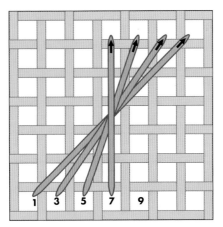

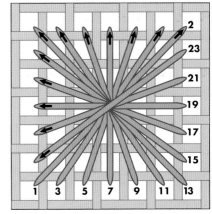

## RAPID

This stitch travels left to right, then reverses for the next row going right to left. Repeat until the area is filled. Use it as a border, working either a single row or a double row of stitches around the area. Like its name, it does work up rapidly. The rhythm is so easy, you will be surprised. It is stunning when a single strand of a hand-dyed twisted thread is used. Keep the stitches even in height.

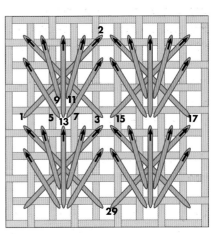

You can use any type of thread or yarn for this stitch.

**Ways to use:** borders, bands, backgrounds, geometric patterns

# FRAN'S TEXAS STAR

This stitch is worked in layers to create a single square stitch unit. The numbers and arrows of each layer must be followed exactly to create the beauty of the stitch. Notice that the 11–12 stitch weaves under the 5–6 stitch. The other stitches in the center will automatically weave over and under as they are worked. Although this stitch appears difficult to work, it isn't. Once you achieve the rhythm of the stitch, it works up quickly.

The layers give this stitch an appearance like no other needlepoint stitch. Of all the hundreds of needlepoint stitches, this is one of the most stunning. Its use in designs is somewhat limited by the size of the stitch. It is beautiful when worked with a flat thread like ribbon floss, silk ribbon, hand-dyed twisted thread, or flat metallic braid.

You can use any type of thread or yarn for this stitch.

**Ways to use:** borders, door panels, corners, bands, backgrounds, geometric patterns

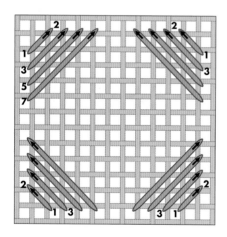
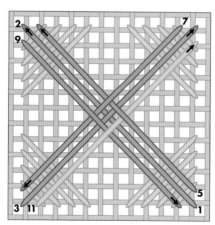
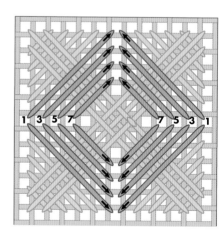

# WAFFLE

This stitch is worked in layers to create a single square stitch unit. Notice how the threads automatically weave over and under to create the waffle. To achieve this woven appearance, the numbers and arrows of each layer must be followed exactly. It is always worked over an uneven number of canvas threads. The size of the stitch can be adjusted to fit an area. Some stitchers like to use two colors, working the last two threads in all four directions in a different color. However, the beauty of the stitch can be lost when another color is introduced. This stitch appears difficult to stitch, but it is easy to work.

You can use any type of thread or yarn for this stitch.

**Ways to use:** borders, corners, gift packages, geometric quilt block patterns

**Also known as:** Southern cross, Norwich

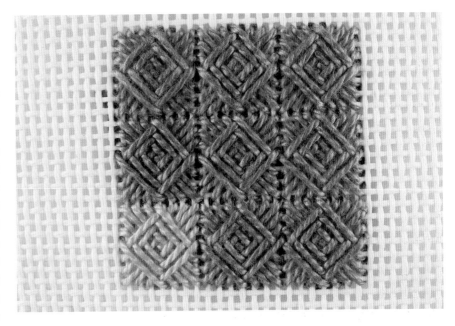

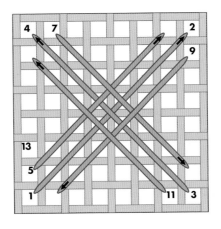

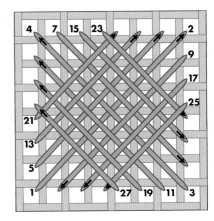

# Flaming Maze Market Basket

This market basket was designed when it was cold and spring gardens were only a dream. The two-way darning became a maze, and as the stitches in the tangerine silk ribbon were worked, they took on the look of a small rosebud. Thus a garden maze appeared in a vision. This is a quick weekend project.

Needlepoint Chart

**Approximate design size:**
4½" x 4½" (11.4 x 11.4 cm)

**Stitches:** 57 x 57

 Leaf motif: shamrock,
100% silk thread

Diagonal knitting (single stitch unit):
shamrock, 100% silk thread

 Diamond ray: med tangerine,
4 mm silk ribbon

 Diagonal knitting and backstitch:
med electric blue, pearl cotton

 Two-way darning: med electric blue,
pearl cotton

Running: lt parrot green,
stranded cotton

Color Key

## Stitching information

**1** Tape and secure canvas on the stretcher bars, following instructions in the beginning of this chapter.

**2** Mark a T (top) at the top of the canvas on the tape. This will keep the stitches going in the correct direction.

**3** Work the design in the order given. Refer to the chart for the placement of each stitch. Refer to the Stitch section of this chapter for information on how to work the stitches used in this design.

**4** Use two strands of silk thread in shamrock and the leaf motif. Find the center of the canvas and work the four leaves.

**5** Use blue pearl cotton and the diagonal knitting stitch to work the green center of the motif. Place a backstitch between the leaves. Notice one diagonal knitting stitch unit is used to create the corner stitches of the small green motif.

**6** Use the tangerine silk ribbon and the diamond ray stitch to work the border around the leaf motif. When ending these stitches, check to see that no stray ribbon from the back can be seen on the front of the canvas. For best results, start on the left side and work to the right. To stitch the next side's row, turn the canvas a quarter turn working left to right across the row. Continue around the area. Refer to the information on how to lay stitches in the ABCs and the Silk Ribbon chapter for working with silk.

**7** Use one strand of shamrock silk thread and the diagonal knitting stitch to work the small motifs in the four corners of the center area.

**8** Use the blue pearl cotton and the two-way darning stitch to work the border around the diamond ray stitches.

## Finishing

**9** Remove the canvas from the stretcher bars. Use a small piece of quilter's tape and mark a T on it. Place this on the open area of the cut canvas to indicate where the top of the canvas is. Follow the manufacturer's instruction regarding how long the tape can remain on fabric.

**10** Check to be sure the canvas threads are still straight. If they are not straight, then dry block the canvas following directions in this chapter.

**11** Refer to the chart to see how the next canvas thread out from the two-way darning runs along the stitch. Trim the canvas to within three threads of the two-way darning.

**12** Use a very small amount of the liquid seam sealant along the edges of the canvas. Sealant is very thin—use with caution. Allow to dry several hours before continuing.

**13** Cut a piece of felt the size of the cut canvas. Baste the right side of the felt to the back of the canvas.

**14** Use five strands of the green embroidery floss and a running stitch to work the last border. Start on the left side of the top of the canvas and place the first running stitch one stitch over from the corner of the canvas. Work two running stitches, skip one stitch, and work two more. Continue in this manner as you work around the area until you reach a corner. Leave the corner stitches blank. Refer to the chart for correct placement of the first stitch. These skipped stitches will be used to hold the canvas to the basket for finishing. See Creative Embroidery chapter for how to work this stitch.

**15** Cut a 12" (30.5 cm) piece of green embroidery floss for the bow. Separate five strands for the bow. Turn the canvas diagonally one-quarter turn. On the bottom point of the diamond, take the needle/thread into the canvas on the right side where the last running stitch will end, and come up on the left side where the last running stitch will end for that side. Pull the stranded thread until you have equal lengths. Use quilter's tape to tape the thread out of the way, securing the tape on the blank canvas area.

**16** Center the diagonal piece of canvas on the basket. Keep the marked T on the right side of the top point of the diamond shape. To hold the work in place, push long straight pins straight down into the basket on the four corners in the middle of the two-way darning. When you place the pins, try not to pierce a stitch. Before continuing, see Alternate Finishing Method.

**17** Work from the inside of the basket to carefully baste the canvas to the basket, using several long stitches. The pins will prick your skin, so be careful. Remove the pins as you baste. If the basket is lined and has inside pockets, keep the stitches from going through the outer fabric piece of the pocket.

**18** Use five strands of the green embroidery floss and a running stitch to secure the canvas to the basket. Work the remaining open stitches around the area.

**19** Trim the felt to match the canvas edge, if necessary.

**20** Tie a bow with the piece of green embroidery floss. Trim the ends of the bow to desired length. Secure the bow knot with a tiny drop of the liquid seam sealant. Allow to dry before continuing.

**21** Use the fabric adhesive to adhere the tips of the diamonds corners to the felt.

## Alternate Finishing Method

Instead of stitching the canvas to the basket, place all running stitches in the final border and create the bow. Secure canvas to the basket using fabric adhesive or hot glue.

# Neat Open Work

For open-weave canvas design: use matching sewing thread to tack any stitching threads on the back that may be showing through to the front of the canvas. Working on the back, stitch through the sewing thread and pull the threads together so only the front stitches are showing. Tie off and clip all thread ends.

# Iris Lace Box

Beautiful iris flowers bloom as the snow melts and spring arrives. The iris hand-dyed threads, metallic braids, and beads highlight the lilac canvas. The beaded center motif gives the hint of flower petals.

## YOU WILL NEED

- 10" × 10" (25.4 × 25.4 cm) piece of 18-count mono canvas in lilac
- 10" × 10" (25.4 × 25.4 cm) stretcher bar frame
- hand-dyed single strand cotton: iris
- metallic braid: amethyst, purple, and holographic purple
- six-strand embroidery floss: very dark blue violet
- seed beads, size 11/0: mercury
- Silamide bead thread, size A: purple
- brass tacks or staple gun and staples
- tapestry and beading needles: size 24 or 26
- square wooden box with a 4" × 4" (10.2 × 10.2 cm) visible open: mahogany finish
- acid-free paper or fabric: lilac

## STITCHES USED

- straight diamond motif
- Smyrna
- Scotch
- upright cross

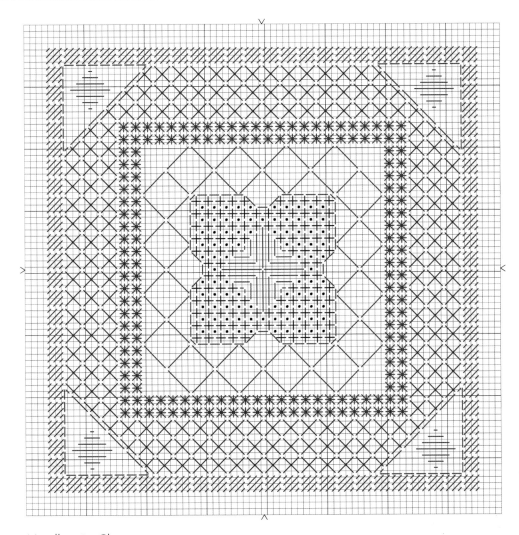

**Approximate design size:** 4" x 4" (10.2 x 10.2 cm)

**Stitches:** 72 x 72

Needlepoint Chart

 Straight diamond motif:
iris, 209 Wildflowers

Straight diamond:
iris, 209 Wildflowers

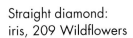 Smyrna cross:
iris, 209 Wildflowers

Scotch:
iris, 209 Wildflowers

Upright cross:
amethyst, 026 fine #8 braid

Backstitch:
purple, 012 fine #8 braid

Large lacy cross:
very dk blue violet, 333 stranded cotton

Beads:
mercury, 00283 seed beads

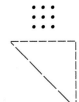 Backstitch:
purple, 012L fine #8 braid

Color Key

## Instructions

1  Tape and secure canvas on the stretcher bars following instructions on page 214.

2  Mark a T (top) at the top of the canvas on the tape using a permanent pen. Refer to this T to keep the stitches going in the correct direction.

3  Use the tapestry needle for all needlepoint stitches. Use the beading needle for attaching the beads.

4  Work the design in the order given. Refer to the chart for the placement of each stitch. Refer to the Stitch section of this chapter for information on how to work the stitches.

5  Optional step: Use a light-colored sewing thread to baste a center line vertically and horizontally. Count from the center basted line for correct placement of each section of stitches.

6  Use two strands of iris single-strand cotton and the straight diamond motif. Use only lighter pieces of the single-strand cotton to work the motifs. Place the motif in the center of the canvas. Start stitching with the top diamond. Turn the canvas a quarter turn to work the second diamond. Repeat for the other two. The four diamond stitches will share holes.

7  Use the amethyst metallic braid and the upright cross to work the stitches around the diamond motif. The braid will have a nicer sheen if the thread does not twist when it enters the canvas hole.

8  Use two strands of iris hand-dyed single-strand cotton and the Smyrna to work the two border rows around the center area. Count up from the center motif and work the border clockwise around the center area. Use the single-strand cotton as it comes from the skein for the correct color flow for this border.

9  Use the purple metallic braid and the backstitch to work diamond-shaped lines in the center area between the Smyrna and upright cross. Work one half of the diamond at a time, starting next to the upright cross. This stitch will share some holes with the upright cross section and the Smyrna cross border.

10  Use two strands of the iris hand-dyed single-strand cotton (matching method) and the Scotch stitch to work the outside border row. Start the border by counting up from the Smyrna border. Work to the left and around the area. At each corner of the border, turn the canvas a quarter turn and continue working to the left.

11  Use one strand of the dark purple embroidery floss and the large lacy cross to work the area between the Smyrna and the Scotch stitch. Notice the corners of the area are not stitched with the large lacy cross. You'll need to compensate the slanted edge along the open canvas. Follow the chart. Some of the large lacy cross-stitches will share holes with the Scotch and Smyrna.

12  Use two strands of the iris hand-dyed single-strand cotton and a straight diamond in each corner of the open canvas in the large lacy cross area.

13  Using seed beads and two strands of the purple Silamide, attach the beads between the upright crosses. The placement is indicated by a dot on the chart. When the upright cross is stitched, it leaves a perfect resting place for a bead between each stitch. Attach the beads so they rest over the opening between the crosses. Come up from the back with the needle/thread, slide on a bead, and go back down through the same hole. Secure the thread on the back after two beads have been placed. Pull the beading thread taut to keep the beads upright. Repeat until the area is beaded.

14  Optional step: Use the purple metallic braid and the backstitch to work the outline stitches around the center upright crosses and around the triangular area in the four corners of the large lacy cross. Notice the backstitches in both areas are worked straight or on the diagonal and cover a different number of canvas threads. These stitches are worked to highlight the area.

## Finishing

**15** Remove the canvas from the stretcher bars. Check to be sure the canvas threads are still straight. If they are not straight, then dry block following directions on page 215.

**16** Trim the canvas and lilac paper to fit the opening in the box.

**17** Place lilac paper or fabric behind canvas in the box, following the directions for finishing that come with the box.

# Hand-dyed Options

- **Color Flow.** When stitching with hand-dyed thread, use the thread as it comes from the skein to keep the color flow of the dyes. When threading the needle each time, use the previous cut for the knotted end of the thread. This way, you'll be using the thread that has the same shading as the last stitch worked. This method is used in step 8.

- **Matching.** For a more intense, consistent look, cut a length of thread and then match this length with the next length on the strand with the same color shading. Matching the thread in this manner will use slightly more thread, but provide a more even color tone. This method is in step 10.

# Resources

## PROJECT MATERIALS

The following product brands and style numbers were used for the projects in this book:

**Indigo Jacket**
Page 66
The Caron Collection Wildflowers guacamole #206
DMC six-strand embroidery floss: avocado green #469, very light topaz #727, and medium electric blue #996

**Azalea Blaze Pillow**
Page 68
DMC six-strand embroidery floss: lemon #307, light lemon #445, light avocado green #470, topaz #728, royal blue #797, very dark parrot green #904, medium parrot green #906, bright canary #973
DMC satin: ultralight avocado green #S472
DMC pearl cotton #8: medium delft blue #799
Pellon stabilizer #30

**Paisleys and Pearls Pillow**
Page 108
Appleton wool in aqua #483, bright yellow #551, orange red #445
Fire Mountain Gems Swarovski #1241P RD 6 mm powdered almond pearls
YLI Silamide beading thread

**Touch of Gold Fedora**
Page 110
National Non Woven Bamboo Xotic Felt: lava rock #1005
Pellon fusible fleece
DMC six-strand embroidery floss: medium old gold #729
brown paper packages: Trio white #T02
Vineyard Silk Shimmer: gold #S-517
Kreinik Fine Braid: gold #002
Beacon Permanent Adhesive Fabri-Tac

**Rainbow of Ribbons Purse**
Page 144
Weeks Dye Works: Iris #2316
YLI 4 mm silk ribbon: medium lavender #101, medium French lavender #118, pinkish red #28, medium peachy pink #104, off-white #12
Fire Mountain Gems Delica beads: opaque rainbow ivory #1501, luster wisteria lavender #1476
Wichelt/Mill Hill Beads 11/0 seed: ice lilac #02009
DMC six-strand embroidery floss: very light topaz #727
Caron Collection Impressions wool blend: olive green #5023, blue purple #6042
YLI Silamide bead thread: purple, light gray, and natural

**Silk Magic Lamp Shade**
Page 148
YLI 4 mm silk ribbon: Mediterranean blue #011
YLI Silamide beading thread: turquoise

**Beaded Bliss Checkbook Cover**
Page 186
Palmetto Purse Company checkbook cover
DMC six-strand embroidery floss
Fire Mountain Gems Delica Beads
YLI Silamide beading thread

**Midnight Shimmer Bracelet**
Page 188
Beacon Permanent Adhesive Fabri-Tac
Fire Mountain Gems beads: silver-lined light purple #0629, purple #1347
Kreinik very fine braid: turquoise #029
Mill Hill 11/0 beads: turquoise frosted #62038
Toho 11/0 beads: silver-lined diamond rainbow #2029
YLI Silamide beading thread: grey
(Ribbon clamp and sequins are available at bead shops or online.)

**Violet Blossoms Candle Band**
Page 210
Violet Blossoms Candle Band
Zweigart 16 count Stitchband7008/11 in antique white
DMC six- strand embroidery floss: light forest green #164, lemon #307, light blue violet #341, light avocado green #470, light parrot green #907, dark forest green #987, forest green# 989, dark grey green #3051, very light golden yellow #3078, cornflower blue #3807

**Springtime Journal**
Page 212
Wichelt Imports Jim Shore perforated paper: flourish spruce #502
DMC six-strand embroidery floss: medium light moss green #166, black #310, dark coral #349, coral #351, avocado green #469, very light topaz #727, black avocado green #943
Barnes and Noble natural hemp Nepal handmade journal
Bazzill Basics cardstock: sugar daddy and painted desert
Beacon Permanent Adhesive Fabri-Tac

**Flaming Maze Market Basket**
Page 254
Zweigart Orange Line Interlock or Mono canvas
Frank A Edmunds stretcher bars
DMC pearl cotton: medium electric blue #996
DMC six-strand embroidery floss: light parrot green #907
Vineyard Silk Classic 100 percent silk thread: shamrock #C-06
River Silks 4 mm silk ribbon: tangerine #11
National Non Woven wool blend felt
Dritz Fray Check liquid seam sealant
Beacon Fabri-Tac fabric adhesive
Kim Agardy Coe Basket in style Becky

**Iris Lace Box**
Page 256
Caron Collections Wildflowers hand-dyed single-strand cotton: Iris #209
Kreinik Fine #8 braid: amethyst 026, purple #012, holographic purple #012L
DMC six-strand embroidery floss: very dark blue violet #333
Wichelt/Mill Hill Beads: mercury #00283
YLI Silamide bead thread: purple
Sudberry House Donna's Box: mahogany finish #99511

# ONLINE SOURCES

**AllAboutBlanks**
*Fine linens for embroidering*
www.allaboutblanks.com

**Beacon Chemical Company, Inc.**
*Fabric-Tac Permanent Adhesive and other glues*
www.beaconadhesives.com

**brown paper packages**
*Silk & Ivory and Trio (wool blend)*
www.brownpaperpackages.com

**The Caron Collection**
*Hand-dyed and solid colored threads in Wildflowers (single strand), Watercolours (twisted), Impressions (wool blend), Waterlilies (silk), Snow (synthetic), Rachel (synthetic tubular)*
www.caron-net.com

**Colonial Needle, Inc.**
*Colonial, John James, Richard Hemming & Sons, and S. Thomas & Sons Needles*
www.colonialneedle.com

**DMC**
*Embroidery floss (six-strand embroidery floss), pearl cotton, metallic (six strand), linen, satin (synthetic), memory thread, tapestry wool, and needles*
www.dmc.com

**Fairfield**
*Quilt batting, pillow forms*
www.fairfieldworld.com

**Fire Mountain Gems**
*Beads including Delica, 11/0, disk, Rondelle, and stranded*
www.firemountaingems.com

**Fiskars**
*Cutting mat, rotary cutters, rulers, scissors*
www.fiskars.com

**Frank A Edmunds**
*Needlework frames, hoops, stretcher bars, snap frames*
www.faersc.com

**It's a Stitch of Charleston Needlepoint Shop**
*Threads, yarn, canvas, painted canvas, various stitching supplies, and accessories*
*(Ships USA and international)*
www.itsastitch.net

**JHB International**
*Buttons*
www.buttons.com

**JCA Inc**
*Paternayan Persian Yarn*
www.jcacrafts.com

**Kim Agardy Coe, Designer (Queen BEA Studio)**
*Baskets (Becky Basket)*
kimacoe@gmail.com

**Kreinik**
*Very fine #4 braid, fine #8 braid, tapestry #12 braid, medium #16 braid, heavy #32 braid, 1/16" (0.16 cm) ribbon, 1/8" (3 mm) ribbon (metallic and flat braids), Silk Mori, Silk Serica, Silk Bella threads (spools, skein)*
www.kreinik.com

**MagEyes, Inc.**
*Magnification in clip-on or head-mounted*
www.mageyes.com

**Mary Jo's Cloth Store Incorporated**
*Fabrics, sewing supplies*
www.maryjos.com

**National Non Woven**
*Felt*
www.commonwealthfelt.com

**Pellon**
*Stabilizers and fusible fleece*
www.pellonideas.com

**PLD Designs, Inc. t/a JulieMar & Friends**
*Painted Canvases (Julie Mar Design)*
www.juliemar.com

**Presencia**
*Finca embroidery floss (six-strand embroidery floss) and pearl cotton*
www.presenciausa.com

**Prym Consumer USA, Inc.**
*Dritz Products: beeswax, embroidery marking pencil, Fray-Check*
www.Prym-Consumer-USA.com

**River Silk**
*Silk ribbon 4mm, 7mm, 13 mm*
www.riversilks.com

**Soft Flex Company**
*Bead wire*
www.softflexcompany.com

**Sudberry House**
*Wood accessories for needlework*
www.sudberry.com

**Gentle Art**
*Sampler Threads and Simply Shaker Threads (hand-dyed and over-dyed)*
www.thegentleart.com

**Vineyard Silk**
*Classic and shimmer (silk) and merino (wool)*
www.vineyardsilk.com

**Weeks Dye Works**
*Hand over-dyed threads, weaver's cloth, wool and linen fabric*
www.weeksdyeworks.com

**Wichelt Imports Inc.**
*Mill Hill beads, Jim Shore perforated paper, linen and cross-stitch fabric*
www.wichelt.com

**YLI Corporation**
*Silamide, silk ribbon in 2 mm, 4mm, 7mm, Susan Schrempf (signature silk ribbon), ribbon floss (synthetic and metallic synthetic)*
www.ylicorp.com

**Zweigart**
*Linen and cross-stitch fabric and needlepoint canvas*
www.zweigart.com

# Stitch Index

Refer to these pages when you need to quickly find the instructions, photographs, and illustrations for the stitches taught in each section of the book.

## Creative Embroidery

## Crewel

# Silk Ribbon Embroidery

# Bead Embroidery

# Cross-Stitch

# Needlepoint

# About the Author

Linda Wyszynski lives with her husband Dennis in Mount Pleasant, South Carolina and is the owner of Hearthside Creations, LLC. She is a professional needle arts designer who has over twenty years experience as an artist creating freelance needlework projects for publication. She began her designing career painting custom needlepoint canvases for local needlepoint shops in Minneapolis. She is an author of needlework textbooks, magazine articles, and multi-author books. Her work can be seen on the newsstands in craft, needlework, and home décor magazines.

Linda has always been active in the art and needlework community including the following: CHA Designer Section Council, Board of Directors Society of Craft Designers, and Outreach After School Project program for a local EGA Chapter, Board of Directors Needlework Guild of Minnesota, Twin Cities Metropolitan Art Council Board, and Polk County NC Community Arts Council Committee.

She is passionate about needlework and continues to be active in both local needlework chapters and national organizations. She is currently a member of the Embroiderers' Guild of America (EGA), American Needlepoint Guild (ANG), the National Needlework Association (TNNA), and the Craft and Hobby Association (CHA).

# Acknowledgments

There are many people who helped make this book possible. I would like to thank the companies that donated supplies and are listed in the Resources. Without their generous support, so many tools, fabric, canvas, threads, beads, and other supplies would not have been available for the photographs in this book.

Thank you to Annette Calhoun, my stitcher of many years for stitching the needlepoint samples and several projects for this book.

Thanks to my designer friends and my sister for giving me the encouragement to write this book and for listening to me as I did so!

Thank you with love to my husband, Dennis, for always being the calm through the storm, always being there, supporting me and creating the graphics, even when I changed my mind a dozen times. You are very dear to me; without you I would not be the designer I am. Your photographs and graphics for this book are awesome. As my designer friends say, you are a peach.

Thank you to my editor, Linda Neubauer. It has been a pleasure working with you.

# Index